Frontispiece
by Susan Hopkins

From time to time the mountains of southwest Virginia call me home. I go there to renew my spirit; to be held up close in a big hug by those mountains and to "take the waters." The sulfur springs have been there forever, but only became the proper "baths" we know today in 1761 for the gentlemen and in 1836 for the ladies. The bath houses, now old wooden structures, haven't changed much, nor has the bathing procedure. Upon arrival, ladies are welcomed and asked by the attendant, "Do you wish to wear your suit, my suit, or God's suit?" I always elect her suit — a soft cotton gingham sack. Most recently, my visit was around noon-time on a Sunday. I had no sooner settled myself comfortably in the deliciously warm 95 degree water, when there was something of a commotion. Looking up, I saw about 15 ladies, all in baggy cotton sacks like mine, enter the pool. As they climbed down those ancient wooden steps, they broke into song — it was Sunday! — and they were part of the local church choir. They sang out their praises. For about 30 minutes, we were treated to a celebration of some of the most marvelous music I've ever heard. The music expressed their joy in sharing music with each other as a way to communicate their appreciation for life, for a power greater than themselves, and for being together to celebrate. The harmony created and the unity built as the women rejoiced in song brought forth the title for this work: *Hearing Everyone's Voice!*

With Gratitude and Affirmation . . .

from Susan Hopkins, Editor

The creation and development of *Hearing Everyone's Voice* was, for me, an incredible lesson in patience, trust, and faith that what needed to be in the book would come to us. It started with a concern for practices in which the people involved, especially children, do not have a voice, are not welcome to share in decision making. But there was also a strong awareness and understanding that many, many people who work and live with children are struggling very successfully to promote practices which do share authority to "hear everyone's voice." As I talked to parents and teachers and children, the stories unfolded of the struggles and the successes, and emerged in such powerful ways that our seven democratic principles were defined. These principles became the foundation for the book. Other sections were developed as people shared their feelings and experiences, their writings, their music — and trusted that all would be used in ways to support others. I express my profound gratitude to all who have had the faith to contribute to this work. From ideas, to encouragement and trust, to acknowledging vulnerabilities and successes — this collaborative work is a gift of affirmation from us to all who are struggling to create a better world.

List of Contributors

Lisa Atkinson — Songwriter; Musician

Bob Barns — Facilitator, Alternatives to Violence Project; Right Sharing of World Resources Committee (FWCC)

Marcia Berman — Singer; Songwriter; Educator

Julie Bisson — Early Childhood Trainer and Consultant on anti-bias and peace issues

Bob Blue — Musician; Songwriter; Storyteller

Jacki Breger — Musician; Teacher; Singer; Recording Artist

Sue Bush — Teacher of 5 and 6 year olds at Sequoyah School in Pasadena, California

Carmen Campos — Peace Camp Parent at Fullerton, California

Julie Carrara — Parent

Anarella Cellitti — Assistant Professor, Child Development, Texas A & M University, Kingsville

Chico Peace Camp — Chico, California

Victor Cockburn — Artist-Educator; Troubadour, Boston, Massachusetts

Sister Janet Corcoran — Coordinator of Santa Maria, California, Peace Week

Mary Daniels — Child Psychologist; Day Care Consultant

Jane Davidson — University of Delaware Lab School

Sharon Davisson — Director, Stepping Stones Preschool, Nevada City, California

Jan DeLapp — Community College Instructor, California; Early Childhood Education Consultant

Louise Derman-Sparks — CAEYC Leadership in Diversity Project; Professor, Pacific Oaks College, Pasadena, California

Developmental Studies Center — Oakland, California

Fundi — Director, Vukani Mawethu Choir

Dolores Garcia — Executive Director, Placer Community Action Council

Chris Gerzon — Kindergarten Teacher; TRUCE member

Betsy Gibbs — Parent; Director of Children's Center, Cal State Fullerton, California

Rosmarie Greiner — Deceased

Joanne Hammil — Musician; Songwriter

DIAGNOSTIC READING/ READING METHODS

AN INVALUABLE TOOL FOR ASSESSING STUDENT READING SKILLS

For over 40 years, pre-service and in-service teachers have used the *Classroom Reading Inventory* to help identify students' reading problems. It is the leading reading inventory in the field and comes in an easy-to-use, spiral-bound format. Unlike other lengthy reading inventories, the *CRI* can be fully administered in 12 to 15 minutes.

FEATURES NEW TO THE 11ᵀᴴ EDITION

Multicultural Themes: Many stories that embrace diverse characters, multicultural themes and global settings have been updated and added throughout the *CRI*.

Online High School and Adult Testing Material: The diagnostic and sub-skills materials for high school and adult education students are now available for downloading from our website, **www.classroomreadinginventory.com**.

Online Video Clips and Explanations: Video clips of the *CRI* being administered, plus explanations of results and other resources for future teachers also are available at **www.classroomreadinginventory.com**.

Online Support and Information from the Authors: Frequently asked questions, case study examples and responses to your emails are available at **www.classroomreadinginventory.com**.

INVENTORY ADMINISTRATION KIT

At the back of the text you will find a master set of the essential *CRI* pages for ease of use during administration. These include the complete Pretest and Posttest Records from Forms A and B. No more copying or printing-out needed!

The McGraw-Hill Companies

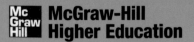
McGraw-Hill
Higher Education

ISBN 978-0-07-313127-6
MHID 0-07-313127-X

EAN

9 780073 131276

90000

www.mhhe.com

List of Contributors
continued

Amanda Heberden — Peace Camper at Fullerton, California

Cathy Higa — Head Teacher, Cal State Fullerton Children's Center

Jill Holt — Parent

Cameron Hostetter — Student at Orangethorpe Elementary School, Fullerton, California

Tom Hunter — Minstrel; Educator

Rebecca Janke — Growing Communities for Peace

Ann Johnson — First, Parent; second, Concerned Citizen; third, Head Start Supervisor; fourth, Songwriter

Karel Kilimnik — Primary Grade Teacher, Mary McLeod Bethune School, Philadelphia, Pennsylvania

Dolores Kirk — St. Louis Peace Camp Director

Alfie Kohn — Author; Lecturer

Pat Landry — Director, Boston Native American Head Start

Diane Levin — Professor at Wheelock College in Boston; Activist and Author; Specialist on children and media violence

Bonnie Lockhart — Musician; Songwriter; Teacher

Jay Mankita — Songwriter; Musician

Elizabeth Matlin — K1/K2 Teacher, Lucy Stone School, Dorchester, Massachusetts

Lee McKay — Instructor, DeAnza Community College

Nicolas Merrihue — Peace Camper at Fullerton, California

Leslie Minium — Reading Specialist; Community College Instructor

Melody Mitchell — Student

Rheta Negrete-Karwin — Peace Camp Teacher; CAEYC Leadership in Diversity Graduate

J. Chris Olander — Poet and Teacher, California Poets in the Schools (CPITS)

Kathy Olmstead — Head Teacher, Infants, Cal State Fullerton Children's Center

Ruth Pelham — Musician; Songwriter; Founder/Director of The Music/Mobile

AJ "Tony" Pellicano — MSW; Welfare to Work Consultant

Alisa Peres — Performer; Music Educator

Mary Perkins — Retired Primary Grade Teacher

Sandra Perkins — Spanish Teacher, K-6; Afternoon Day Care, 3-5 year olds

Julie Peterson — Growing Communities for Peace

Sarah Pirtle — Children's Musician and Songwriter; Director of The Discovery Center

Rosi Pollard — First Grade Teacher at Jefferson Elementary School, Pasadena, California

Lee Quinby — Head of School, State College Friends School, State College, Pennsylvania

Bailie Reither — Peace Camper at Fullerton, California

Resource Center for Non-Violence, Santa Cruz, California

Cindy Santa Cruz — Teacher, Silver Springs Head Start, Grass Valley, California

Peggy Schirmer — Founder and Coordinator of Concerned Educators Allied for a Safe Environment (CEASE)

Janice Sheffield — Head Teacher, Four Year Olds, Cal State Fullerton Children's Center

Marilyn Shelton — Associate Professor, California State University, Fresno

Patricia Shih — Singer; Songwriter

Tania Simirenko — Parent

Ben Silver — Musician; Songwriter

Robin Song — Consultant to Child Development Division, California State Department of Education

Sarah Speakman — Peace Camper at Fullerton, California

Lucy Stroock — Preschool Teacher/Director, Haggerty School, Cambridge, Massachusetts

Kate Sweeney — Early Childhood Educator

LuAnne Venham — Child Development Specialist, Orange Coast College Early Childhood Lab School

Jeffry Winters — Parent; Macintosh Enthusiast; Consultant

Barbara Wright — Preschool Special Education Teacher

Table of Contents

Table of Contents
continued

Dedication —

To the children:
      Those who have gone before,
      Those here now,
      And those yet to come . . . we dedicate this work.

Hearing Everyone's Voice

Building Democracy — Nurturing Community:
Educating Young Children for Peace and
Democratic Community
Edited by Susan Hopkins

Introduction

Hearing Everyone's Voice is a collaborative manual which coordinates stories and songs around the theme of building democratic community with young children. We are defining young children as children within their first eight years of life. Democratic practice includes concerns of peace and justice, caring about and inclusion of others, relationships and power. In this work, we share our thoughts and ideas about how children can be supported in their awareness, understanding, and actions around these issues. Young children are beginning to know when something or someone is unfair, and they need adults to help them sort out their concerns about how to take action to bring about fairness for all. This manual integrates peace education, the anti-bias perspective, and democratic practice. Connections are made between conflict management alternatives in the culturally relevant context and how one's choice of actions relates to solutions. Peace, anti-bias perspective, and democracy cannot really be separated if one is to do the best possible work with children and families around full participation in the community. Teachers and parents and children tell the stories of their struggles in making the connections to hear everyone's voice. Participation in this work crosses many barriers including age, ethnicity, class, culture, gender, and others as we do our best to learn from one another about the many good ways to really hear each other.

Our hope is that this manual will serve different purposes for different readers. If you are looking for theoretical discussion around children's social development, you'll find sections one, two, and three useful. If you are looking for program ideas, sections four, five, and six describe numerous strategies. If you need to restore your confidence in children's capabilities to solve problems, to develop relationships, to clarify their concerns, read their own voices in section seven. Some of your own doubts and barriers may find resonance in section eight. And additional resources and supplemental information are in sections nine and ten. While the manual has been edited to provide certain continuity for the reader, most sections may be taken on their own. The many contributors to our manual hope their writings will be used to enhance the work to build community with children. Enjoy these stories, songs, and contributions, and use them as inspiration to create your own best ways to "hear everyone's voice."

Key to Graphics

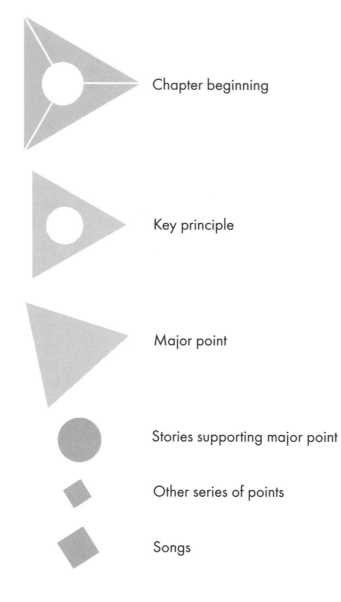

Chapter beginning

Key principle

Major point

Stories supporting major point

Other series of points

Songs

Credits

Design: Margie Bloch
Cover photograph: Bonnie Neugebauer
Production editors: Sandy Brown, Carole White
All Rights Reserved • Copyright © 1999 Exchange Press
ISBN 0-942702-26-3 • Printed in the United States of America

I. Stories to Illustrate Theories of Children's Social Development

In offering theoretical foundation to our work on building democratic community with young children, Jane Davidson has woven together theories of children's social development with stories to demonstrate effective strategies. Her stories describe how adults can support children's best social growth by combining knowledge of children's developmental needs and strategies which meet those needs.

Working with Very Young Children to Build Social Equality, Respect, and Community
by Jane Davidson

When I heard that a new book was being written to bring together stories and ideas for helping young children learn about democracy, I felt uncertain. To me democracy is a complex form for government at a level of abstraction way above the understanding of young children. Since voting is a part of democracy that is simpler to understand than the whole, people often have children vote on things to help them to understand the meaning of democracy. I was not comfortable with exploring democracy in this way either. Young children do not manage competition well. Voting for them would be a way of winning or losing, not an equitable way to make a decision. I delved further, feeling there must be something I was missing about democracy and its relevance to young children.

I looked up democracy in the dictionary and found my first two responses to democracy — government by the people, and majority rule. However, the third definition of democracy explained its pertinence to young children: "principles of social equality and respect for individuals within a community" (Encarta 97). Both of these principles encompass areas of social development which are being constructed by young children.

Social equality, at its most basic, deals with issues of fairness. From an early age, children are concerned with fairness. Anyone spending time with children will hear refrains such as these: "It's not fair!" "But I need it!" "He has more!" and "It's mine!" At the beginning, the concern is for their own needs: "It's mine" and "I want it." One might assume that the child who is more possessive of toys has fewer social skills, yet in a toddler class possessiveness may in fact indicate higher level social understanding. Levine (1983) found that two year olds with stronger self definition were more possessive about objects. Declaring "It's mine" – either verbally or physically by grabbing or clutching a desired object – says that I am an individual who can have something. "Rather than being a sign of selfishness, early struggles over objects are a sign of developing self hood, an effort to clarify boundaries between themselves and others" (Berk, 1997, p. 425). The children who are possessive have developed a clear sense of themselves as separate entities with needs.

Since ownership is an important step in the process of developing self identity, parents and teachers will want to support the toddler's need to possess things. Therefore, it is important to have many similar toys and materials in group settings so children can own things without depriving others of that same opportunity. Early social interactions revolve around imitation, so similar materials will also foster more social interactions.

Carlotta, two years old, is pretending to give a bottle to a baby doll. The caregiver, Chris, comments, "Carlotta, you are taking such good care of your baby." Wilson comes over and is about to take Carlotta's doll so he can take good care of it too. Chris hands Wilson another baby saying, "This baby is also hungry. There is a bottle on the table to feed your baby." The two children smile at each other as they feed their babies. Chris comments, "Now you are both feeding your babies. It is fun to take care of your babies together."

Chris has encouraged social interaction by pointing out Carlotta's actions, by offering Wilson a way to engage in the same type of action, and by recognizing their enjoyment of each other. This simple support lays the foundation for emerging concepts of social equality.

Carlotta and Wilson are sharing an activity. They are engaged in the simplest form of sharing where both children have their needs met. It is easier to share when there are ample materials, and sharing means each having some of the available materials.

As children spend more time with others, they begin to be concerned about having a "fair share" and getting a "turn." First the concern is for themselves, but it begins to extend to wanting what is fair for their friends as well. As children get older, the meaning of "fairness" broadens beyond just possession and equal division of materials to wider issues of fulfilling the needs of all individuals in the community.

Sharing a single desired object requires more advanced social skills than all using similar toys at the same time. "To take turns successfully a child must be able to postpone her [his] wishes, understand that taking turns is expected and normal in the social context, and behave appropriately when her [his] turn finally comes" (Katz & McClellan, 1997, p. 3). Two other social skills which facilitate turn taking are empathy for others and the ability to resolve conflicts. In fact, these social skills are necessary for emerging concepts of social equality and respect for others, beyond the limited area of sharing.

There are many ways that adults help children to build these social skills. Let's look at stories that illustrate some of these techniques. Postponing wishes is hard for young children. What they need is so clear to them. Many times children will demand something over and over, because they are sure if you just understand their need you will see why it is essential to fulfill.

Jocelyn has just begun attending child care. She is unaccustomed to sharing toys with so many other children. When another child picks up a toy and starts playing with it, she always wants the same toy. It looks like so much fun when others are using it. Jacob has just gotten on the swing and is commenting on how high it is going. "I want to swing," demands Jocelyn.

Tracy, the teacher, explains, "Jacob is using the swing right now; you can swing when he is done."

"But I want it!" Jocelyn insists.

Tracy sees that for Jocelyn describing turn taking is not enough. "It is really hard to wait for a turn when you want something." Jocelyn relaxes a little. "What should we do while we wait for your turn?"

Later, when it is Jocelyn's turn to swing, Tracy comments, "Look, Jacob is giving you the swing now. You did such a good job of waiting for your turn."

Tracy helped Jocelyn by recognizing that it IS hard to wait, by helping her find something to do to make the time go faster, and by recognizing that she did manage to wait even though it was hard.

Humor can often help children deal with unfulfilled wishes. Another day Jocelyn was again having a hard time dealing with the needs of others.

Jocelyn is playing in the block area. She has lined up about 10 small rubber cats and dogs on the wall she has made. There is still some more space, but all the other animals are being used by Neelima and Cole. Jocelyn starts taking animals from Cole's truck. "They're mine," he tells her.

"But I NEED them!" Jocelyn explains. Cole grabs them back and Jocelyn starts to cry.

Nnamdi, the teacher, empathizes, "It's hard when there aren't enough animals for everyone to have as many as they want. Wouldn't it be great if we had enough to fill the whole block area?"

"What if we had enough to fill the whole room?" asks Cole.

"Would there be room enough for us?" asks Nnamdi.

"There would be so many it would break down the windows," adds Jocelyn.

"They would fill up the whole world," Cole says.

"Yah, they would go all the way to the moon," chimes in Jocelyn.

The humor of the discussion helps to temper Jocelyn's distress. Nnamdi might also have suggested alternative means for filling the wall, such as making paper animals, finding different animals or people to fill the wall, or decorating the wall with blocks around the animals. For some children, learning to postpone wishes is much more difficult than for other children, thus the amount of adult support and help required will also vary.

In the story about the swing, Tracy not only helped Jocelyn to wait, she also set the expectation that children need to take turns with toys. Adults communicate this to children in many ways.

◆ Helping children to understand that others are waiting. *"Carlos, when you are done with the bike, please let Jessamine know. She would like a turn too."*

◆ Valuing when children do take turns. *"Peri, it was so kind of you to let Nick use the baby doll."*

◆ Clarifying that all will get a turn, and helping children to keep track of turns when many are waiting. *"Jackson is filling his bucket with water first, then Kevin will go, then Carly."*

◆ Teaching children techniques for getting a turn. *"Binta, did you tell Tommy you want a turn with the truck when he is done?"*

◆ Realizing when there are many of an item some should be left for others. *"Wow, Andrew, you have a lot of people. Why don't you take just two more and then leave the rest for your friends."*

Another aspect of social development which underlies social equality is empathy and concern for others. It is only through recognizing that others also have needs that we can work towards social equality and respect for others in the community. Berman (1997, p. 21) states that for a long time it had been a "commonly accepted view" in the field of moral development that "children prior to age ten are egocentric, [and] unable to take the perspective of others." He found it fortunate that in the last ten years researchers have begun to question this assumption. Dunn (1988) found that children as young as seven or eight months were starting to respond to expressions of feelings in the people around them.

Hoffman (1988) also saw empathy as beginning to develop at a young age. He describes four phases in the development of empathy. The first phase is "global empathic distress" seen in infants. When others are distressed, the infant will also act distressed and respond with his/her own distressed behaviors such as crying, thumb sucking, and so on. In the second year, children will display "eccentric empathic distress." Children now recognize that it is the other person who is distressed, but see the distress through their own perspective. Hoffman tells of an 18 month old child who brought his own mother to help a crying friend, rather than bringing the friend's mother who was also present. The child would have wanted his own mother, so he assumed that the friend would want her as well. Between the ages of two and three years, children begin to feel empathy for the feelings of other people. They become aware that the other person's feelings are different from their own and respond to that person's needs. The fourth phase is seen in late childhood. This is when children can see beyond the immediate and empathize with a person's life situation.

Adults can facilitate the development of empathy. The techniques needed will vary depending on the age of the children and the level of their empathetic development. For infants, who cannot yet tell personal distress from the distress of others, adults must provide comfort and reassurance. Thus, if one infant in a group cries, other infants may need to be held and soothed. The children whose distress was empathetic will begin to recognize that, although they hear crying, they themselves are still safe. Of course, the child who is actually in distress would need to be helped as well. Having others respond empathetically to their distress helps children learn that people do, and therefore can, respond in a more differentiated way, that when someone cries, the response is one of comfort from others.

As children get older, there are many ways adults can facilitate the development of empathy. Let's look at some stories to illustrate appropriate techniques. Providing adult comfort for those in distress is still an important method for supporting empathy in children. However, the adult's manner of providing comfort would be a bit different.

Wendy bumps her knee on the cupboard and begins to cry. Hannah, the adult, picks up Wendy, saying, "I am so sorry you hurt yourself. Let me give you a hug to help you feel better."

Hannah not only comforts Wendy but she verbalizes that we feel sorry for others when they hurt themselves, and that we can do something (in this case give a hug) to help people feel better when they are sad.

Before children can respond to feelings in others, they must first be able to recognize those feelings. Often this is done by first learning to recognize their own feelings. Adults can label feelings for children.

Sachi is crying because her mother left. The adult comments, "You are sad because your mother left. Let's read a book to help you feel better."

Neelima is upset because it has gotten cold and Mr. Harshorn told her she has to wear her jacket outside. She is sitting under the climber shouting and biting her jacket. "I will rip all the jackets in the world."

Mr. Harshorn says, "You are angry that you have to wear your jacket. If you come play, you will feel better."

In both cases, the adult not only labels the feeling but also suggests ways to alleviate the unpleasant feeling. Sometimes children do not want to give up their sadness or anger. If Neelima rejects Mr. Harshorn's suggestion to play, he might ask, "Would you like to stay angry, or would you like help cheering up?" Mr. Harshorn has recognized Neelima's feelings and helped her to see that she can choose to continue feeling the way she does or work to change the feelings. If the anger about the jacket is directed at Mr. Harshorn, he might try less direct ways of enticing her into play.

Alerting children to the feelings and needs of others is an important technique for building empathy, according to Katz and McClellan (1997). In order to respond to the feelings of others, children must first learn to recognize how others feel.

A group of four year olds are playing detective. They are charging around the room looking for clues. Raymond has made a gun-like creation with a building toy. Ms. Lee, the teacher, expresses her concern about guns. Raymond reassures her, "It's not a gun, it's a hornet squirter. It kills hornets so they won't sting you." Soon others have made copies of this intriguing device. The detective play builds in intensity. Joshua begins to follow the group. Raymond makes spraying noises as he sweeps the area with his hornet squirter. Joshua looks terrified and begins sobbing when the squirter seems pointed at him. Raymond either does not notice or does not care. Ms. Lee stops Raymond gently and says, "Look at Joshua, your squirter is scaring him. Be careful where you aim it."

Ms. Lee helped Raymond to notice Joshua's feelings and to realize that such awareness is valued.

Children learn about emotions from watching other children who are struggling with their feelings. Adults can help others learn and grow through watching what is happening with others. When Sachi is crying for her mom, other children might observe with interest and concern. Rather than shooing them away, the adult can say, "Sachi is sad now, she misses her mom. Do you ever feel sad when your mom is gone? What do you do?" It is often easier for children to talk about their own feelings, and how they deal with them, when they are not in the middle of an emotional crisis themselves. Of course, it is important to discuss distressed children's feelings in a respectful way that does not put them "on show" but instead looks at their needs as human needs that we all have and must respond to.

Katz and McClellan (1997) say that adults can do more than help children recognize and respond to needs; they can also help them to be concerned in advance. "The goal is to develop children's dispositions to speculate and anticipate the response and feelings of peers to various events, thereby deepening their knowledge and understanding of others" (p. 86).

A class of four year olds had been learning about book making. They were going to make their own book. Each child was making a page, then using the ditto machine to make copies for everyone's book. Each child was going to collate a set of pictures and use the spiral binder to punch holes and bind the pages into their own book. Leeza had been sick for a week and had not yet had a chance to make her picture. Tomorrow was to be the day for punching and binding.

At snack, the children were talking about binding their books tomorrow. Rena, the teacher, asked, "What should we do about Leeza? She hasn't had a chance to make her picture yet."

Ricardo suggested, "We could make one for her and take it to her."

Rena wondered out loud, "Do you think she would be sad that she does not have a picture in the book?"

"She could make the picture at home and we could copy it for her," suggested Orion.

This idea seemed to please the children until Cassie said, "But then she can't use the copier and that's the most fun." In the end, the children decided to make cards to send to Leeza, but to postpone the book making until she could participate.

This discussion took place at the end of the school year. This group had close bonds to each other, and had previous discussions of this type, so the teacher help needed was minimal. Earlier in the year, or

with a different group, the teacher might have had to point out that the copying was the fun part and ask how Leeza might feel about missing it.

Adults can also help children to reinterpret their perceptions of others. Matthew, almost five, was one of the largest and oldest in his class. His language skills and social skills were more like that of an early three year old. He moved in an awkward way as though he was not quite sure where his body was going. He loved spending time with other children but did not know how to begin interactions. He would often run up to classmates and throw his arms around them to give them a hug, in the process accidentally knocking them over. Many of the children were scared of him. As Matthew was running up to Evan, Evan seemed to be shrinking back, as he told Ms. Sachar, "He's mean."

Ms. Sachar explains, "Matthew really likes you, he is coming to give you a hug. Sometimes he does not know how to do it softly. Let's tell him." She reaches out a hand to slow down Matthew. "Matthew, Evan is worried you are going you give him a hard hug. Can you give him a gentle one?" Matthew does and both boys smile.

Ms. Sachar is redefining Matthew's behavior as affectionate, rather than mean. She also stays by Matthew to insure that when he is being affectionate he does not accidentally hurt children and reinforce their perceptions of him as "bad" or "dangerous." Over time, the other children know how to tell Matthew, "I don't want a hard hug." Not only did Ms. Sachar help Evan to reinterpret this particular behavior, she also set the expectations that we should think about alternative interpretations for assessing the behavior of others.

Adults not only help children to recognize feelings but also help them find a way to offer empathy. In an early example, Wendy bumped her knee and received comfort from Hannah. If another child — Marcus, for example — was nearby, Hannah might have included him in the comforting process by saying to Marcus, "Let's give Wendy a hug to help her feel better." This tells Marcus that not only do adults offer support when someone is hurt but that he can do so as well. It also offers Marcus a specific way to offer empathy to Wendy.

Children will also reach out on their own to offer comfort to unhappy peers. Adults can support such actions through recognition and praise. In the earlier example of the child who offers his own mother to a friend, the adult could say, "It is so kind of you to try to cheer up your friend." If the helper is ready, the adult can also extend the help by offering additional ways to offer support. "Maybe he would also like his own mother." This offers the helper another action, without negating the value of the first action.

We have looked at how children develop principles of social equality through building an understanding of fairness and developing empathy. Let's now look at the other principle involved in democracy: respect for individuals within a community. Empathy is an important aspect of respecting individuals. By recognizing and responding to the feelings of others, children are showing respect for them as individuals.

Building an ability to redefine how we view others is essential in order to respect the wide range of differences that occur in every community. When the teacher helped Evan to view Matthew's behavior as seeking affection, rather than as aggression, she allowed Evan to come to respect Matthew. It is often difficult for children to understand that a behavior that is bad when they do it might be viewed differently when another child does it. Adults must work hard to help children accept peers who have special needs that result in what is commonly perceived as "bad" behavior.

Miro, four years old, was adopted from a Rumanian orphanage two years ago. He still suffers many social delays and differences. It is the third day of school. He is trying to build a ramp, but the block is too heavy to stay at the angle he desires. The block slides down again. Miro begins kicking the blocks. "You ugly, stupid blocks, I hate you, I am going to kill you," he shouts. The teacher, who had been helping him, comments that it is upsetting. She tries to redirect him to something which will result in more success. Miro continues shrieking at the top of his voice. He kicks blocks and rips pictures off the wall. As his tantrum builds, other children in the class become quiet and watch him. The teacher comments to Alora, who is also in the block area, "Miro is angry. Have you ever been angry?"

Alora nods, "Yes, but not THAT angry." They talk about how upset Miro must be and things that can be done to calm down when people are angry. Similar discussions are occurring all over the room between other teachers and concerned classmates.

The teachers helped the class to understand that Miro is angry, not BAD. The teachers demonstrated that they were not scared of his angry behavior. They were close to the other children offering security, so that children did not feel their safety threatened by Miro's anger. Throughout the year, his behavior continued to be more out of bounds than his classmates. He would shout out "stupid head," "ugly," and "I hate you!" even when he was playing happily. The teachers made sure to shield the other children from any harm that might come from Miro's actions when he was out of control.

Teachers, children, and Miro had repeated discussions about how Miro is working to control his anger and how he is working to use better words to talk about how he feels. Teachers offered suggestions for ways children could help Miro. The teachers were careful to not label his behavior as bad. If he was loud at group time, they would help him to calm down, rather than removing him. By the middle of the year, the children came to see Miro as someone who had wonderfully creative play ideas but could not always control his anger or communicate well with words. They no longer saw his aberrant behavior as "bad." If other children shouted out "stupid head," classmates were upset. When Miro did it, they accepted it as part of who he is.

Many of the children gave a great deal of thought to why he was behaving the way he was. Cailey frequently watched his behavior and discussed it with teachers. She drew her own interesting conclusion about Miro.

In the spring, Miro is drawing a road for the bikes with chalk. He is directing the activity while a number of other children help. Cailey is watching from the swings. She comments, "Miro is getting older; he is using his words now." Later that day, Miro is upset and screaming. Cailey remarks, "Miro's getting younger again."

Cailey has justified Miro's immature behavior by deciding that he is younger when he acts out but older when he is able to control himself. Although her conclusion is not the correct one, it allows her to view Miro with respect. She has developed the disposition to look beyond the obvious characteristics to see the person who is underneath.

Every group of children is composed of unique individuals. As in the above example, adults can help children to view all differences with openness — whether in race, gender, family composition, age, national background, physical abilities, social skills, or emotional stability.

Becoming an active participant in communities is an essential part of learning about democracy. It is within a community that we come to care about and empathize with others. According to Berman, "Social understanding and social responsibility are built on the children's desire to understand and feel effective in the social world, to initiate and maintain connections with others, and to reach out to those in distress" (1997, p. 22). It is within a community that we can come to work towards a common good. With isolated individuals, there is no "common" group whose well being can be observed, understood, and supported.

In the past, children, parents, and extended family shared a connectedness to a local community. With shifting work styles, smaller families, and job mobility, families experience less shared community (Katz & McClellan, 1997). "Parents no longer share a common center of community with one another and their children. In the past, children's need for a sense of community and belonging, emotional and social bonding, and nurturance were met by family, extended family, and larger community." (p. 24)

Schools, churches, and other group settings can play an essential role in providing the community setting for children and their families. This is a logical role for them. Not only are they fulfilling a societal need for the children and families in their care but a sense of community is essential in order for adults to facilitate the development of children's social skills.

Building community in the group setting is a complex process. It is not as simple as planning a few activities, providing some toys, or making an addition of "community building time" to the schedule. Instead, it is ingrained into everything that happens. It involves creating a climate that fosters community, cooperation, and caring. "It is not something that the teacher does for the children; it is something she helps the children to do with and for one another" (Katz & McClellan, 1997, pp. 26-27). In broad terms, the adult sets expectations that each group of children will build their own unique community, the adult fosters the development of community rituals, the adult provides and supports opportunities for social interaction, and the adult considers community building when planning all aspects of the environment.

From the moment children enter the group setting, adults help children to see themselves as a part of a community. Let's look at some stories which illustrate this point.

It is the first week at school. Children in the class are just starting to get to know each other. Tihomir is "driving" by turning the wheel on the climber. Jamal is sitting behind him. Kenyatta approaches looking uncertain. They ignore her. She seems ready to depart. Ming Chang, the teacher, stands by Kenyatta. "What are you driving?" he asks.

"Our train," Tihomir replies.

"And where are you driving to?" Ming Chang asks.

"Disney World, and it's going to take 20-17 hours," Jamal explains.

"Slow down, I see the station coming. Kenyatta has a ticket to go to Disney World too," Ming Chang informs them. They stop and Kenyatta gets on.

Ming Chang did not ask the boys if Kenyatta could play. This would have given them an option of including or not including Kenyatta. Instead, he communicated the expectation that, of course, Kenyatta is welcome.

Children are coming over to circle time. They all want to be near the teacher who is leading the singing so they push forward towards the center of the circle area. After half of the group is seated, there is a tight circle with little room for others. Gertha, the teacher, comments, "Look how crowded we are. Can everyone move back a few scoots so all our friends can sit in the circle?" The children comply. As additional children come over, the children already seated begin pointing out spaces. "I love the way you are helping your friends to become part of our group," Gertha remarks with a smile.

Gertha makes clear the expectation that all children should be part of the group. She suggests a way to make this happen. The children move back as requested but also extend the suggestion by actively helping the newcomers to find a place where they are included.

It is the third week of school. Akihito is surrounded by a group of children waiting for him to suggest what to do. He is enjoying his popularity. At home he has to give in to his domineering older brother. He proclaims, "Let's be lions. I will be the boss of the game and you can do what I say."

The teacher, Carl, is standing nearby and hears this exchange. "Lions sound like fun. But why do you want just one boss? That is easy. Having lots of bosses is REALLY cool. Then there would be lots of good ideas. But it's pretty hard work."

Akihito thinks for a minute then — still with the leader voice — proclaims, "We know how to do it. We will be a family of lion bosses." As the game continues, Akihito maintains the leadership, but others feel empowered to contribute ideas by their new found status as "bosses."

When Akihito's brother comes at the end of the day, he demands of Akihito, "Were you the boss today?"

"We were all bosses," he said with great pride.

Carl helped set the expectation that working together is "cooler" than having a boss. He allowed Akihito to still lead the play but to give the others important roles in the play as well. The fact that Carl stepped in so quickly helped the children to build a cooperative play pattern that could continue to develop over the school year.

Teachers help create this feeling of community by helping to build routines and class customs. Again, some stories will illustrate how this is done.

At circle time, the children help the teacher to count how many children are here today. They then think about who is missing. If the teacher knows why a child is missing, she will say, "Margie is sick" or "Henry went to see his grandma." If the teacher doesn't know, she will say, "I don't know why Keisha is missing today." The children offer possible reasons why she is not at school. "We'll have to ask her when she comes back," the teacher suggests. By the second month of school, children are announcing who is missing before the counting even begins. They are waiting at the door to question Keisha about where she has been.

This routine of counting children and noticing missing friends has encouraged children to own the process — they now independently notice when friends are missing. It also encourages them to express interest and concern for the missing children upon their return. When children are sick for more than a day or two, classmates will suggest the need to write get-well cards. This small routine (taking attendance) with support from the teacher has become an important community event.

At the snack table, Nicholas has a tendency to get loud and silly. He will encourage other children to join him in rocking back and forth in their seats, singing bathroom words, and laughing meanly at whatever is said. The teachers have decided to be proactive and start constructive activities before things get out of hand. As Ms. Marlow sits down, she says, "I bet you can't guess who I am thinking of." She proceeds to describe one of the children at the table. Nicholas listens eagerly and proclaims, "It's Marcy."

Ms. Marlow is amazed that she could not trick them. The game continues throughout snack, without a hint of the usual disruption. The next day, Nicholas demands the game again. Soon the children are initiating it on their own and doing their own describing.

The introduction of the "people game," as the children came to call it, not only prevented the disruptive behavior but became an important community event.

Singing together strengthens community feeling and builds shared rituals. Groups will develop favorite songs they want repeated. They often invent their own variations to favorite songs that make the songs unique to them. Regular group events such as lunch and snack bring children together to share time and build routines such as the "people game."

Remembering and repeating favorite activities also fosters a feeling of community.

The favorite activity of the afternoon class is to jump off the climber onto a mat on rainy days. If they come to school and it looks cloudy, they proclaim excitedly, "Climbers!"

The joy of anticipating a favorite class event turns the usually dreaded rainy day into an anticipated community happening. Teachers can reinforce this by helping the class to remember and celebrate favorite shared activities. Favorite books can be read with great fanfare. Books can also be revisited using felt boards, puppets, or reenactment (Davidson, 1996). Children can be encouraged to request the return of favorite toys and activities.

Play, especially pretend play, offers wonderful opportunities for building rituals and group customs (Davidson, 1996; Katz & McClellan, 1997). It also provides a forum for stretching social interactions.

After an ambulance came to visit the play yard, doctor and hospital became a favorite theme of play. One day Sasha pretended to fall off her bike. At first, Ben, the teacher, thought she was hurt. When he realized that Sasha was pretending, Ben suggested that another child be the ambulance driver and bring the wagon to take her to the hospital. Soon there were a myriad of accidents and ambulance drivers. This continued for many weeks. When a child would "crash," a teacher would call, "We need an ambulance," and someone would run to get the wagon. Soon the children took over the role of calling for the ambulance.

Doctor play and ambulance continued to be a favorite theme of the class for the rest of the year. It was a game that included all the children at various times throughout the year. Even the least skilled children socially could bring a wagon or pretend to be ill. In fact, some of the children who had trouble joining the class community found that they could be the center of interest by just laying down on the ground.

Basically everything that teachers do can have an impact on the construction of classroom community. In *Fostering Children's Social Competence: The Teacher's Role,* Katz and McClellan spend a chapter detailing how we support development through designing space to support social interactions among groups of varying sizes and by providing time enough for social interactions to develop, materials that foster interactions, and rich opportunities for play, especially dramatic play (1997, pp. 34-48).

Let's look at one example of how something as simple as selecting toys can impact community building. When rearranging toys and materials, it is important for teachers to leave out materials that have meaning for that class. Sometimes a toy becomes so important that children squabble over it. Everyone may want the "cool" sunglasses, the "detective bike," or the "mommy's dress." These are not designations set by the teacher but labels children have placed on certain toys. Because these toys have gained great value in the class community, they also create conflict. Teachers may be tempted to put away these toys to prevent conflict. This would be a mistake. Instead, teachers can look for ways to offer other toys that will supplement the favorite ones:

provide extra sunglasses that are cool in the same way, add special detective license plates to a number of the bikes, and add some new dresses which might also become "mommy dresses." Teachers can also facilitate discussion with the children about how the materials can be shared, and about how equally valued alternatives can be found.

Building a sense of community requires the adults to value community, and to support and nurture its growth with the children in their care. Building democracy with children requires adults who have a vision of what they want for children — a world that values social equality and respect for individuals within the community. This vision is an essential first step; the second is helping children build the skills and values that allow them to contribute to such a world.

Bibliography

Berman, S. (1997). *Children's social consciousness and the development of social responsibility.* Albany, NY: State University of New York Press.

Berk, L. (1997). *Child development.* Boston: Allyn and Bacon.

Davidson, J. (1996). *Emergent literacy and dramatic play in early education.* Albany, NY: Delmar Publishers.

Dunn, J. (1988). *The beginnings of social understanding.* Cambridge, MA: Harvard University Press.

Hoffman, M. (1988). Moral development. In M. H. Bernstein & M. E. Lamb (Eds.), *Developmental psychology: An advanced textbook* (pp. 479-548). Hillsdale, NJ: Erlbaum.

Katz, L., & McClellan, D. (1997). *Fostering children's social competence: The teacher's role.* Washington, DC: NAEYC.

Levine, L. E. (1983). Mine: Self-definition in 2-year-old boys. *Developmental Psychology, 19,* 544-549.

II. Principles to Promote Democratic Community

Creating and developing ways all people in the community can participate is the primary goal of democracy. We can think about this participation as speaking out and taking action when appropriate. People are to be included in such participation, no matter what their differing abilities, cultural and ethnic context for viewing the world, or age. Hearing everyone's voice gives us the benefit of a wide diversity of ideas. Those of us who work with young children are figuring out how to empower our youngest members of society to become people who can take action, who can advocate, who can make a difference. What skills and attitudes are necessary to be able to fully participate as members of their communities, and therefore to be included? What can we do, as grownups, to better hear their voices? How can we best create caring communities?

Friendships are basic to creating community. Young children are eager to figure out how to make and be friends with one another. Their often awkward attempts may provide challenges to the grownups in their lives. However, a variety of useful strategies to support children in their work of building relationships are described in the stories following. Both the sections on "Strategies" and "Children's Issues" offer many ways to enhance building community through friendships.

The previous section of this work takes a concentrated look at very young children and how they develop social equality and respect for individuals within a community. Stories support the adult role in helping children learn the social behaviors of taking turns and sharing, of caring about and for others to promote and develop empathy, of developing the skills to problem solve, as well as of respecting individuals. These social behaviors are basic to everything we do to create, live, and work in communities. They are the foundation pieces upon which our work builds; these are the pieces upon which the seven following principles are developed.

The seven principles are important to focus upon and to integrate throughout children's daily experiences as they learn and develop at home and school. We can think in terms of a tapestry — a model in which we weave the needs of the individuals within the community together with the seven principles which promote participation from all members. Adults who are responsible for children plan for them to have opportunities to establish and practice:

◆ Developing self identity within the community
◆ Establishing safety and trust
◆ Taking responsibility for our own actions: dependability
◆ Cherishing diversity: respect for and inclusion of same and different
◆ Sharing control and decision making
◆ Promoting problem solving and choices
◆ Sharing resources and helping

One day a number of years ago at Cal State Fullerton Children's Center, the four year olds ran outside for their usual play time. They discovered their teacher in distress talking to a groundskeeper from the university who had been told to cut down the liquid amber tree by the back door. The tree was much valued for its shade, leaves which turned a beautiful yellow in the fall, and as the pet chicken's evening roost. The four year olds stopped in their tracks upon seeing the electric saw which the groundskeeper held and demanded to know what was going on. Upon hearing the problem, they all spoke at once telling the now also distressed groundskeeper why he must not cut down the tree. With 20 four year olds and their teacher giving reasons such as "the chicken will have nowhere to sleep," the astounded grounds-keeper said he would discuss the problem with his boss. He told the children the name of his boss so that they could "write" a letter to him. The teacher took dictation from the children and the letter was sent. To this day, the liquid amber tree still lives at the Children's Center.

In what ways had the teacher been working all year to enhance the children's ability to speak out — to make their voices heard? Clearly the seven areas presented above were significant. The children's identities as members of the community permitted them to speak up with confidence; they knew they had to take responsibility for the safety of the tree. It wasn't someone else's job — they were there at that time.

They trusted their own ability in the process of taking action. The children had many experiences with inclusion and fairness for all; therefore, saving the tree for the chicken seemed only natural. It never occurred to the children that they did not have the power to stand up to the groundskeeper in the face of an injustice — shared power had been practiced all year. The children were obviously adept problem solvers: they wrote a letter to the boss. And they certainly understood the need to share our resources. Children who can speak out for justice will become adults who can use democratic practice to make our world a better place for all to live.

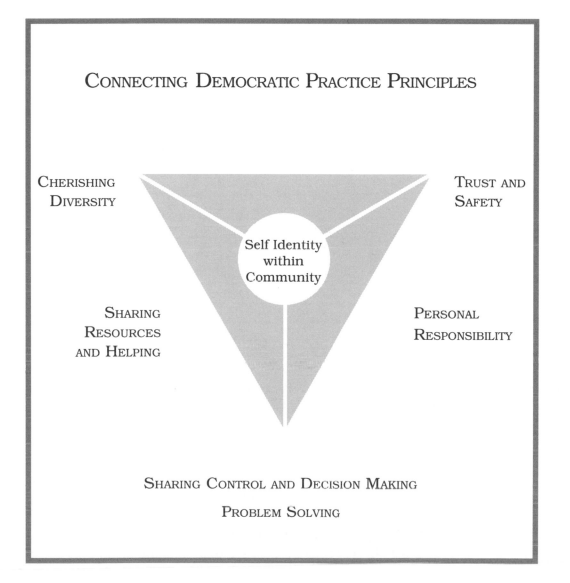

CONNECTING DEMOCRATIC PRACTICE PRINCIPLES

CHERISHING DIVERSITY

TRUST AND SAFETY

Self Identity within Community

SHARING RESOURCES AND HELPING

PERSONAL RESPONSIBILITY

SHARING CONTROL AND DECISION MAKING

PROBLEM SOLVING

Following are the seven principles, each defined with a story explanation.

Developing Self Identity within the Community

Self esteem has been defined by the California State Task Force on Self Esteem as:

"Appreciating my own worth and importance, and having the character to be accountable for myself, and to act responsibly towards others."

"You Can Ask Us!"
by Janice Sheffield

In our classroom at California State University Fullerton Children's Center, the children select jobs to do each day. One job is for a child to open and hold the door for everyone when it's time to come inside from the play yard. I, the teacher, can never remember who opens the door for the day. So I asked the children to please help me. "Today Jason is going to open the door. Let's all say, 'Jason.' Now, when I ask, 'Who is the door opener?' what do you say?" The children knew and responded enthusiastically, "Jason!" The children are great helpers. But to top it off, the other day we had a new university student intern join our class. We said his name several times to help everyone remember. We have discovered that the children will talk more to a new person if they know his or her name, so it is really important for us to remember. I asked the children, "What if I forget his name? What could I do?" (I was expecting an answer such as "You could ask him his name.") Instead, as if someone was holding a cue card, four or five children said in unison, "You can ask us!" (Of course!)

"Wyatt Fix It"
by Cathy Higa

It was the beginning of the semester and the two year olds at California State University Fullerton Children's Center were gathered by

our enclosed tortoise pen. One of our tortoises has only three legs, as the result of an infection years ago. This tortoise walks in a much more slow, elaborate stride.

Wyatt was watching the tortoises, when he suddenly left and ran towards the sand pit. He ran back with a small stick. "Wyatt fix it," he said, as he came to the edge of the pen. He threw the stick towards the three legged tortoise and then ran back to the play yard. This time he picked up some dirt, returned to the pen, and threw it near the tortoise, once again saying, "Wyatt fix it."

After observing this, I made a comment, "Wyatt, it sounds like you want to fix something." He said, "The turtle has five, six, seven legs!" I responded, "Let's count them." We counted to three, pointing to each leg. "Oh," replied Wyatt. Then I told Wyatt about how the tortoise had a sore on his leg and the doctor needed to take his leg off so the tortoise could be healthy again. Raven, who was nearby and had heard this story before said, "But he is happy. He can walk." Wyatt replied, "Yeah, he can eat too!" He then added, pointing to the other tortoises in the pen, "That's the mom, that's the daddy, and that's me, Wyatt!" as he pointed to the three legged tortoise.

This story is especially precious to me as Wyatt is the third of five children in his family. He loves to help. I think that young children who feel capable are do-ers and that they internalize the world which is around them. We, as teachers and parents, are so fortunate to be able to view their delicate understanding of their environment. By thoughtfully listening and watching, without intruding, we can share their world.

"What Are You Good At?"

Tom Hunter, storyteller and songwriter, tells about talking with children and grownups about what they are good at. Tom says, "We all need to pay attention to the things which nourish us — the things we're good at." Some of the responses to his question — "What are you good at?"— (from children and grownups) include:

"I'm good at purple."

"I'm good at applesauce."

"I'm good at sadness." The grownup who shared this one said that she had had a lot of sadness in her life; therefore, she was really good at helping children who are feeling sad. She could really listen to them *with empathy; she could really hear their feelings, and then help them move on as needed.*

Establishing Safety and Trust

For people — including children — to develop trust, there must be an environment of safety and respect. These two foundation pieces are so basic to trust that they must be kept foremost in our thinking at all times as we interact with people. In thinking about an environment in which children and adults will be spending significant time together, it is helpful to have a discussion which includes everyone involved to establish ways to have a safe and respectful time with each other.

Two questions to ask about how we want our home, class, or camp to be are: "What will I see?" and "What will I hear?" What actions and words will promote trust in each other as we go about the daily business of living together?

Trust is central to being able to work and play together. As adults who are responsible for the best possible development of young children, it is critical that we focus our attention on the children's concerns around safety and trust.

The following story tells how a sensitive teacher supported a very young child, as well as his friends, in the process of creating an environment in which he could feel safe and therefore able to trust.

Persona Dolls
by LuAnne Venham

Jenny and Jeff are special dolls who live in LuAnne's infant/toddler classroom at the Orange Coast College Early Childhood Lab School. LuAnne made the dolls when her children were young and Cabbage Patch Dolls were very popular. She brought them to school to help the children listen to stories about each doll's hurts, joys, conflicts, and successes in order to learn more about similarities and differences within all of us.

Each doll is like a classmate; they come to the snack table every day. Jenny has a new baby brother, just like several of the children in the classroom. Jeff cries when his mom leaves him at school, and sometimes he sits near the door with his blanket.

LuAnne experiments by sharing Jeff and Jenny's stories with the children, and the results are very interesting. Here are a few highlights:

It is Hunter's third day of school. During the first two days, he spends most of his time near the door with his blanket over his head. On the third day, Hunter is crying in the block area when Jordan comes over and starts rubbing Hunter's back; Mitchell stands by the puzzle area watching with a look of concern.

LuAnne brings Jeff over to the group and says, "Jeff is so sad! It's his first day of school and he's missing his mom." (Suddenly, Hunter starts to cry really hard and LuAnne wonders if she has made a BIG mistake!) She continues, "Jeff brought his blanket from home, just like Hunter has his Mickey Mouse. Jeff likes to sit by the door, just like Hunter."

Hunter stops crying, Jordan fondles Jeff's blanket, and they all just look at Jeff for awhile. LuAnne sets Jeff on the file cabinet next to the door and says, "I'm putting Jeff here so he can watch the door." As soon as she returns, Hunter moves over to the garage and cars, and begins playing. Jordan plays alongside him.

It seems that Hunter found comfort in Jeff's feelings and similar experiences. With Jeff at the door watching for the mommies, did Hunter feel free to stop watching and begin playing?

On another day, Hailey seems to create her own persona doll. She brings a doll from the pretend area to LuAnne, stating, "She's afraid."

When LuAnne asks what the doll is afraid of, Hailey answers, "I don't know."

LuAnne asks, "Are YOU ever afraid?"

"No, never," Hailey answers.

But as for Dolly, Hailey says, "She's afraid of the giant." Hailey goes on to describe the giant in great detail, including the marks on his face, his size, and his clothing. "But he's FRIENDLY," Hailey says.

LuAnne asks if they should tell Dolly she doesn't have to be afraid of the giant. "Yes!" Hailey says.

LuAnne holds Dolly, looks her in the eye, and says, "Dolly, you don't have to be afraid of the giant, he's friendly." Several times throughout the rest of the day, Hailey brings Dolly back for the same reassurance.

When LuAnne shares the story with Hailey's mom at pick-up time, she learns that Hailey has been having trouble going to sleep at night. Is there a giant she's been seeing and thinking about, wondering if he's friendly or not? Although it's hard to know for sure, it seems plausible.

The Persona Dolls present an interesting way of talking about feelings and experiences with the children. From the very first day when Jenny brought animal crackers to school for her birthday snack, the children have seemed to welcome Jeff and Jenny into the classroom community without question.

Taking Responsibility for Our Own Actions: Dependability

People who participate effectively in a democracy take responsibility for themselves and their actions. They understand that it is not up to someone else to solve their problem, to advocate for justice, or to make change. They understand that they are responsible for making their own choices, and for the consequences of those choices. From the time children are tiny, they can learn to take responsibility. They can speak up. They can help with simple family jobs which need to be done. They can learn to be a dependable member of the family and/or classroom community. They can make choices which have been carefully framed by the adults to be manageable and acceptable. They can learn to solve problems — and they can learn to discern whose problem it is. As they get a little older, they can participate in family and classroom discussions which plan, carry out, and evaluate the work of the group.

Karel Kilimnik's class of first graders from Mary McLeod Bethune School in the northwest area of Philadelphia learn to take responsibility by helping with the classroom tasks. The children do not generally need to be reminded after the first few weeks of school and they do the work with obvious pride in their contributions. When visitors come, the

*children graciously welcome them, show them their classroom, bring
them chairs to sit on, and invite them to go along on excursions to the
school office. These children clearly love to be helpers; they take
pride in their dependability. Their pictures of how they like to help are
included later in this work as a book on helping in the section about
"Children's Issues."*

Cherishing Diversity: Respect for and Inclusion of Same and Different

Inclusion involves deepening our awareness of the value
of many different cultures, perspectives, ideas, ways of living
our lives, and much, much more. Inclusion means both really
opening ourselves up to "hear" unique perspectives, as well as finding the "common ground" we share. The ways we communicate
play a big role in how our perspectives are shared, and they may
vary considerably depending on our ethnic, cultural, and other
unique histories. By coming together to share of ourselves and to
hear each other, we can learn how to trust one another.

*At the Fullerton Peace Camp in California, an activity to develop
people's awareness of inclusion was incorporated into the overall camp
theme of advocacy. The children, ages five through eleven, were given
instructions that collages were going to be made using pictures from
magazines which were to represent different kinds of people. The
collage would show the wide diversity of people. The children were
looking for pictures of people of color, older people, people differently
abled, and so on. However, they were getting very discouraged by the
lack of representation other than people of the dominant culture. As
frustration grew, the teacher focused a discussion first on their feelings,
then on their concerns, and finally moved it on to what the children
would like to do about their concerns.*

*Joseph, an 11 year old of Hispanic background, suggested
writing letters to the magazines. In his letter, he wrote: "I think you
should include more pictures of people of color in your magazine.
When you don't show people who are different, it makes you look
prejudiced."*

Sharing Control and Decision Making

One of the most difficult things in the world for grownups to do is to share control with children. What are the issues around sharing power and authority? What are the perimeters of responsibility when it comes to sharing control? Issues of trust, power, responsibility, and who is in charge all can get in the way of giving children appropriate opportunities to make decisions. Children need lots of practice to learn to make good decisions; they need guidance and support from those more experienced. They need to be able to take risks — even to fail at times. They will make mistakes, hopefully not big ones. They need affirmation to feel they can bounce back and try again, and they need to be able to learn from the experience.

The story below, about decision making, looks at different ways decisions may be made. Children can learn early that there may well be more than one way to do something — looking at options and choices is part of decision making and problem solving.

At the Peace Camp in Kingsville, Texas, the children were offered a challenge to name one of the Persona Dolls who was brand new. After an introduction, they were asked, "Who has an idea for a name for our new doll?" They called out lots of names and these were placed on a long list for consideration. The children were asked how to select a name from the list, but no one had an idea. They were asked to think about the problem of how to select the name and then to discuss it later.

After awhile, Joseph, age ten, asked one of the teachers which name had been chosen. She explained that no name had yet been chosen because it wasn't up to the teachers to figure out which was the best one. That was the job of the whole group. Joseph was a little surprised, probably because he was used to the grownups making most of the decisions. But then he said he had an idea for how the name could be decided. He suggested that it could be voted upon. The teacher affirmed that indeed it could, but also commented that voting doesn't always work out well to select the best choice because it just shows what some people want, but leaves out all the others. In this case, with so many beautiful names suggested, most people's ideas would be rejected and people could feel hurt that most people didn't like their ideas. Joseph considered this thought and said that wouldn't be good.

Then he asked, "If each child put a sticker next to their favorite name, would that be the same as voting?" The teacher asked him what he thought, and he decided it would be.

He was quiet for a few minutes and then said, "Now I've got an idea — how about if we put all the name ideas from the list into a hat and someone can draw out a name to be the one — that's not voting." The teacher agreed and said the new idea could be discussed with the group at the next meeting.

Later in the day, Joseph's idea was brought to the group as a way to decide which of the many names could be the one. The children thought it was a good plan and someone suggested that they use one of the Peace Hats which had been made that day to put the names into. One of the dads who was assisting was asked to draw out the name. In the end, while only one name could be chosen, the children did seem to feel that the selection process was fair. No one felt hurt. They showed respect for Joseph's idea, and they worked with the process of decision making which resulted in compromise.

Promoting Problem Solving and Choices

"How you live your life amounts to how you solve problems." This challenging thought is an opportunity for creative growth. Life is full of choices and problems. Our attitude towards them may be one of discouragement or optimism. It's our choice!

When young children are challenged early on to become problem solvers, they also become empowered to take charge of choices in their lives, hopefully within reason. When the adults who care for them carefully consider how children learn to make choices and offer only those options which are acceptable under the circumstances, children will experience success in their work as choice makers. When they can make choices successfully and speak out for their choices, they become empowered to live productively in a democratic society.

Problem solving includes verbalizing, identifying whose problem it is, articulating needs, creative thinking, and making choices. These skills take lots and lots and lots of practice, and children need many opportunities for such work. It's important that we consider problem solving a major component of the work we do with children, and recognize the opportunities we have to encourage their growth in this important life skill.

As adults, we have a significant role to play as facilitators — but foremost in our minds must be that the role we play is NOT that of the problem solver. After all, whose problem is it when two children want the same bike at the same time? Our role is to facilitate the problem solving process in an atmosphere in which everyone feels safe and respected. Our job is to help people calm down if necessary, to support the listening to each other, and to facilitate moving through the process of working toward a solution, as needed. It is helpful to remember that sometimes it is not necessary to resolve a problem; it may be enough to simply "hear it out" — to listen reflectively and to affirm the speakers. Feelings shared and really heard by the listeners are powerful communicators. Hearing the worries and concerns of another and affirming their importance may be all that is needed to bring resolution to the issue for the people concerned.

This Peace Camp story shares the role of the adult as facilitator, and the negotiation skills of the children involved, ages five to ten, which did lead to the resolution of the problem. The children's feelings were heard, respected, and acted upon in the work done by the group.

"Visit to the Mountain or the Tree?"
Peace Camp, Fullerton, California
by Rheta L. Negrete-Karwin

"We're going to be explorers! We're going to check out this place called the Arboretum." Their eyes grew wide with anticipation. It was our small group exploration time, and we had plans!

"I'm looking for hidden treasures!" announced a child holding his bag tight in his hand, his eyes fixed on the path.

"I want to show you the big mountain, you'll love it there," declared another child as he led the group up a path none of us had seen before.

It was our fourth day at Peace Camp and we thought we had seen it all, so to me the possibility of finding a new place was intriguing.

"No! I want to go this way!" a child called out.

"But you'll love the top of the mountain; come on," the first child explained. The group stopped walking. The two children in conflict faced me as if to find a solution to their problem.

Being certain they could work through this issue together, I said, "You both have different ideas!"

Looking back at each other, they began to talk it through. "There's lots of neat stuff up there; you'll find lots of treasures!"

"But I'm not looking for treasures; I want to go to the big tree because today is my last day of camp and I want to go there." She forces back the tears and continues, "You can go to the top of the mountain tomorrow, but I can't!" A moment of contemplation for both children.

"Yeah, but I've been looking all week to find this mountain!" They both stand staring at each other as if to find the right words. "Come on, let's go," he says convincingly and tugs on her hand in an attempt to guide her up the hill. She pulls away, standing firm in her position. "Come on, it's really neat!" He looks at the group as he takes a step on the path toward the mountain, his forehead wrinkled as if asking for help. The group stands still and watches him as he inches away. Then he stops moving.

A third child sighs, saying, "I'm hot; let's go!"

"Where to?" another child asks.

The child who is hot turns to me, asking, "Can we go to the mountain AND the tree?"

Our mountain climber hops over to me, saying, "Yeah, we could do both!" looking at me in anticipation. Concerned for time, I hesitate looking down at my watch.

The children's excitement rings in their voices, "Yeah, let's go to both! That's a very good idea!"

I think to myself how I can tell them, after all this hard work, that I don't think we have enough time to do both. Of course, my thoughts are moving faster than my words and they grow impatient with my hesitation, as well as fearing the worst in my response. "Well, let me tell you what I'm thinking. We have 15 minutes until it's time to be back with the group for snack. I don't know if that's enough time to do both the mountain and the tree."

"We could hurry! The mountain is just up this hill, really, it's not far!" declares our mountain climber.

"And the tree is on the way to the snack!" adds our friend whose last day it is. The group agreed that we would hurry and off we went up the mountain, and then on over to the tree.

In the story *Visit to the Mountain or the Tree?*, it is worth taking note that the original framing of the problem was in terms of either/or thinking. It took a child's creativity to reframe it in terms of *both/and* thinking. Whenever we can frame problems and choices as *both/and*, not *either/or*, we can break out of the box and think in terms of many more options and compromise. So often we face paradoxes and think we must do this thing or that thing; a shift in the way we look at problems to find the *both/and* solutions may work out to satisfy everyone.

Sharing Resources and Helping

Sharing and helping may be considered to be intertwined because helping is a way of sharing yourself. Young children cannot be expected to "share" in the same ways as do older children and adults. They simply do not yet have a sophisticated understanding of other people's needs and perspectives. For example, their earliest efforts at making friends are usually very awkward, and may even appear to be "aggressive" to the distress of many adults. We can provide support to learn how people like to be approached, and how they like to be treated. Taking turns with a friend is a useful strategy to introduce to young children who want to make friends, who want to connect to others. The practice of taking turns playing with an object may be facilitated by an adult and set in an atmosphere of enjoying each other. Making friends is a complex process which goes on throughout our lives.

"Helping" is another way that young children can learn to interact with others in positive ways. Doing a useful task together connects people and gives them something in common. Sometimes there are choices and problems to be worked through which can also bring people together. Providing ways that young children can help with useful work is very important in supporting them in the business of making friends, of sharing themselves and being included.

Friendships
by Janice Sheffield

School at Cal State Fullerton Children's Center was in the fourth week and the four year olds have a new friend joining our classroom group. Westley was very quiet, and seemed a bit afraid of all the new faces and the environment. Of course, we were a noisy bunch of four year olds and it does take awhile to get used to us. I thought we were making some headway; he seemed to be opening up and relaxing a bit. Yes, a wee bit of a smile did I see at group time. Then, at lunch time, Westley spilled his milk and his neighbor's at the same time. He got a terrified look on his face and I felt certain he was going back into his shell. I quickly tried to reassure him that spills happen at school and we just clean them up. But, before I could say another word, Jason found two cloths and was handing one to Westley. "Here, I'll help you." A friendship was formed!

Another time, I had a cooking project for a small group. I could only find six cutting boards; and, as often happens, seven children wanted to participate. I told the children I had a problem . . . I had hunted and hunted, but could only find six cutting boards. We have seven children and only six cutting boards. Before I could say another word, Leilani said, "Oh, Crystal and I can share one!" They put the cutting board between them and each one used an end. Leilani got finished slicing her apple first, and then waited for Crystal to finish. Together they picked up the cutting board and scraped the sliced apples into the bowl of water. Then they looked at each other and said with smiles, "Let's do that again! Jan, can we have another apple?"

And, to summarize the basis for our principles, a wonderful Joanne Hammil song about affirmation follows.

My Own Way

by Joanne Olshansky Hammil
© 1993 JHO Music

I'm gonna walk in my own way
I'm gonna walk in my own way
I'm gonna walk in my own way
I've got a lot to say in my own way

I'm gonna live (gonna live) in my own way
I'm gonna live (gonna live) in my own way
I'm gonna live (gonna live) in my own way
I've got a lot to say in my own way (in my own way)

I'm gonna trust . . . etc.

I'm gonna dream . . . etc.

I'm growin' strong . . . etc.

You walk your way, I'll walk mine,
I'd like to try walkin' with you sometimes;
You put that in, I'll put this in,
With all of our voices the world's gonna listen!
(world's gonna listen! world's gonna listen!)

I'm gonna sing (in my own way)
I'm growin' strong (in my own way)
I'm gonna dream (in my own way)
I'm gonna trust (in my own way)
I'm gonna live (In my on way)
I'm gonna walk in my own way!

◆ ◆ ◆

"My Own Way" can be heard on *The World's Gonna Listen!*
available as Cassette, CD, and Songbook from
JHO Music, 70 Capitol Street, Watertown, MA 02472 • (800) 557-7010

My Own Way

Words and Music by
Joanne Olshansky Hammil

1. I'm gon-na walk in my own way _ I'm gon-na

walk in my own way _ I'm gon-na walk in my own way _

I've got a-lot to say _ in my own way _ 2. I'm gon-na

Hearing Everyone's Voice

My Own Way

My Own Way

III. Convergences and Connections Between the Democratic Principles, and Goals of Peace Education and Anti-Bias Education

In 1984, Rosmarie Greiner and the Resource Center for Non Violence in Santa Cruz, California, published *Peace Education: A Bibliography Focusing on Young Children*. Each of the six sections of the bibliography includes a short description of the topic and its relevance to our work with young children in peace education. This work, started by Rosmarie, became the foundation upon which Concerned Educators for a Safe Environment (CEASE) created the peace education manual *Discover the World: Empowering Young Children to Care for Themselves, Others, and the Earth*, published by New Society Publishers in 1990.

PEACE EDUCATION GOALS
by Rosmarie Greiner

Peace Education: A Bibliography Focusing on Young Children. Used with permission from the Resource Center for Non Violence in Santa Cruz, California.

Peace is living in a cactus reading a book. Terrence, 6

Peace is having a toy,
Peace is feeling joy,
Peace is taking a run,
Peace is having fun,
Peace is feeling free,
Peace is you and me. Darrell, 12

Self Awareness

A positive self image lies at the root of trusting human relationships. Children's self awareness grows tremendously in the early years, the time of recognizing the self as autonomous. Many factors contribute to this process. The most basic is security, a feeling that comes with having had many experiences of being accepted rather than rejected, of feeling safe and nurtured rather than threatened and ignored. Trust is built when a child knows that, no matter what, she is valued and accepted and that, no matter what, adults will set reasonable limits and keep the world safe. From this base, children reach out, acquire skills, and become competent. This learning by doing, if it is to build self confidence and independence, requires unrushed time, room for mistakes, patient adults, and plenty of opportunities to experiment and express feelings. Along with this learning, children can cultivate positive feelings about their sexual and ethnic heritage, thus developing a healthy body image. Altogether, a positive self image brings feelings of trust, competence, and joy and reduces helplessness, apathy, and inability to respond. Furthermore, acceptance and love of self prepare the ground for accepting and loving others.

Peace is love that is passed on from generation to generation.
Clifford, 8

Peace is caring for those around you
Peace is all nations joining hands
Peace is not destroying God's creation
Peace is knowing the meaning of love
Peace will only happen if everyone works together. Silena, 10

Awareness of Others

Consideration of others is a valued characteristic of children and adults in our society. The concern with self, so pronounced in young children, does not exclude a developing concern for others. All along the way, children show high awareness of others and practice empathy and friendly interactions, helping, and caring. First within the family, children experience the pleasures and difficulties of human connectedness. They learn about acceptance, change, and differences as well as special relationships and treasured moments. They discover the benefits of cooperation and mutual helping. Their positive social actions increase with age and exposure to the larger world. Friends, neighbors, people in the wider community enrich their social fabric and bring new opportunities for giving and taking. Concrete noncompetitive adult support of these positive tendencies enhances children's efforts to share and care. Furthermore, children learn that to behave in a friendly way toward others brings friendliness in return. The actual practice of helping brings them a solid sense of competence.

Paper Crane
I will write peace on your wings and you will fly all over the world. Sadako Sasaki, age 12

True peace suggests the triumph of justice and love among men; it reveals the existence of a better world wherein harmony reigns. Dr. Maria Montessori, 1943

Global Awareness

Racial and sexual prejudice and discrimination are forces tearing at the foundation of all nations, profoundly dividing groups everywhere. They are based on misconceptions, fear, and ignorance. Children are continually exposed to these influences. Stereotypes and misconceptions, so prevalent in our media, can be deeply ingrained at an early age. Children's natural ignorance and fear of the unknown make them vulnerable to instillment of dislikes of certain people and nations. The value of reducing and counteracting such negative cultural influences is indisputable. In fact, it is an important aspect of helping children gain a sense of who they are and their place in our multicultural world. As a first step, we must help children to cultivate a positive feeling about their sexual and ethnic heritage. From this base, respect for people from a variety of cultures and races can be built. Children's curiosity and interest in all that's new and different aid greatly in the exploration. Concrete experiences as close to home as possible provide the best learning ground. Hearing different languages, observing different customs, eating unusual foods, listening to stories of far-off places, and traveling across any borders are some ways children can discover that people are similar in many ways and different in others. The understanding that differences bring beauty and richness to one's life starts to grow.

At this point, children can also discover that differences have or are still causing hardship to others. Positive actions and views of adults are crucial here and directly shape children's budding sense of social justice.

Books of other cultures are part of this opening up of the world. They contribute to the world family sense of interdependence so much needed today.

Peace is birds because they hardly ever fight. Allan, 10

Peace is a big circle of people doing each other favors, like scratching someone's back or a cat's neck. But another kind of peace is not war, it's when the whole world is being friendly to each other. This is broken when one nation argues with another. John Morris, 12

Conflict Resolution

The complex web of human interaction inevitably brings along conflicts. Children experience conflicts over needs not met, things taken, attention not given, and clashings of ideas. They also witness conflicts among adults, groups, and nations. In fact, our culture is prone to exhibit many violent patterns in the streets as well as in the media.

Thus feelings of hostility, aggression, fear, and resentment arise. The problem of what to do with these feelings is a difficult one for children as well as adults. Children struggle with ways of getting heard, getting things, and asserting their personalities. Much of this is part of a healthy growing-up process. Learning how to express those feelings in nondamaging ways and learning how to accept what cannot be changed is also part of this process. To successfully develop personal power, recognize unsocial impulses, and gain ability to work things out mutually with others takes much practice. Children at a young age understand that violent solutions carry harmful consequences and that it feels better to redress any harm done to others.

Young children strongly feel good and bad impulses struggling in themselves. Therefore, it is not hard for them to understand that those on the good side have to try to convince those who do not share their views.

To actually work out win-win solutions, compromises, and agreements is the most difficult task. With help from adults, young children will begin to experiment with peaceful conflict resolutions. Positive models, in life and in stories, contribute to their store of non-violent ways of seeing and acting and encourage them to look for new solutions.

Peace is smelling a tree. Carrie, 6

It's a small world. Let's keep it together. Lisa, 10

Love of Nature

The understanding and feeling of connectedness with nature starts at an early age. Children from birth on are naturally intrigued about their environment. Touching, looking, tasting, hearing, and smelling are their ways of scientific discovery. Animals and the out-of-doors especially attract them without fail. To touch a kitten, taste sour grass, and splash in the waves are some of the delights of early childhood. To grow plants, even if only on a windowsill in an apartment, is a favorite activity and teaches about the wonders of transformation.

Responsibility for tending grows out of a garden project and taking care of animals. Participation in recycling efforts gives children a sense of self reliance, competence, and stewardship and teaches about rudimentary environmental concerns. Opportunities to explore the natural environment in all seasons lessens children's fears about the unknown on one hand, and on the other opens up doors to beauty and enjoyment. Encouraging children to respect and enjoy the earth is a way of encouraging respect for all life.

Peace is people talking together with a heart in between them.
                                                    Siri Guru Dev Kaur, 5

Peace is a friendship dance that everyone holds hands in.
                                                    Dana, 9

Imagination

Our complex world requires much creative thinking and imagination to solve problems, whether they are problems of personal relationships, relationships between countries, or technological problems. In our culture, we tend to look at imagination as something extra, something to be tamed or at least reserved for the stage, something to be turned into rational thinking. This view limits us all.

Children naturally rely on their imaginations, especially in their early years. Through interaction with people and materials, they create their original ideas about relationships and scientific concepts. Imaginary friends, elaborate theories about rain and lightning, ever-changing play themes, and original imagination helps them express their experiences and feelings, change unpleasant parts in it, and magically add whatever matches their wishes. Understanding the situation of another being also requires much imagination, especially if the other is perceived as an enemy.

As adults, we can cherish children's intuitive, spontaneous imagination and creative thoughts; we can support them by inferring and judging as little as possible. By providing a great variety of self expressive materials as well as imaginative books and stories, we actively encourage the creative processes so apparent in children.

This emphasis on the creative process teaches children directly that there are many ways of doing things, many ways of looking at something. Of special value are the books without words, since their images foster original stories and thoughts, thus preventing rigid and patterned thinking.

ANTI-BIAS EDUCATION GOALS
Used with permission from Louise Derman-Sparks

In 1992, Louise Derman-Sparks and the ABC Task Force published *Anti-Bias Curriculum* (revised, 1997). The goals for anti-bias perspective, which follow, closely link with the peace education topics which Rosmarie Greiner defined in 1984. The anti-bias goals extend the peace education goals and define inclusion, understanding of bias and stereotypes, critical thinking, and taking action. The anti-bias perspective is critical in peace education work as well as a foundation for promoting democratic practice.

The anti-bias goals are for ALL children. The specific issues and tasks necessary for working towards these goals will vary for children depending on their cultural backgrounds, ages, and life experiences.

■ ONE: Nurture each child's construction of a knowledgeable, confident self identity and group identity.

This goal means creating the educational conditions in which all children are able to like who they are without needing to feel superior to anyone else. It also means enabling children to develop biculturally — to be able to effectively interact within their home culture and within the dominant culture.

■ TWO: Promote each child's comfortable, empathic interaction with people from diverse backgrounds.

This goal means guiding children's development of the cognitive awareness, emotional disposition, and behavioral skills needed to respectfully and effectively learn about differences, comfortably negotiate and adapt to differences, and cognitively understand and emotionally accept the common humanity that all people share.

■ THREE: Foster each child's critical thinking about bias.

This goal means guiding children's development of the cognitive skills to identify "unfair" and "untrue" images (stereotypes), comments, (teasing, name-calling), and behaviors (discrimination) directed at one's own or other's identity (be it gender, race, ethnicity, disability, class, age, weight, etc.) AND having the emotional empathy to know that bias hurts.

■ FOUR: Cultivate each child's ability to stand up for her/himself and for others in the face of bias.

This "activism" goal includes helping every child learn and practice a variety of ways to act: (a) when another child acts in a biased manner towards her/him; (b) when a child acts in a biased manner towards another child; and (c) when an adult acts in a biased manner. Goal Four builds on Goal Three: Critical thinking and empathy are necessary components of acting for oneself or others in the face of bias.

These four goals interact with and build on each other. Their combined intent is to empower children to resist the negative impact of racism on their development and to grow into people who will want and be able to work with others to eliminate all forms of oppression. In other words, the underlying intent is not to end racism in one generation by changing children's attitudes and behaviors but to promote critical thinkers and activists who can work for social change and participate in creating a caring culture in a world of differences.

Anti-Bias Goals and Music
Stories from Musicians

Looking more in depth at the four Anti-Bias Goals, Bonnie Lockhart, musician and songwriter, has shared her unpublished thesis. She has interviewed some children's musicians and related their work to the goals of anti-bias practice. We have selected and adapted portions of her interviews to expand upon the relevance of each goal to the work of creating democratic communities for young children. Artists interviewed by Bonnie include:

Victor Cockburn   Jacki Breger
Fundi   Patricia Shih
Marcia Berman   Alisa Peres

ONE: Nurture each child's construction of a knowledgeable, confident self identity and group identity.

(The parenthetical notations contained in this section refer to the cited reference within Bonnie Lockhart's unpublished thesis.)

The Light of Recognition

Many of the participants told stories about the delight and pride children took in finding themselves — their culture, their language, their traditions — in songs. Victor Cockburn tells this one:

In a kindergarten class, I had a little Japanese song about a rabbit in the moon — rabbit in the moon is a common theme throughout Asian culture. This student, she was Japanese; the song was Japanese. I started to sing it (in Japanese) and she just SAT UP! She was new to this country and she didn't have a lot of English under her belt. But she knew that song. She was the only one in the class who could sing along with it. Whereas the other songs I was singing with her classmates — she just sort of sat there looking around. She'd clap her hands, but she couldn't get the words. But with this song, she was the only one who could sing. It was just the two of us singing this song. And it really affected her classmates and they looked at her a little different after that. "Wow, you know that song?" And then they started to learn from that. Everybody in the class learned (about the rabbit). And it was a very wonderful little moment. (page 70)

Hearing the Child's Voice

Victor also talks about working with children he describes as "students in crisis — where their language skills are very low and their self esteem is very shaky." He tells this story about his process and how he tunes it to the child's need for self esteem:

When I'm going into a school that has, say, a high population of African American students, I might bring songs, blues, maybe poems by Langston Hughes, Maya Angelou, maybe a little Nikki Giovani. But basically to show different voices — to say that it really starts with the oral tradition. I really focus on showing how people talk about the world, and see the world, and complain about the world, and praise the world. (page 76)

Jacki Breger discusses achieving strong affirmation of students' ethnic identity by collaborating with them to rewrite a contemporary song. In preparation for a holiday program, she was teaching Ruth Pelham's "Under One Sky" (a call and response that names a number of nationalities and ethnicities) to a performing group of three third and fourth grade classes.

I thought, let's do it in relation to where their families actually came from. We spent a couple of weeks talking about it. The first day, many of the kids did not know where their families had come from. So, we made it a homework assignment to find out by the following week, when I came again. Out of 90+ students in the group, there were more than 60 countries of origin. And many of them — I'd say a good third — were themselves the immigrant generation. Now you can't have a more relevant multicultural (she states the quote, unquote) lesson than that! We spent weeks on it, with all the talk and practice. There was great joy in the discovery, in the discussions, and of course in the singing. We sang every country, and when the audience answered back it was pretty wonderful! (page 72)

TWO: Promote each child's comfortable, empathic interaction with people from diverse backgrounds.

Countering Stereotypes

The construction of stereotypes facilitates scapegoating and putting down. Several of these musicians argue that music is uniquely powerful in dispelling such stereotypes because it compels the body and emotions as well as the intellect. Fundi put it like this: "Education via music had much more of an impact. Maybe BECAUSE the children were responding on a visceral level and they were participating emotionally and rhythmically." Jacki Breger sees it like this: "The idea of stereotyping — doing the we-they thing, that we are good and they, all the 'theys', are bad — comes from a place of dehumanizing those 'other' people. If you don't think of those 'other' people as human beings with the same feelings you have, you can inflict any

Hearing Everyone's Voice

kind of pain and suffering on them. But the minute you begin to see those 'other' people as a mom who has kids, and a child who's afraid of the dark like you're afraid of the dark, you can no longer treat them quite as separately from yourself as you might have otherwise. I think that music really helps to make that connection because it offers a powerful emotional link to the world of other people.   It (authentic folk music from the lives of real people) is so valuable because it helps you understand those people and their culture from the point of view of that culture. You can talk about the statistics of famine and say, 'Too bad.' But when you sing a song sung by hungry people, you might begin to feel a little hungry. It makes all the difference!" (page 78)

Some Stories from Classrooms and Camps

Musicians talked about using songs to help children develop empathy and understanding for people different from themselves. Sometimes they spoke of contemporary songs that deal with diversity, prejudice, and inclusion. Patricia Shih speaks of a song she recorded, "Courage" by Bob Blue, whom she describes as "one of the best songwriters in the world." "Courage" is sung in the persona of a junior high girl who comes to understand the connection between her excluding Diane ("she's strange, like she doesn't belong, we don't like to be with her") and "what people have done, with gas chamber, bomber, and gun at Auschwitz, Japan, and My Lai." (page 86) "Courage" is included in this manual in the section on "Children's Issues."

Marcia Berman remembers the many songs, traditional and contemporary, that built cultural bridges for the kids she sang with in Peace Camp during the 1980's — "Paz Y Libertad," "May There Always Be Sunshine," "Hine Matov," "This Little Light of Mine." She has a vivid memory of how the meaning of one song grew out of interactions in the camp: "The kids would bring snack and we'd put all our snacks together. And somebody brought grapes and we put that out on the table. One of the little six year olds was complaining because of the grape boycott — he knew from his family that we shouldn't be eating grapes. So we had to get into that and talking about the farm workers and 'What about that?' It became a wonderful discussion. And then all the songs you can connect up, 'De Colores,' the favorite song of the farm workers. And then any songs about growing food became important and related to that."

Victor talks about making similar connections. "You can say, 'Now let's talk about a song like 'De Colores.' It's a really pretty song in Spanish, but it's also the anthem of the United Farm Workers.' 'Oh, what's that?' 'Well, how many of you have an apple today, how many of you ate an orange? Where did it come from, other than the supermarket? It had to get there.' You know, it opens up other issues. You can talk about immigration, about workers, farm workers, talk about civil rights, through songs. Just open up the world a little more." (page 80)

THREE: Foster each child's critical thinking about bias.

Real, Meaty Issues

Patricia Shih articulates an assumption that seems to underlie the work of all the participants (in this project). "You can use music as a tool for social change, especially with children. They can be taught — through many means, music is just one of them — about tolerance and differences, about the world, and issues, real, meaty issues. You get pretty heavy issues like racism and homelessness and peace and things like that with kids pretty easily through music. It's important to feed our children nourishing culture, not just the empty junk food culture, not just the pop pap."

As she reflects on the importance of choosing songs that "never talk down to kids," Patricia recalls a small incident that illustrates how children's lives are so routinely trivialized.

As an aside, I was waiting and this ice cream truck went by playing the most inane tune. There were no words or anything, but it was just, "OK, this is a children's song." It was just this little "nee, nee-nee, nee nee" (she chants a sing-song melody and laughs). I guess that's what people think when they think of children's music.

Alisa Peres also talks about the importance of "songs that are about real stuff." She begins to describe such songs as "political,"

but opts for the description "reality oriented material." She reflects that "there's something very powerful about sharing folklore," but that such power "gets to the content of the songs." She elaborates on this point by telling about a song from Ecuador. "It's about a girl that's poor, and she has to wash other people's clothes. So we talk with kids about that. There are no washing machines — so (we talk about) where she has to go (to do the laundry) and so on. I'm really glad we do that song and I really hope that kids think about that — that not everybody has a washing machine, not everybody gets to go to school. Music is a good way to do that." (page 88)

FOUR: Cultivate each child's ability to stand up for her/himself and for others in the face of bias.

"The Power of Songs Can't Be Taken for Granted"

Many of the participants spoke of the power of songs and of group singing to inspire conviction, courage, and action for change. Victor argues that the act of finding one's own voice in song and poetry is a kind of empowerment in itself. "I'm very focused on the importance of language — as a vehicle for expressing yourself and for changing situations that you don't like to see happen. Changing your environment or changing your personal situation." He tells a story to illustrate the far-reaching consequence of the creative work of song writing. A group of his students some years ago collaborated to write a song, "Hunger," which he liked a great deal. Some time after that writing, Victor had the opportunity to sing the song for Pete Seeger, who shared Victor's enthusiasm for the students' composition and sang it publicly. Aside from being what Victor laughingly refers to as "the fulfilling moment of my life," this musical exchange made a story that Victor now tells to his students to persuade them that creative acts may have impact beyond our immediate circumstances. "The power of songs can't be taken for granted. Write something from your heart and it will spread like ripples to other people, inspiring others and creating a change in the world." (page 99)

Marcia Berman talks about the impact of her work on cultural consciousness and social change. Her understanding of that impact has developed over time: "In the beginning, I hoped that people would want to know more and more about the culture (from which the songs came) and that it would somehow bring good feeling toward people. Somehow I thought I had gotten it that way so I thought that maybe that's the way people get it. Now I think I realize it's gonna take a lot more — living with people who have differences, living with people who come from different cultures day in and day out, with much more exposure, is part of it. You can't just learn one Japanese song and then you understand what happened during the war, and Manzanar, and all those things. I mean that's just not going to happen with learning one Japanese dance and one Japanese song. It's gotta be more than that. At the time (in her early days as a singer of international folk song), I think I probably felt good about what I was doing. Maybe I hadn't really thought it through — I was just doing it. I was going in a direction." (page 101)

Part of that direction led Marcia to become a co-founder of Peace Camp. Here Marcia was not only the music specialist, but part of a team with a shared philosophy. Central to the camp project was "the experience of getting to know people from diverse communities. We knew that it was going to take more than songs. We had to get the children involved at their level where they could really experience what it's like to stand up and speak for yourself, integrating the music into it. Or if there was a situation where we could tie in, where something was not just and the children could understand it, and we could devote ourselves to doing something about it."

Marcia's vision for integrating songs, ideas, and action for social change hearkens back to her memories of being a camper during her own pre-teen and early teen years, in the 1940s:

We used to swim in this lake. And we had an African-American woman who helped with the cooking at the camp. And this woman was not permitted to go into the lake. And so, none of us went in the lake. That was our activity; and everyday we picketed that lake. That was a great education. It was real work and responsibility. (page 102)

Charting the Goals:

Peace Education, The Anti-Bias Perspective, and Democratic Practice

The time is right to look at ways to define and promote appropriate democratic processes in our work with young children. When we think about the developmental needs of children and how best to prepare them to live effectively in a democracy, the connections among peace education, the anti-bias perspective, and democratic practice must be integrated. The overlap and connections are apparent as shown in the following chart. The chart connects the goals of education for peace, anti-bias perspective, and democratic practice in developmentally appropriate ways for young children. The chart should be read across as well as down.

PEACE EDUCATION	ANTI-BIAS PERSPECTIVE	DEMOCRATIC PRACTICE
Self Awareness	Identity: One's Self and Group	Self Identity and Responsibility
Awareness of Others	Groups: Similarities and Differences	Trust and Safety
Cultural Understanding	Awareness of Bias and Stereotypes	Cherishing Diversity
Conflict Management	Empathic Relationships	Shared Power and Decision Making
Creative Thinking	Action/Advocacy/ Critical Thinking	Problem-Solving and Choices
Love of Nature	Action/Advocacy	Shared Resources

Linking Peace, Anti-Bias and Democratic Practice Through Music

Four songs follow which express the writers' thoughts about the relationships of peace, harmony, and the interconnectedness of us all. They bring together all the goals and principles of peace education, anti-bias, and democratic practice.

"Under One Sky" by Ruth Pelham

"The Color Song" by Patricia Shih

"Dreams of Harmony" by Joanne Olshansky Hammil

"Circle the Earth (with Peace)" by Joanne Olshansky Hammil

Under One Sky

Words and Music by
Ruth Pelham

CHORUS

2. Well, we're plumbers, we're doctors,
   We're farmers and teachers, too. (Repeat)
   CHORUS

3. We're lions, we're elephants,
   We're puppies and kangaroos. (Repeat)
   CHORUS

4. Well, we're daisies, we're tulips,
   We're roses, chrysanthemums. (Repeat)
   CHORUS

5. Well, we're Americans, we're Russians,
   We're Italians, and Vietnamese.
   We're Israelis, we're Irish,
   We're Africans, and we're Chinese.
   CHORUS

Note: Where teacher or leader wishes to use the song with the "echo effect" the song
      may be sung by the leader or by one section of the class with the "echo" s
      ingers coming in at the appropriate points. Example, Verse 1:
      1. Well, we're people (people), we're animals (animals),
         We're flowers (flowers), we're birds in flight
                                  (birds in flight), (Repeat)

◆ ◆ ◆

THE COLOR SONG

c 1984 Patricia Shih
Fragile Glass Music Publishing, BMI

Verse: Why do they call you yellow man? You're not yellow at all

Yellow is the color of the morning sun and dande - lions and chicken soup and

legal pads and fearful minds Yes

Yellow is the color of all these things But people are not the same

You re - mind me of the Gold- en Rule when - e - ver I say your name - O

Bumbumbumbumbumbum...

Why do they call you red man? You're not red at all
Red is the color of the climbing rose and traffic lights and
  tomatoes and chicken pox and bloody nose and
Angry words
Yes, red is the color of all these things
But people are not the same
I can see the rosy future whenever I say your name-O

Why do they call you black man? You're not black at all
Black is the color of light not there and Daddy's shoes and
  Mommy's hair and bowling balls and question marks and
Blind despair
Yes, black is the color of all these things
But people are not the same
I have had the deepest thoughts whenever I say your name-O

Why do they call you white man? You're not white at all
White is the color of the petticoats and Elmer's glue and
  billy goats and falling snow and
Burning shame
Yes, white is the color of all these things
But people are not the same
I can see the clearest light whenever I say your name-O

So what do you call your fellow man if color doesn't matter at all?
Anything! So long it's in the name of love and forgiveness and
  hopefulness and lasting peace and dignity and
Brotherhood (sisterhood too!)
For many are the colors of all these things
But people are all the same
We're each other's brothers and sisters and we all have one name-O

Dreams of Harmony
by Joanne Olshansky Hammil
© 1988 JHO Music

The languages in this song are English, French, Japanese,
Spanish, Swahili, Chinese, Russian, German and Hebrew.
One world full of harmonies from all our glorious differences — that's my dream.

Goodnight, bonne nuit, oyasuminasai,

Buenas noches, lala salama, wan an,

Spokoinyu noche, gutte nacht, lila tov.

Wherever you rest your head tonight —

We are all one family, let's hold tight

And fill the world with dreams of harmony tonight!

◆　◆　◆

Dreams of Harmony

Words and Music by
Joanne Olshansky Hammil

Hearing Everyone's Voice

Dreams of Harmony

Dreams of Harmony

no – ches, la – la sa – la–ma, wan an, spo – koi–nyu noche, gut–te nacht, li – la

tov. Good – – night.

Circle the Earth (with Peace)
by Joanne Olshansky Hammil
© 1994 JHO Music

Peace, peace, peace,
Peace the whole world over,
Building friendships, sharing our worth, [Building, sharing,]
Take my hand, let's circle the earth with [Take my hand with]
Peace, peace, peace.

Spanish or Portuguese:
Paz, paz, paz,
Paz the whole world over,
Building friendships, sharing our worth, [Building, sharing,]
Take my hand, let's circle the earth with [Take my hand with]
Paz, paz, paz.

Swahili:	Amani	Indian:	Shanti
Hebrew:	Shalom	Greek:	Iri'ni
Japanese:	Heiwa	Italian, Rumanian:	Pace
Arabic:	Salam	Dutch:	Vrede
Chinese:	Ho Pinh	Polish:	Pokoj
German:	Frieden	Hungarian:	Beke
Russian:	Mir	Swedish, Danish, Norwegian:	Fred
Vietnamese:	Hwa Bing	Turkisk:	Sulh
French:	Paix	Indonesian:	Pordamaian
Finnish:	Ruaha	Esperanto:	Paco

◆ ◆ ◆

"Circle the Earth (with Peace)" can be heard on *The World's Gonna Listen!*,
available as Cassette, CD, and Songbook from
JHO Music, 70 Capitol Street, Watertown, MA 02472 • (800) 557-7010

Circle The Earth (With Peace)

Words and Music by
Joanne Olshansky Hammil

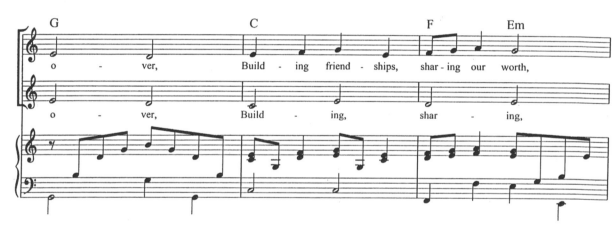

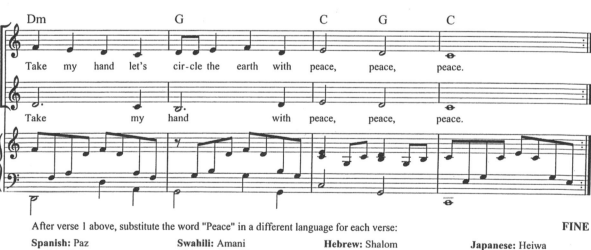

After verse 1 above, substitute the word "Peace" in a different language for each verse:

Spanish: Paz	**Swahili:** Amani	**Hebrew:** Shalom	**Japanese:** Heiwa
Arabic: Salam	**Chinese:** Hou Pien	**Italian:** Pace	**German:** Freiden
Russian: Mir	**Vietnamese:** Hoa Binh	**French:** Paix	**Indian:** Shanti

FINE

Circle The Earth (With Peace)

On the companion recording to this songbook, a native instrument is added on each verse as follows:
Spanish verse - zampoña, Swahili verse - marimba, Hebrew verse - dumbek, Japanese verse - koto.
All instruments join together in end.

IV. Strategies to Build Community Through Democratic Practice

There are a number of strategies which can be implemented at home and at school to promote the goal of developing children's skills in speaking out and participating in a democratic society. Use of these strategies will promote a caring community, that is, inclusion of all members. The power structures in our relationships with each other will be addressed as we explore and practice the seven principles of democratic practice.

The development of the democratic principles discussed previously can be supported through careful thought and planning around the strategies described. The strategies include ways for children and adults to be recognized, listened to, and heard in a variety of ways. When real "hearing" happens, people are affirmed in their own value and worth. *High self esteem and identity within their community* develops.

People who feel valued are more able to *trust*; they feel confident that they can share and be open with others. They feel safe. They trust that their vulnerabilities will not be exploited. Therefore, *taking responsibility* for one's own actions and the risks involved follows naturally.

Cherishing diversity is one of the great pleasures in life if one is comfortable with oneself and can accept that people will be different. Respect, in spite of, and perhaps because of, our differences is essential. Finding common ground is important, but so is valuing diversity of thought, ideas, customs, and even values. Enjoying both our samenesses and our differences gives opportunities for creativity as ideas are shared and explored. By welcoming and including those in our lives who are different, we can grow and develop in ways we never dreamed possible.

Sharing control and authority are basic to practicing inclusion if we are to hear from others, to include others. When the control and power are held by one person or group, others may not have opportunities to bring their unique ideas forward. *Decisions* made with thorough input from others will naturally become broader and deeper in scope. *Choices* will be explored and *problem solving* will have creative input with a variety of ideas. We deserve to hear from each other; we all have so much to offer.

Sharing resources and *respectful helping* of others naturally follow sharing control in the development of caring communities. If we are willing to share power with others, i.e., adults including children in goal setting and problem solving, etc., then it follows that such willingness would also include being willing to offer assistance, aid, and resources for caring about one another. Issues around respectful helping are addressed in several areas of this book, as it is a complex subject.

Stories follow about some of the strategies parents and teachers have used and the success experienced. In most examples, more than one strategy is being used; many are woven together to create the tapestry of learning. And additional strategies are unlimited!

First Steps to Constructing Knowledge

Learning is built upon our previous experience and knowledge. We construct our understandings from compiling many experiences built upon each other. We link them together in our attempts to make sense of the world.

Young children think in terms of the here and now, not the abstract. How can we know what they understand in our complex world? What about the more abstract issues such as justice, peace, and diversity concepts? How can we best make decisions about putting such issues into practice in ways which are appropriate to the development of the children and which meet their needs?

As always, our first step in making decisions about what's best for children's growth is to observe and listen. What are children really saying when they say, "That's not fair!"? When they are problem solving to get their needs met, what strategies are they using? And when they use stereotypical language, what do they really mean? What are they thinking, believing, knowing? Our careful, supportive listening — in nonjudgmental ways — can go a long way to give us the information we need to give children the experiences they need to build upon previous understandings.

The strategies as described in this section build first upon the careful observation and listening by the adults. The adults then support the children in constructing knowledge around their previous experiences. The strategies described here through stories put these complex issues into the framework of development of young children. They define and describe techniques which have worked with children when the adults are in tune with the children's needs and development. They support ways we make decisions about best practices for children.

Teacher Research on Topics of Interest to Children
"What Can You Tell Me About Indians?"

This survey was done to find out what non-native children knew about Indians. The children were all four years old and attended Cal State Fullerton Children's Center. A small group time format was used as the children were used to and comfortable with these intimate discussion times. It was explained to the children that some grownups wanted to know their ideas about Indians and that we would write down their words to send to the grownups. The transcript of the interview questions and the children's responses:

Teacher: *What can you tell me about Indians?*
    They ride horses.
    They wear belts.
    They pat drums.
    They have bows and arrows.
    They play guitar and drums.
    They have guns and they shoot animals.
Teacher: *What kind of animals?*
    Cows, sheep. They wear Indian feathers.
Teacher: *What does an Indian feather look like?*
    It's red, white, and black.
Teacher: *Have you ever seen an Indian?*
    Just on TV. Me too. Me too.
    I see Indians pick up trash and eat corn.
Teacher: *Where could I look to find an Indian?*
    In the forest.

Teacher: The kids thought it silly when I asked them if I might see an Indian in the grocery store or the library.

Teacher: Can an Indian be a fire fighter?

No, because they have to stay Indian and someone might burn their house. No, because fire fighters can't even wear feathers.

(Laughing) No, because!

Indians blow things up.

No, but some live in brick houses.

Teacher: Can they be fire fighters?

No, just can't. They might hurt someone.

Teacher: What do you know about Indians?

Indians live in tents with sticks on top. That's called a tepee.

Indians have brown, yellow, and green coats.

They wear feathers in their hats. They wear headbands.

They make fire.

Indians live in tents.

Indians use bow and arrows.

They eat corn. My mom told me they eat hot dogs too.

They scare people. I saw on Woody Woodpecker they run and catch people.

They have hats — hats with a circle with feathers in back.

Once there was an Indian and he was trying to kill me and I got my sword out.

They dance, they do drums.

They wear Indian hats and they wear feathers.

After the interviews, we realized how much work needed to be done with the children about the stereotypical images they had formed regarding Indians. We gathered photographs of current Native Americans from a wide variety of tribes and nations, as well as those living in urban and reservation settings. The pictures showed people going to school and work, playing, sharing family times, and celebrating together. After three weeks of intensive work on stereotypes such as "scary" and " feathers," the children understood (at some level) that those people with the feathers are either cartoons or preparing for a special ceremony such as the Corn Dance.

Observation and Listening

Throughout all our work with children, it is critical that we observe and listen carefully to hear the messages the children send to us. When they are heard, children are empowered. The affirmation of empowerment leads to further growth and development in speaking out.

Probably there is no other skill more needed in our work with children than real listening. Perceptive listening includes keen observational skills as well. The key to really listening is to be nonjudgmental. Describe, but do not judge. When you are focused on what a person is really saying, and on the feelings behind the words, then you can really hear what is being said. However, when you are trying to figure out what you'll say next, or solve the problem, you'll probably miss the real meaning being expressed. We have so much to learn from one another, please don't miss an opportunity!

Once upon a time, at a Peace Camp in Northern California, there was a young boy who came because his mother wanted him to be there. He was very angry about it, and told us right from the moment he signed in. He went so far as to kick the table where people were gathered to register. One of the perceptive adults calmly took him aside and asked him if he wanted to talk about why he didn't want to be at Peace Camp. He told her that he wanted to stay home. According to him, his mother was always making him go places and he was tired of being "dragged around." The adult listened to his words and affirmed the feelings he expressed. She acknowledged what he was saying and accepted his need to have some say in what he wants to do with his time.

She then asked what he would have liked to do if he could have stayed at home. By now, since he was really feeling listened to, he had calmed down enough to be able to talk and think about something he would like to do. He said he would love to have time to do nothing — maybe to lie under a tree and look at the clouds go by through the leaves. The adult asked him if he thought he could do that at Peace Camp. He looked puzzled, as if getting to do what he wanted was an unusual idea to him. Then he looked at a huge oak tree nearby with its branches and green leaves reaching towards us, and said, "There's a tree for me to lie under to watch the clouds. Can I do that now?" He spent about 20 minutes just

doing what he wanted, then he was willing to join the activities of Peace Camp.

We all deserve to be listened to; we all deserve to be respected. A few moments of listening and respect can often work miracles.

Guidelines for Listening and Observing

Make the time to be involved at a serious level.
Listen for the feelings behind the words.
Be empathetic rather than sympathetic.
Concentrate on the other person's point of view and/or distress.
    Forget yourself for the moment.
Observe nonverbal clues to gain genuine understanding.
Validation of feelings may be all that's needed. Not all problems
    must or can be resolved.
Describe rather than judge.
Avoid the "roadblocks" to opening communication:
    Judging: "You made a mistake."
    Ordering: "Stop crying."
    Admonishing: "You should . . ."
    Using logic: "What you need is . . ."
    Interpreting: "You feel this way because . . ."
    Praising: "Good girl, nice . . ."
    Reassuring: "Don't worry . . ."
    Advising: "I suggest that you . . ."
    Preaching: "When I was your age . . ."

Child Initiated Questions

Our best listening skills are challenged at those moments when children ask us the "hard" questions, or want to talk about things not easy. So often their timing doesn't work into our busy schedules, and they may feel pushed aside when we can't take the time to really open dialogue with them. As this story tells, time in the car is frequently good focused time to listen and share together.

A Story of Courage
by Robin Song

It was a bright summer day. My two daughters, Jane (age eight) and Nancy (age ten), and my younger daughter's friend Rhonda were sitting in the back of our station wagon busy talking while I drove us into San Francisco for a trip to the aquarium. Rhonda was a constant addition to our family and my daughter was a constant addition to Rhonda's family. For weeks, my younger daughter had been talking to me about her need to tell Rhonda that her mother is a lesbian. She did not want to keep secrets from her very best friend, but was worried about how Rhonda would react. We talked about many ways she could tell Rhonda, and exactly what she wanted to say. I suggested that she be clear and direct and simply say, "My mother is a lesbian." And I told her that when and if she wanted to tell her that she would know when it was the right time.

Evidently the time was right on that bright summer day. My hearing was drawn to the back of the car when I heard my daughter say the words, "My mother is a lesbian." My heart skipped several beats waiting for Rhonda's response, which was not long in coming. "Oh, my uncle is gay!" The breath that I had been holding was released on the wind of relief. As I listened, they were deep in discussion about differences. Their conversation was filled with acceptance of those different from themselves. They included those from different cultures, races, those differently abled, and I sat in wonderment at how easy it had been for them.

But it had not been easy for my daughter to take the risk of revealing the truth of her mother's lifestyle. For her to take the step and "come out" as a lesbian's daughter to her best friend had been a great struggle for her. She did not want to keep secrets from her buddy. Her courage was wonderful to see. I was happy that the outcome had been so positive. It has not always been that way for her. It will be a wonderful day when children will not have to blink an eye when telling their friends, "I have two moms" or "I have two dads."

"What Do You Get When You Become a Grownup?"
by Tania Simirenko

One day not long after Christmas, I was driving my daughter Kaitlin over to visit her grandparents. In three months, Kaity would be seven, and she had been growing more and more excited about her upcoming birthday.

Suddenly she turned to me and asked, "What do you get when you become a grownup?"

I was a little stunned. What did she mean? "What do you think you get, Kaity?"

"I don't know, Mom! That's why I asked."

"Oh!" I said, "Do you mean what do you get to do?"

"NO, Mom, what do you get? What tells you how to be a grownup?"

I suddenly understood. After some further discussion, I discovered that not only was Kaity hoping that there was a guidebook with a job description and what the responsibilities were, but she also figured that since it was such a big deal, that there should be a definitive age, a moment in time, that one "grows up," and a suitable celebration to go along with it.

As I think back to my own childhood, I also expected there to be a special day when it was clear that I was a adult. Maybe at 16, or 18, and at those ages, at times, I did think I knew it all. I, too, wanted a party, an exact moment to measure my maturity by, an acknowledgment that I really was all grown up. Through careful listening until I understood Kaity's question for what it really meant, I was able to respond to her with authenticity. We opened a conversation then, long to be continued. I was able to connect her thinking and growth to my own experience in trying to understand this business of becoming a "grownup." We created yet another bond between us.

Joanne Hammil shares a song/playlet which helps us to gain understanding of another person's perspective, an essential skill in "hearing" another person's message.

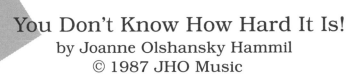

You Don't Know How Hard It Is!
by Joanne Olshansky Hammil
© 1987 JHO Music

playlet and four-part round:

girl: You don't know how hard it is to be told to eat your vegetables for 10 years!
          Well, I do!

father: You don't know how hard it is to feed a child vegetables for 10 years!
          Well, I do!

boy: You don't know how hard it is to be told to go to bed every night for
          10 years! Well, I do!

mother: You don't know how hard it is to put a child to bed every night for 10 years!
          Well, I do!

girl: You don't know how hard it is to be told to clean your messy room for
          10 years! Well, I do!

father: You don't know how hard it is to live with a child and her messy room for
          10 years! Well, I do!

boy: You don't know how hard it is to be told what to do every day of your life
          for 10 years! Well, I do!

mother: You don't know how hard it is to take care of someone else every day for
          10 years! Well, I do!

[sing first two lines in a four-part round, with two children on girl line and two adults
on father line]

ending —
all: You don't know how hard it is to listen to the words you say and understand
          — but we can try.

◆ ◆ ◆

JHO Music, 70 Capitol Street, Watertown, MA 02472 • (800) 557-7010

Meetings

Meetings are very useful strategies for solving problems, making decisions, imparting information, and so on. However, meetings must be structured in such a way that everyone can "have a voice." If one or two people have the control or power, then others will not feel free to express their thoughts. Trust must be built so that maximum participation will generate a variety of ideas. There is a need for someone to chair the meeting simply to bring order. Many groups rotate this job among participants. Following are stories of solving problems, sharing leadership, and imparting information.

Desiree's Bubbles
by Susan Hopkins

A few years ago, in our group of four year olds at the Children's Center, California State University, Fullerton, there was a little girl named Desiree. She had long blond hair, a ready smile, an eagerness to enjoy life, and scars over about 17% of her body. She was the survivor of a fire. Part way through the year, her doctor decided that skin graftings were needed. He tried a then very new technique of helping Desiree grow her own new skin by making two "bubbles" within her skin. These "bubbles" would grow bigger and bigger until such time that grafting could take place.

Desiree's mother explained the situation to the teachers and we decided not to tell the other children until the "bubbles" were obvious because it seemed difficult to imagine what they would look like. What we didn't know was that from one day to the next, Desiree's "bubbles" would enlarge and be very obvious. Naturally the other children were quite distressed when they saw Desiree. We wondered how best to handle the situation and called Desiree's mother for her thoughts. She wanted the children to understand as well as possible, so we talked to Desiree about how to tell the children about her "bubbles." Did she want to tell them, or did she want the teachers to tell them?

As so often happens with children who have been trusted to create their own best solutions, she came up with a third choice. She would tell

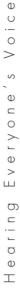

the children at circle time by whispering what she wanted to say into the teacher's ear and then the teacher could repeat it. Everyone sat down and the teacher explained that Desiree would be telling them about her "bubbles." The children were respectful and full of questions as Desiree and the teacher proceeded to jointly communicate to the group . . . but for one statement only! Then Desiree got carried away answering their questions and forgot she "needed" the teacher. Once the children understood what was happening with Desiree, they no longer were distressed and fearful. They wanted to play with her as usual.

When the hospital stay got closer, the teacher brought out the dramatic play props and, together with Desiree and the children, set up a hospital. During class meetings, they jointly planned what was needed in the hospital through discussion and hearing stories about hospital visits. The dramatic play continued all through Desiree's hospital stay and afterwards as she taught the children about her experience. The children communicated with her in the hospital by making get well cards and a book. The teacher telephoned her directly with Desiree's mother's help. Through the involvement of the teacher and the children, with the mother's support, the experience Desiree had was a growing, learning, empowering time for her and all the children in her class.

Looking back, the important aspect of this experience is clearly the need for the children and adults to understand difficult situations as best they can. Knowledge is critical in dealing with fear. Once the children had the opportunity to learn and understand what was happening to Desiree, they were no longer afraid. This is an example of adults taking action, rather than remaining silent and ignoring the problem. They restructured the morning to include this very important group discussion, and trusted the children to learn with each other. Desiree found her voice, at first with the teacher's support, but soon enough all by herself. She felt the affirmation of the group, was able to trust the teacher to be there for her, and therefore was empowered to take charge of the discussion. Desiree took the action needed within this carefully structured environment which supported her needs.

Desiree's mother wrote the following note to us in response to seeing the story above. At the time of this communication, Desiree was 13 years old.

This one instance where Desiree was encouraged to speak made a big impact on her and how she relates to her burn injuries and other people. She is not afraid to speak out, she's not afraid of being stared at or pointed at. She initiates discussions. She also doesn't wait for the boys to ask her to dance — she asks them!

The Sprinkler
by Rheta Negrete-Karwin

It was hot that day at Fullerton Peace Camp in California — really hot! In the later part of the day, we turned on the sprinkler — one of the freestanding ones that rotates back and forth. The children stripped down to their underwear and joyfully ran through the sprinkler. They clumped together on one side and waited for the water to reach them — then squealed in delight. They jumped over the sprinkler and had such fun . . . until one child decided to challenge the fun and put his foot over the sprinkler head. No water!!! The children let out a roar of disapproval and pulled the child off the sprinkler. He insisted on disrupting the fun and things were about to explode when the teachers intervened. By then, all the children were yelling and pushing each other, so the teachers turned off the water.

At first, the teachers themselves weren't sure quite how to handle the situation. They talked among themselves for a minute, and then called everyone together for a meeting. They all sat down in a circle and the teachers spoke about conflicts and how difficult they can be to work through. They told the children that they often have a hard time with conflicts too, and sometimes even have to ask for help. Then they asked the children what had happened. The children wanted to talk all at once, but were asked to speak one at a time to better be heard. They said that Jason put his foot on the sprinkler so they couldn't have any water. The teacher asked Jason about what the children had said. He said, "Yes, I want all the water." The teacher commented that there's a problem here. One person wanted all the water and the other people wanted some too. Everyone agreed that this was a problem. What to do? Jason was quite definite that he should have the water because he was the hottest. The children let him know with their words that this was not fair because they were all hot. The teachers gave them opportunities to tell Jason how they felt and what they needed so he could hear them.

After a "go around" when all was said, the teachers asked what could be done — ideas for solutions.

No one said anything for a couple of minutes. The teacher suggested, "Because everyone has to be safe at Peace Camp, we'll keep the water turned off. That's one idea." Then the children suggested several ideas, which came together as turning on the water and everyone who wanted to jump over the sprinkler could as long as no one stopped and put their foot on it. Since there had been much talk and discussion of feelings and needs, everyone, including Jason, was willing to try the solution. It was still hot, so the water went back on and the children eagerly cooled off in the sprinkler again.

A meeting such as this one, although spontaneous, was carefully structured to hear everyone's ideas. Jason could hear that other people were hot too. While he would have liked the water all to himself, it was clear that the children were not willing to give up playing in the water. The teachers had to keep everyone safe, so the best way to work it out was for everyone to be able to play together. Jason has lots of growing to do in the area of hearing other people's points of view — true of most young children. The teachers made the most of this opportunity for a meeting to hear each other and to problem solve.

Guidelines for Meetings

Adapted with permission from *Ways We Want Our Class To Be: Class Meetings that Build Commitment to Kindness and Learning*, by the Child Development Project of Developmental Studies Center.

The guidelines shared below have been created for use in classroom settings. However, since we believe that family settings can also be used for meetings such as those described, we have adapted the guidelines to fit both settings.

Purposes of Meetings:

Planning and Decision-Making Meetings to discuss:
- "Ways we want our home or class to be"
- Planning for special events
- Discussions around how we can build community in our family or school

Check-In Meetings to talk about:
- ◆ "Is this the way we want to be?"
- ◆ "What did we learn?"

Problem-Solving and Consciousness-Raising Meetings to work on concerns such as:
- ◆ "My friends won't let me play"
- ◆ Tattling versus needing assistance from an adult
- ◆ Sharing materials

Discussion and Facilitation Strategies:

Use of positive modeling by the adult
Questioning and Response Strategies:
- ◆ Use of a "go around" process to give everyone the opportunity to speak: address each person individually and allow people to "pass" if they wish
- ◆ Allow adequate wait time
- ◆ Use follow-up questions which promote discussion — use of open-ended questions rather than "right and wrong" questions

Strategies to Encourage and Manage Participation:
- ◆ Brainstorming — use a "go around" to include all ideas
- ◆ Small group discussions
- ◆ Partner chats
- ◆ Partner idea list
- ◆ Collected ideas
- ◆ Individual reflection — use of silence

Decision Making through Consensus — Five Steps:
- ◆ Define the problem or issue in concrete terms, including stated needs
- ◆ Brainstorm solutions, involving *all* participants in sharing if they wish
- ◆ Discuss solutions and consequences
- ◆ Reach consensus by combining, developing, or compromising on ideas — all voices need to be heard in the reaching of consensus
- ◆ Evaluate the decision after it has been implemented

"Agreements"

One of the most effective ways to share authority and control with others is to jointly establish "Agreements" as to how you want to maintain safety and respect as you work, live, and play together in community. The foundation pieces are safety and respect, but the specific behaviors can be defined by the people in the community. Even young children can, with support in small groups, create their own "Agreements." It is useful to discuss with children *how we want to be together to create a safe and respectful community or family* and to frame the behaviors in the following way:

SAFETY

"What will I see?"	"What will I hear?"
"I will see people cleaning up."	"I will hear people using words, not hitting."

RESPECT (KINDNESS)

"What will I see?"	"What will I hear?"
"People sharing." "Paying attention."	"Thank you." "Please." "You're cool."

The "Agreements" are written with all participants in the community or family present and giving input, perhaps going around to hear each person, one at a time. All can share in the development of the Agreements — everyone given opportunities to speak to each Agreement. If the children in the group speak more than one common language, the languages represented should also be included in the writing. The Agreements can be written on large pieces of paper and posted in the classroom or at home. All participants sign the Agreements. They can be referred to as needed for reminders, or to adapt and change as the needs of the participants change. A constructivist approach to the process will help the Agreements evolve and grow with the community. They are a way of building community together and working out how to meet everyone's needs within the setting, family as well as classroom.

A caution here: Agreements are not a punitive technique. However, when children make poor choices to break the Agreements, there will need to be consequences. Because safety is a priority, children may need to be removed from the situation. Education is important in both safety and respect, but especially in respecting differences. Children can and must learn to take responsibility.

Family Peace Circles

Getting Your Needs Met! Adapted and used with permission from Growing Communities for Peace.

Family Peace Circles can be fun and productive. They can be an opportunity for adults and children to create a more harmonious family, and they can provide fertile ground for practicing democracy and demonstrating respect. Even with the best of intentions, sometimes we create situations of "power over" rather than "power with" our children, which, of course, fosters resentment. Here are some tips to help "share authority" in the family meeting context:

◆ *Discuss that family circles are an opportunity for everyone to have input on family decisions.* No one is required to attend. The family can decide whether or not overnight guests are invited to family circles. If children don't want to participate, or need to get up and leave, ask them to stay nearby so you can get their feedback when needed. Remind them that their ideas are important in the decision making process.

◆ *Establish "Agreements" with all members as to how you will be making decisions in the family circles.* Will you use a decision making process in which everyone must agree? How will you listen to one another? How will you include everyone in the discussion? These questions can be decided by the group, using democratic process of making these decisions, to help establish "how you want to be together" in your family circles.

◆ *Have family circles at a time when everyone is usually home.* The time and day may vary based on other commitments and events. At the end of one family circle, set a time for the next.

◆ *Focus the first family circles around fun topics for discussion* — like planning family vacations and other special events. Save boring tasks or difficult agenda items, like household jobs, for later on.

◆ *Provide a special treat for family circles only!* The provision of something special creates a satisfying ritual or tradition for your family.

◆ *Start the circles with something children won't want to miss,* once again a family tradition may be established. Music, prayer, jokes, moments of appreciation — whatever fits for your family.

◆ *Demonstrate responsive listening to each other.* Re-frame ideas and incorporate into the discussion and decision making process. If needed, move into "active listening" when feelings are running high and need to be reflected and affirmed.
◆ *Use a calendar to schedule meetings and family events and commitments.*
◆ *Consider using a Talking Stick so everyone has opportunities to speak.*
◆ *Use consensus process for decision making.* Decisions need to work for everyone in the family.

You may want to evaluate at the end of each family circle by:
1. Asking your family to record answers to these questions on paper or in a family journal:
   ◆ What decisions did we make? What did we agree to do?
   ◆ Who is taking responsibility for _____? When will it be done?
2. Then ask:
   ◆ What needs to go on the agenda for the next circle?
   ◆ Who is willing to be our facilitator for the next circle?
   ◆ Who would lead us in a celebration or fun activity for the closing?
3. Did we follow a democratic process?
   ◆ How did we show respect for one another?
   ◆ Did we include everyone in our decision making?

Evaluations need not take long, usually a couple of minutes is enough. If topics come up again at the evaluation time, they may need further discussion at the next meeting. Evaluation is a special time to listen to each other and to consider how the process of being together is working.

Interviews with Children

Interviewing children is a great empowerment technique because children, like everyone else, like to talk and tell you their ideas. When interviewing them for a project or research, it is useful to take notes. The children feel

really "heard" when we write down their words on paper. A "go around" process includes everyone in the discussion.

Topics of Special Concern to the Children

When we talk directly to young children about topics of deep interest to them such as friends, courage, and helping, we ask specific questions:

◆ Who do you like to play with? Why?
◆ Tell me a story about a time you showed courage, or bravery.
◆ How do you like to help other people?

Talking About Friendships

In talking to the younger children under age six, we phrase our questions very concretely and specifically to start the conversation and to keep it focused. As questions are answered, we are able to encourage more sharing of thoughts and information by referencing previous points made by the children. Starting with the question "Who do you like to play with?" works well to initiate the discussion. Moving into "Why?" furthers it. They also respond well to the question "What do you like to play together?" The "who" and "what" questions often generate lists as the children name the people they see and the toys they like in the classroom. And, with many children, we have found we are able to move into some of the questions we typically use with older children once they have been grounded in the concrete and specific ones.

With older children ages six and up, as well as some younger ones, we have found we can ask more abstract questions such as:

"Tell me about your friends, who do you like to play with?"
    (Identity and Self Esteem)
"How can you tell someone likes you?" (Trust Building)
"How do you help your friends?" (Helping and Taking
    Responsibility)
"How are your friends the same as you, and different from you?"
    (Cherishing Diversity)
"How do you and your friends decide things like what you want
    to play together?" (Decision Making)

"What if you don't agree on what you want to play? What do
you do?" (Problem Solving and Sharing Authority)

As noted by the topics in parenthesis, these questions were framed
around the seven principles defined throughout this book. The exercise
of framing the questions to correlate with those topics was one which
was interesting as a way to think about organizing interviews with
children to further our understanding of their awareness of the principles of democratic practice.

And with eight year olds and older, we have found we can simply
ask them to tell us about "Friendships" and that they have a wealth of
information, as written in the section on "Children's Issues." The
children tend to be organized in their thinking and able to express their
thoughts to the interviewer using a style similar to an essay. They also
respond well to the interview questions listed above, but specific questions sometimes seem to inhibit their creative use of thinking and words.
Transcripts from interviews are located in section seven on "Children's
Issues."

Persona Dolls

Persona Dolls take on qualities, characteristics, and
personalities which compliment and enhance the
group of children they join. They are dolls in appearance,
but are treated as members of the group or community. They
are not played with in the usual way we use dolls; rather, they
are used to bring various issues, concerns, and problems to the
group. They have names and consistent characteristics such as family
background, physical differences, and concerns about identity issues.
Below are guidelines, ideas, and stories which further explore the
effective use of Persona Dolls.

◆ Persona Dolls are effective for telling stories about real people and concerns.

◆ Children connect and identify with them, both physically and emotionally.

◆ Children really identify with the feelings through the recognition of common feelings and issues. Use of the dolls help children learn empathy and develop an understanding that their feelings are not so unusual.

◆ Development of social skills and problem solving also result when the dolls are carefully used in settings which promote such skills.

◆ Use of the dolls can help prevent, or recognize and stop, hurtful behaviors.

Stories do not need to be lengthy and/or too involved. They are built over time, using events in the classroom and homes, or the community.

"THINK ABOUTS" FOR PERSONA DOLLS

Consider the group you work with:

Is your group diverse? In what ways: group identities like ethnicity, race, gender, language, physical abilities, socioeconomic status, religion, as well as individual differences like family patterns, size, and physical appearances?

In what ways is your group similar? What things do they have in common: likes, dislikes, feelings, favorite activities?

What are the ages of the children in the group? Is there a wide range of developmental differences?

What kinds of questions/issues have you heard the children bring up or talk about? What are they noticing or wondering about? Have you observed any of the children getting teased about anything specific?

What kinds of dolls might you need to reflect the diversity in your class?

What kinds of dolls might you need to add to your group to provide different representation, or to focus on issues that may not be reflected in your group?

How to Use Persona Dolls
Adapted by Jan DeLapp
from *Anti-Bias Curriculum* by Louise Derman-Sparks

When developing an identity for your doll, consider:
- his/her name;
- his/her ethnicity and cultural background;
- his/her family structure.

Pick only one issue, or problem when introducing the doll to the children. These issues/stories may arise from:
- the children's everyday interactions and relationships;
- events that are currently happening in your community or the world;
- information that the teacher wants the children to have; or
- history.

When introducing the doll at group time, also be ready to:
1. Tell the story and inform the children of how the doll feels. Dialogue with them about how the doll may need help. Encourage the group to talk about this problem by asking questions such as:
   - "How do you feel about this?"
   - "What do you think he/she can do about this?"
   - "What could we do to help her/him?"
2. Be prepared to model appropriate ways to be supportive, such as with words and body language.
3. Focus on a specific issue and appropriate behavior.
4. As time goes on, you may be focusing on other issues that may present themselves, possibly as extensions of discussion from the children themselves, or issues that come up from the children and families you are working with.

Social Problem Solving Using Persona Dolls
by LuAnne Venham

Another way to use the interview strategy is in problem solving with Persona Dolls. LuAnne Venham has shared some pages from her journal which record how interviewing around a classroom problem worked. These children were four years old.

Karima, Jeff, and Jenny are all Persona Dolls who live and play in LuAnne's classroom. They have identities which remain consistent and are used to introduce issues and problems which merit serious consideration and discussion.

Karima and Jeff were playing in the top of the climber. Jenny wanted to go up too.
Karima said, "You can't come up!"
Jeff said, "We don't want to play with you!"

Monday, June 9
Teacher to children: "What do you think about this?"
Everett: "It's not fair!"
Anders: "I think that's bad."
Zachary: "I think I know the answer. Maybe they don't know her so well. Maybe they are next door neighbors so they just want to play by themselves."
Jared: "It's not fair!"
Shelby: "It made her sad, really sad, she cried."
Sean: "Someone's crying."
Melanie: "It made me sad."
Marshall: "One time it happened to me and I felt bad."
Hailey: "That's bad — she would be sad."

Tuesday, June 10
Katie: "I think it made her sad."
Taren: "I think it made her sad too."
Katie: "I think it made her angry."
Ian: "It's not good. They are supposed to let her up on the climber."
Shelby: "Karima and Jeff wouldn't let Jenny on the climber. She's sad. It made Jenny cry. They let her up — she's happy."
Ian: "Jenny's a girl, Jenny likes girls."

Wednesday, June 11
Jack: "It feels kind of sad. It makes me feel like saying, 'One person can't say that.' Everyone can play!"

Thursday, June 12

>Jack: "It sounds like they hurt her feelings."

Monday, June 9

>Teacher to children: "How could they solve their problem?"
>Everett: "She could say please and they might change their minds."
>David: "I could tell her to get down cause I'm a big guy."
>Anders: "They could say, 'I just don't like you.'"
>Zachary: "Maybe you could take those two off and put her up."
>Bryant: "Tell them to play nice."
>Jared: "I think they should be arrested by the police. I think they could play together."
>Emily: "Let Jenny come up."
>Everett: "She could go play somewhere else."
>Shelby: "I'd make them play. They could ride bikes and hold hands."
>Everett: "Once Jennifer said I couldn't come up in the climber — I went up on the other side."

Tuesday, June 10

>Katie: "They could use their words, like please and thank you."
>Taren: "I think they need a friend. They could work it out."
>Ian: "I think they got down."
>Katie: "Jenny could play with another doll."
>Shelby: "You could make her play."
>Ian: "Go on her own climber."

Wednesday, June 11

>Everett: "Jenny could say, 'I can play with you, please!'"
>Jack: "They should let the other person play in here."
>Shelby: "I make her happy. Make her have fun."
>Jack: "Would tell Jenny to make all the kids play."
>Shelby: "Make her draw with colors."
>Jack: "Something she would like to have would make her happy. I don't want anyone to say you can't play up in the climber."

Thursday, June 12

>Devon: "Tell them there is enough room for everyone up on the climber."
>Christopher: "They have to let other people come up."

Joey: "If everyone can come up, all the people can come up."

Devon: "If everybody wants to come up, they can come up."

Christopher: "They should let her up."

Devon: "Jenny could tell a teacher."

Christopher: "Tell her there's room for everybody. She could find some other friends."

Jared: "They should all go play with dinosaurs from the lost world, because dinosaurs are amazing."

Tuesday, June 10

Teacher to children: "What would you do if someone wouldn't let you up in the climber?"

Katie: "It would make me feel sad and I would tell a teacher. Say please and thank you and ask them if you could come up."

Ian: "I would go on a different climber."

Shelby: "I would go on a different climber."

Taylor: "I'd make my own climber."

ASSORTED OTHER COMMENTS:

Monday, June 9, 1997

David: "I'm a big guy and I can tell new guys to put things away."

Bryant: "My brother didn't let me share his legos because he's mean to me. My brother hates me and doesn't like me. That problem I told you before is important."

Emily: "My sister was hitting me and she's wrong."

Tuesday, June 10

Everett: "LuAnne, we better go in and talk about those dolls." "They said, 'I don't want to play with you, Jenny,' and she felt sad."

Hailey: "Are they dolls?"

LuAnne: "Yes, they are dolls. They are Persona Dolls. They have real stories. The problem in the climber has really happened to real children on our yard."

Katie: "I help my mom and dad clean up."

Thursday, June 12

Shanel: "Jeff and Jenny play." Shanel carried and hugged each doll. She danced them on the bench. "Dance, play." She sat

*on the bench with the dolls and put Jenny on Karima's lap.
"Lap, lap." She offered Jeff's hand to the teacher to shake.
"Hi." When Jeff fell off the chair, she brushed him off, hugged
him and sat him back on the chair.*

Discussion Groups

Discussion groups differ from meetings primarily in
that they are not necessarily used for problem solving. A
topic may be talked about, but there may not be a problem
associated with it. The following story describes a discussion
which developed around an interview question, a combination
interview-discussion.

An Anti-Bias Success Story
by Elizabeth Matlin

*Many of my students at Lucy Stone School have seen the movie
"Pocahontas." During a discussion about Pocahontas with my five year
old class, we were discussing the stereotypes that the movie had taught
my students. We talked about the fact that Pocahontas was a Native
American. Then I asked them, "Do you think Native Americans are
'good' or do you think they are 'bad'?" I asked the question in this
manner because I wanted to frame it in the way children themselves
often categorize characters in movies, that is, either as 'good' or 'bad.'
Very young children tend to think in concrete terms which allow for little
digression from the extremes. It's also hard for them to think about
several aspects simultaneously. In other words, something or someone
can be "good" or "bad," but not both! Fifteen children out of 18
responded quickly, "They are bad!" The children continued to explain
that the native people were hurting the white people. Immediately,
three other children exclaimed, "No! Native Americans are good! They
were on the land first and people came to take it away. They helped
the white people learn how to plant and get food." I was surprised that
these children were so knowledgeable and adamant about their*

thoughts. Then I realized that I had had these same three children last year in my four year old program. I had incorporated a year long curriculum which focused on Native Americans living in our area: the Wampanoags. We learned about their history, contributions, culture, and how they live today. We learned the ways in which they are similar to all of us.

From my observation, I can conclude that children are very impressionable. If children learn only negative or positive ideas about a culture, they will inevitably establish stereotypes around "good" and "bad." Due to the thinking patterns of young children, which are not yet flexible enough to allow them to work through the complexities of several conflicting ideas at once, they will think in terms of only one aspect. However, if children learn about people and their culture in ways which make connections for them in their world, then they may be able to use the information to challenge stereotypes when presented. They may also be able to extend these understandings to resist other stereotypical images in the media.

Discussions such as the one described above are very useful to determine what the children know about a topic so that further planning will be appropriate to develop their knowledge and thinking. By using terminology which the children use, the adult leading the discussion is connecting with the children in how they are currently thinking. She then knows how to expand that thinking by bringing in knowledge and understandings which the children can grasp. And she can go beyond the "good" and "bad" judgmental thinking to "both/and" thinking."

Partnering

Partnering work with children can be effective in helping them start to develop awareness of others: their needs and perspectives. Two children can create a boat when singing "Row, Row, Row Your Boat" and that's an easy way to start partnering. Have them sit opposite each other on the floor, put their feet together, hold hands, and then rock back and forth as the song is sung. They will enjoy the movement as well as the awareness that two are needed to create the boat. Other opportunities

to work together as partners may be encouraged through setting up the environment in such ways which support looking at books together, walking down the hall with a partner, and asking a friend to help with a job. As children become more skilled in working together, mirroring movements done with partners to gentle music becomes an exquisite method to practice leadership and followship, as well as communication. The ideas are endless!

Cooperative Learning and Games

Cooperation is learned through much practice, and our family and classroom settings are wonderful opportunities to set up such activities. When competition is removed from the environment, the children then can learn to come together in common purpose and community instead of worrying about who will be the "loser" this time. Children will learn that when we work together on a game, activity, or project each person contributes in his/her special way and the end result is much more diverse and creative than when only one person has input. Games develop with interesting outcomes, sometimes totally unexpected.

Thoughts On Competition
Used with permission from *No Contest: The Case Against Competition* by Alfie Kohn

Alfie Kohn has studied the effects of competition on people's self esteem and ability to envision themselves as successful. He strongly advocates the abolishment of competition which promotes a winners and losers way of thinking. If we are all to be winners, our thinking will need to focus more on *both/and* as a way to include all participants, as a way to "hear everyone's voice."

Strip away all the assumptions about what competition is supposed to do, all the claims in its behalf that we accept and repeat reflexively. What you have left is the essence of the concept: mutually exclusive goal

attainment (MEGA). One person succeeds only if another does not. From this uncluttered perspective, it seems clear right away that something is drastically wrong with such an arrangement. (page 9)

Why do we feel a need to compete?

Specifically, I would offer the proposition that we compete to overcome fundamental doubts about our capabilities and, finally, to compensate for low self-esteem. (page 99)

In sum, the security that is so vital for healthy human development is precisely what competition inhibits. We are anxious about losing, conflicted about winning, and fearful about the effects of competition on our relationships with others — effects that can include hostility, resentment, and disapproval. (pages 123-124)

And, finally, competition in the classroom pits one child against another. Do we really want children to learn that they are losers?

Cooperative Games
Musical Chairs — Two Different Ways
by Janice Sheffield

In the old fashioned way of playing musical chairs, chairs are removed when the music stops along with the people who didn't get a chair to sit on. By the end, there is one chair for two people and they rush to sit on it. The last one is the loser.

The four year olds played the game and then talked about how it made them feel to be out and not able to play. Some children were very angry when they didn't get a chair, hurt because their friends were playing but they could not. There was an argument because two children felt that they each got to the chair first. Neither one wanted to be out. "It's not fun to be out." A few children said the game was great or okay. Then the teacher asked them if they wanted to play again. "No, it makes me feel sad." Only the few who had lasted to the end wanted to do it again. This game encourages people to think about how they can get to the chair first, often at the expense of others.

Later the teacher and children played musical chairs to cooperate. The chairs are still taken away, but if one cannot find a chair to sit on, a lap of someone on a chair will work as well. No one is out. There was lots of talking and laughter going on. After the children had played it once, they started sitting more on laps than chairs because it was more fun. Children called: "Sit on my lap" or "Sit here with me" or "We have room for you." Sometimes there were full laps and empty chairs! Sometimes the laps were four or five or six children deep. When the teacher asked, "Do you want to play again?" the children eagerly responded, "Yes!" The teacher asked, "Which musical chairs do you want to play?" The response, "The fun one — the one with the laps!" In this game, people must think about others. There is touching and hugs, and children who have a hard time working in groups may forget about themselves and be able to be part of the fun.

When we play the old fashioned musical chairs and then the cooperative musical chairs, it always amazes me how much the attitudes, behavior, and togetherness grow toward the positive. It does not take very long for the change to happen and is such a sharp contrast. Changing one little thing in the game makes a huge difference. Little things do make a big difference!

Descriptions of Cooperative Games

1. CATCH THE DRAGON'S TAIL

Players line up with arms around the waist of the person in front. The last one has a handkerchief in his/her pocket. The player at the head of the line tries to grab the handkerchief. Participants in the middle of the line need to follow the movements of the person in front of them. No part of the dragon may break. *Variation:* Two dragons attempt to catch each other's tails. Rotate the players.

2. BLANKET VOLLEYBALL/COLLECTIVE BLANKET BALL

Players hold the edge of the blanket. They place a ball on the blanket, toss the ball up by cooperatively manipulating the blanket, and try to catch it in the middle of the blanket. *Variation:* Use volleyball, beach ball. Change blanket size, define boundaries, use net. Pass ball between two groups with blankets. *Special Hints:* Switch positions on blanket — make sure little ones do not get hurt. Greatly helps energetic ones to center on cooperation.

3. ROPE RAISING

Take a soft rope about 30' in length and tie both ends together very tightly. Place the rope on the ground in a circle. Seated in a circle all around the rope on the ground, all pull on the rope with their hands so that they stand at once. *Variation:* Stretch rope out in a line and make two equal teams at ends, pull together so that everyone stands up. *Special Hints:* Coach the children to pull *together*; watch out for the energetic children criticizing the less active ones. This is a cooperative activity, not one to see who can stand up and who cannot. It provides very real opportunities for group problem solving as everyone contributes ideas as to how to support each other in the process of raising the rope together.

4. DOWN THE HOLE

Cut a small hole, just big enough for the ball, in the center of the bedspread or sheet. Children hold the edges of the sheet and try to get the ball to go through the hole. *Variation:* Use several balls, try a parachute instead of a sheet. *Special Hints:* Great fun, brings group to a center.

5. WALKING TOGETHER

Four leather straps (or ropes) for footholds screwed into two studs, 6' long, and 2" x 4". Four people slip their feet into the straps — left feet in one *sandal*, right feet in the other *sandal* — and they try to walk as a unit. *Variation:* Move over or through obstacles, dance, move sideways. Try various lengths of 2" x 4" studs. *Special Hints:* Make sure to practice before trying difficult maneuvers. Be safe.

6. HULA HOOPS

Have various sizes of hula hoops. Have everyone in a circle holding hands. Place one hula hoop over a person's arm and ask him/her to pass the hula hoop to the next person. The next person puts his/her body through the hula hoop and passes it to the next. *Variation:* Have more than one hula hoop (different sizes) being passed simultaneously.

7. BALL IN THE CIRCLE

Have everyone sit on the ground in a circle with feet touching in the middle and hands on the outside of the circle propping them up. Be sure to have everyone sit close together. Put a ball in the circle. Have the participants pass the ball around the circle with only their legs and/or bodies. Their heels need to remain on the ground. *Variation:* Use various size balls, use more than one ball.

8. STRAW AND PRETZEL RELAY

Have the participants form lines or circles. Each participant receives a straw. One of the participants holds a container of small pretzels, while a participant at the end holds an empty container. Participants pass the pretzels down the line on their straws. Hands should be behind their backs.

9. BEACH BALL BALANCE

Have the participants divide into pairs of similar height. Place a beach ball between one set of pairs (i.e., head to head). The pair needs to pass the beach ball to another pair without using their hands. *Variation*: Different body parts can be used to pass the ball (i.e., backs, legs, top of heads). One pair can challenge the next to think of a different way to pass the ball.

Conflict Management

Conflict is a reality in everyone's life. While many people may wish to avoid it as something unpleasant, which it can be if handled inappropriately, it is important to help people face conflict and learn how to deal with it in productive, nonviolent ways. This is not to say that one should necessarily go about encouraging conflict, but when it occurs naturally, attempt to work with it to build practice in problem solving.

It is important to help young children learn the processes of problem solving which include verbalizing feelings and needs, communicating what the problem is, creating several solutions, discussing solutions, making a choice, trying out possible solutions, and evaluating the results. Skills such as verbalizing, listening, remembering, making choices, and following through are critical life skills. It is our responsibility to encourage and support the children and adults who touch our lives to use them.

Steps to Conflict Management

1. DEFUSE ANGER

Anger is such an intense feeling that it must be defused before any negotiation can happen. Supportive, active listening may help, pounding the play dough may help, hugs may help. Using everyday songs in new, simple ways can also help: "Gee I'm mad, skip to my loo. . . ." There are many productive ways to defuse anger; it's important to model and practice them.

2. LISTEN TO PEOPLE'S FEELINGS WITH RESPECT

Help children become aware of their own feelings, as well as those of others, by listening to and reflecting the feelings expressed. Acknowledge and support the feelings; after all, the feelings are real and it is critical that we pay close attention to what the children express to us. Their feelings must be validated. It may, in some situations with older children and adults, be useful to ask the question, "What worries or concerns you about this issue or problem?" In some cases, simply identifying the *worries* may clarify the issue enough that there is no need to move into problem solving. And, very often, such identification results in being able to think more objectively about the concerns. The listener takes the role of validating the importance of the concerns expressed. Common ground may also be expressed if possible. Problem solving can then be used to resolve what choices and/or decisions to make.

3. PROBLEM SOLVE

Once anger is defused and feelings are respected, then one can settle into problem solving, as needed. Help by:

- ◆ Collecting information from both parties: "What happened?"

- ◆ Stating the problem clearly, including everyone's concerns.

- ◆ Finding common ground: "Do you both have the same worries or needs?"

- ◆ Thinking of solutions so everyone's needs can be met.

- ◆ Looking at possible consequences of the solutions.

- ◆ Planning the solution and helping to implement as needed.

Supporting growth using this guide will help people become negotiators in conflict management and will encourage their indepen-

dence. As they learn to problem solve, they will need less intervention and they will grow in confidence.

"Out On A Limb" — Together
by Susan Hopkins

I looked up into an old oak tree when I heard two six year old peace campers hollering at each other from up in that tree. It appeared that they both wanted to be in the same tree on the same limb at the same moment. It wasn't working out for them, so they were starting to push and yell at each other. I told them it was not safe to be yelling and pushing each other in the tree. They would need to come down so we could talk about the problem. They came down with reasonable willingness and we started to talk. I commented that since I saw pushing and heard yelling there must be a problem to solve. They immediately started calling each other names. I tried to get at the feelings behind the names, but the name-calling continued. Then I said firmly that we had a problem to solve and that calling each other names wouldn't solve it. I said, "I think the problem is that you both want to be in the same place in the tree at the same time." Both children agreed. I commented, smiling, "You both want the very same thing." They looked at each other and grinned. We had found common ground — a much needed component to problem solving. I asked who had an idea to suggest to solve this problem. One child suggested that they each go up different trees — not the original one at all.

The other child then said, "And once we get up there we could wave to each other." Clearly, pointing out their common ground helped these two children realize they really could be friends and they could solve the problem together.

Problem Solving at Stepping Stones Preschool
by Sharon Davisson

Nestled among lush green cedar and pine, in the foothills of Nevada County, California, is a small rural school, Stepping Stones

*Preschool. Stepping Stones offers a developmental preschool program
for children ages three to five. The children enter the program at three
and attend the Tuesday/Thursday nursery program. They then move on
together to the three day a week preschool program.*

*Spending this significant block of time together sets the stage for
meaningful relationships to develop. The children learn to adapt to
each other's personalities, temperaments, and skills. A genuine community forms with the children learning to problem solve, respect others,
and feel respected.*

*We usually begin teaching conflict resolution skills around the third
month of school. By then the children have developed a trusting relationship with their teachers, are comfortable with the daily schedule,
and are beginning to shift from solitary and parallel play to group play.
These three year olds do not have words yet to solve problems (it is
unproductive to say "use your words" if they do not yet have the concept!). Usually the children are used to creating a conflict and having
an adult rush in and solve it for them, so the teachers begin gradually to
introduce the idea that conflicts can be solved by the children themselves. By the end of the first year, teachers no longer have to offer
suggestions as the children have developed confidence in their own
capabilities.*

*A wonderful development unfolds as the children develop compe-
tency in problem solving. We find that once the children realize that
their teachers EXPECT them to resolve their own conflicts, then they
experience a sense of empowerment and self esteem. We see a dramatic reduction of negative defense reactions, and the conflict resolution process creates an environment of safety.*

*An easy way to observe how conflict resolution works with the very
young is to observe children over a year's time. Last year, we observed
a dramatic leap in competency and confidence particularly in two of
our little ones.*

OCTOBER 10 (a month and a half into the school year)
*We are in the midst of making applesauce. The children are
taking turns using a large spoon to scoop the pulp from the cooking pot
into the grinder. Skylar is carefully scooping and Emily, with furrowed
brow, grabs the spoon out of his hand and says, "My turn." The
teacher says, "Oh my, Emily, I know it is hard to wait, but you need to
ask Skylar if you can have your turn now." Skylar grabs the spoon, and
a tug-of-war proceeds. The teacher removes the spoon and puts it*

behind her back (removing the object of contention helps shift focus) and says, "It looks as though TWO children want ONE spoon! Emily, you may tell Skylar what you want." Skylar says, "I have a Batman!" The teacher says, "We are thinking about the spoon, Skylar." Emily frowns and stomps away from the group. The teacher says, "Emily, if you do not wish to talk to Skylar about the spoon, he will finish his turn now." No response from Emily. Later, after the activity was completed, the teacher had a talk with Emily, letting her know she understands how hard it is to wait, and asking her what she could do next time instead of grabbing the spoon.

JANUARY 25

A rainy, indoor day. Two children are in conflict on the block rug. One teacher holds and soothes a crying child, waiting for her to be calm enough to express herself. Emily begins a little dance march, followed by a pal, and begins bringing small blocks to the crying child. Emily sings, "We have to fight the problem, we need to do the solution." The teacher continues rocking and soothing the crying child as Emily and her pal continue piling small blocks around the sad child (who by now has taken an interest and ceased crying). Skylar tosses a pteranodon in the sad child's general direction, saying, "I don't need that one." It is obvious to the teachers that both Skylar and Emily are aware that (1) there is a problem and (2) they are capable of offering solutions. A wonderful moment in a classroom! After the original two children in conflict have come to an agreement, the teachers thank everyone who helped.

APRIL 4

Emily and Skylar run to the one empty swing. A tug-of-war ensues with Emily crying, "I wanted the swing," and Skylar shouting, "I got it first!" The teacher says, "Oh dear, I see TWO children want ONE swing! Does anyone have an idea on how to solve this problem?" Bystanders begin making suggestions as the teacher holds the swing. Emily says, "I know, let's use the sand timer!" Teacher asks if they both agree, they both grin and nod their heads "yes!"

JUNE 11

Emily is hiding under a blue tarp. Skylar runs up, grabs the tarp, and pulls it across the play yard. A tug-of-war ensues (again!). Emily shouts, "I want to hide behind the tarp!" Skylar looks at her and shouts,

"It's mine!" The teacher asks, "Do you two children need help solving this problem, or do you think you can do it yourselves?" Emily looks at Skylar and says, "I know, we could use the sand timer!" Skylar looks at Emily and says, "No way!" Emily is silent. A bystander offers that since Emily had it first, she should have the tarp. The teacher asks Emily if she agrees, which she does. The teacher asks Skylar if he agrees. "No!" Emily offers, "We could take turns. I could have it first and then you could have it!" Skylar answers, "We could get those sticks off the high tree!" The teacher reminds the children they are thinking about the tarp. Skylar looks at Emily and says, "I know, we could make it into our swimming pool and we could both swim in it." Emily grins and says, "Okay!" Several children help straighten out the tarp, they jump in and SWIM until lunch is called. They DRY OFF after getting off the tarp and run indoors grinning.

Both these children are only three years old! They have at least one more year together. Judging from past experience, the teachers expect that these two will need little or no adult intervention next year. They will hear the words "Do you need help solving this problem?" or "Are you listening to each other?" and automatically know they are expected to and are capable of solving their own problems.

Some of the Guidelines the Teachers at Stepping Stones Use

Never moralize when children are in conflict! They will not move forward with confidence if they are feeling defensive or ashamed. There are plenty of opportunities throughout the day to model acceptable behavior or to talk about it in a general sort of way.

Begin the process ONLY when emotions are NOT running high (comforting, calming, soothing from the adult first). Children are unable to think while they are emoting!

Have children say what happened and how they feel, without blaming or scolding. The very young child may need the adult to verbalize for him/her.

Have the children LOOK AT EACH OTHER, rather than at the adult, while speaking. Remind the children to focus on the ISSUE. It's important that the adult redirect the discussion back to the issue if the

children digress from it. Have all the children involved LISTEN to the speaker. Have the children take turns offering solutions. During this brainstorming it is critical that the adult not try to influence the outcome. If a solution seems just right, give it no more weight than an illogical solution. During the brainstorming of solutions keep turning to each child and ask, "Do you agree?" If not, just keep on trying.

The solution is stated clearly by the adult, affirmations given to all participants such as "good listening" or "We made it!"

Conflict As an Opportunity
"Playing" with Conflicts
by Susan Hopkins

Chico, California, has been developing children's Peace Camps within the elementary school district. The Peace and Justice Resource Center and the Chico Police Department have collaborated with the schools to help create a program in which children learn the skills of peacemaking. At Peace Camp we talk about conflict with the children — what it is and some ideas for how to handle it. They eagerly become engaged in this work because they have all experienced conflict in one form or another. We role play strategies and discuss some of the real conflicts children want to share.

Toward the end of one of our Peace Camp days, two boys (third graders) came up to me with big grins on their faces to tell me what good conflict managers they'd become. They had created a game of inventing conflicts/problems to be solved. Then they proceeded to solve each conflict. They told me of complex conflicts in which they had enjoyed the challenge of solving the problems. These young boys clearly have developed an attitude about conflict and problem solving which is optimistic, confident, and creative. These boys will be well equipped to meet the challenges of their lives.

How can we as teachers and parents set up the environment so that children will have opportunities to create problems and conflicts which challenge and interest them? Many of the strategies suggested in this manual give children the empowerment skills needed to think creatively and critically.

Children who are given appropriate choices, are trusted to make good decisions, and are genuinely included in the community of the

home and school can be empowered to take charge of learning what they feel they need to know.

Children's Literature Used to Teach Conflict Resolution Skills
by Chris Gerzon

Children's literature can provide us with an opportunity to teach the skills of conflict resolution in a way that fits into our family discussions or existing curriculum. Children love to listen to stories and often identify strongly with the characters. Here are some suggestions to help when reading books about conflict and cooperation. These steps will help children learn to identify a conflict and recognize the actions and statements which escalate it. Using stories is a nonthreatening way to practice brainstorming and problem solving skills.

For Books with Themes of Conflict

1. Read the book up to the point of conflict.
2. Ask how the characters are feeling.
3. Have the children identify the conflict(s). Choose the one conflict that seems to be the most central to the story. Discuss the behaviors and statements of the characters that made the conflict escalate.
4. Brainstorm ways the characters could solve the conflict. Discuss which one the children think the character in the story will use.
5. Read the rest of the story. Discuss the characters' solution to their conflict. Was it a good solution? Why or why not?
6. How do the characters feel now?

For Books with Themes of Cooperation

1. Read the story.
2. Discuss how the characters in the story cooperated with one another. Ask how the characters are feeling.

3. Ask why it benefited each character to cooperate. Did the characters get what they wanted? How are they feeling?

Follow-Up Activities

1. Use problem solving puppets to act out common conflicts that occur at home or school.
2. Have the children draw pictures/write stories of conflicts that have escalated.
3. Have the children draw pictures/write stories of cooperative activities in which they have been involved.
4. Discuss the feelings the children had in each of these situations. Make a list of feeling words.
5. Have children re-tell or re-write the ending of a story with one of their own endings. They could choose a win/win, win/lose, or lose/lose ending.
6. Have the children play *conflict detectives.*
7. Ask the children to keep a conflict journal about conflicts they witness at home or school. Younger children can dictate if they are not yet writing. They can answer these four questions:
    Who was in the conflict?
    How did the conflict escalate?
    How did the conflict end?
    Was the solution a good one?
8. Older children can put on skits of their conflict stories for younger children.
9. Older children can re-write well-known stories from another point of view. Suggestions: *Jack and the Beanstalk* from the giant's point of view, *Goldilocks and the Three Bears* from Goldilock's point of view, *Little Red Riding Hood* from the wolf's point of view, etc.

Problem Solving Puppets
by Chris Gerzon

Using puppets in your setting is an ideal way to teach the skills of problem solving. The advantage that puppets have over using children's books is that the problems the puppets act out can be custom made to fit the needs of your children. For example, if sharing toys is an issue, the puppets would act out this problem.

Remember the problem solving process:
◆ Define the problem the puppets are having.
◆ Discuss possible solutions to the problem.
◆ Choose a solution to the problem and put it into practice.

In my classroom, the problem puppets are kept in the meeting area in a decorated shoe box. Once a week, I act out a problem with the puppets for the children to solve. During the rest of the day, the children are free to play with the puppets on their own to act out problems that they make up. When the children become proficient at solving problems, I send home the puppets for the weekend with one child at a time. At home, the parent and the child make up a problem for the puppets. After they act it out, they discuss possible solutions and the child draws a picture about the problem while the parent writes down the solution they like the best. Following is a copy of the form I send home to families to give them some structure in this process. At school, we keep these drawings in a notebook. When the child brings the puppets back to school, we act out the problem with the puppets during meeting time.

For successful problem puppet sessions, it is important to:
◆ Focus on one problem at a time.
◆ Keep the problem simple.
◆ Limit the problem to one to two minutes.
◆ Act out the problem up to the point of escalation and then ask the children for solutions.
◆ Do not have the puppets hit each other.
◆ Encourage the children to address the puppets directly.
◆ Finish the session by having the puppets act out the solution the children like best.
◆ Practice using the puppets ahead of time.

Other possible questions to ask the children:
◆ How are the puppets feeling?
◆ What could they do differently next time to keep this conflict from happening again?

Other activities include:

- Having the children make their own problem puppets out of socks, paper bags, construction paper, and paper towel rolls, etc.
- Putting on puppet shows of some of the children's books you have read together such as:
  - *Six Crows*
  - *The Owl and the Woodpecker*
  - *The Rainbow Fish*

Letter to Parents
from Chris Gerzon

Dear Parents:

Our class has been practicing problem solving so that when we have a conflict with each other, we can learn to talk to each other rather than hit and fight. We use the problem puppets to act out common problems that we experience in school. Then we brainstorm solutions to the problems.

The children have enjoyed watching me *play act* with our puppets so I thought each of them could show you what we have learned in school by acting out a problem with the puppets at home.

Can you please:
1. Talk about a problem your child might have had at school — or one he/she observed other children having.
2. Help him/her act it out with our puppets — Greeny and Orange.
3. Brainstorm some solutions to the problems and choose one you and your child like best.
4. Have your child draw a picture about the problem. It does not have to have the puppets in it.
5. Put the drawing in the notebook and return it with the puppets in the bag within two school days so another child can take the puppets home.

Here are some suggestions for problems:
1. cutting in line
2. sharing a book, toy, ball
3. taking turns at the computer

4. when someone wrecks your Legos or blocks
5. deciding what to play with a friend

Thank you for your help!

Problem Solving with the Puppets
(form which goes home with the puppets)

Here is a problem for the Problem Puppets . . .

This is how they solved their problem . . .

Name:_____

Mediation with Young Children

Peace Table
by Dolores Kirk
Adapted and used by permission, *Discover the World:*
Empowering Children to Value Themselves, Others
and the Earth, edited by Hopkins and Winters

The Peace Table, a method of conflict resolution with young children, is one of many ways to take peace making from the abstract to the concrete. Problem solving, compromising, and thinking through alternatives are learned skills. As teachers and parents, we must find a way to give them the opportunity to experience the process, be responsible for their actions, and to be a part of the solution.

WHY
There is a need for children to learn problem solving and alternatives to fighting in their lives, from the earliest age possible. Authoritarian methods keep all power, decisions, and enforcement in the hands of adults.

GOALS

To have children view the Peace Table as an opportunity for them to be heard and understood. If this method is used for punishment, it cannot work. The most difficult aspect of the Peace Table process is relinquishing adult power. The Peace Table can become the most freeing experience that can happen for you as a teacher or parent.

THE ONLY RULES

You must touch the table to talk, teachers and parents, too! (Children love it when adults must touch table.) This gives control to the process. If someone says something that has already been said, ask to hear that person's special ideas. We want to encourage lots of thoughts and ideas to be expressed.

HOW

- ◆ Any table or designated spot, e.g., rock, leaf, handkerchief, can be a Peace Table.
- ◆ Any place and any time.
- ◆ Adult acts as the Moderator/Facilitator.
- ◆ Children involved in the conflict come to the Peace Table and tell what happened from their point of view. Use of a "Go Around" structure works well to hear from everyone. If invited, anyone in the larger group can add to the presenting of the problem.
- ◆ After the problem has been stated from all points of view, the children of the group are asked to give alternatives on how the problem could have been solved.
- ◆ At this time, the Adult/Facilitator needs to accept only real solutions or alternatives, e.g., child says, "They should be nice to each other." Adult/Facilitator, "How could they do that?"
- ◆ Adult/Facilitator restates the alternatives but never declares which option they should take or what to do. Adult/Facilitator never asks them to say they are sorry or force adult solutions on them.
- ◆ If an audience gathers, ask Peace Table problem solvers if they feel comfortable with others listening.

TIME AND COMMITMENT

Approximately ten minutes, depending upon the attention span of the children. Some adults may object to stopping activities and calling the group together for a Peace Table because of schedules and time. To make peace a part of children's lives, both a commitment to the concept and a willingness to invest what is necessary to build successful practice are essential.

NOTE
I have used the Peace Table and other methods of teaching peace in my classroom for over five years. After the first of the school year, children call for Peace Table themselves.

Talking Stick: Learning to Listen
Adapted and used with permission from Growing Communities for Peace

Young children love to use a Talking Stick during group and family discussions. It gives each child a chance to speak and encourages careful listening. By reducing competition for time and attention, the routine helps children relax and build trust.

Introduce the idea of the Talking Stick by explaining that the ritual was used by some Native American tribes during council meetings. The council members were able to discuss their problems peacefully by passing an object around a circle. Only the person holding the object was allowed to speak; the others had to wait their turns.

To make a Talking Stick, take the group on a nature walk and look for a sturdy 12" to 14" stick and objects to tie onto it such as feathers, stones, acorns. Yarn, ribbon, and other items can be added later.

At discussion time, explain the purpose of the decorated stick and how it will be used. You might say, "Because each person's feelings and ideas are important in our group (or family), we use the Talking Stick to remind ourselves whose turn it is to speak while the rest of us listen from our hearts."

Help the children understand that the stick will be passed around the circle, giving each person a chance to speak. If they would rather not speak, they may say "Pass" and hand the stick to the next person. Remind them to listen carefully to the person who has the stick.

The stick is passed around as many times as necessary to air concerns or solve a problem. If time is short, pass the stick around the group once and then put it in the center. Anyone wishing to speak again may retrieve the stick and return it to the center when finished.

There may be times when the problem cannot be solved in one session. Explain, "Sometimes it takes a long time for everyone to express their feelings. That's okay. We can stop for awhile and come back later. It's important to keep talking until we've heard what everyone has to say."

The Talking Stick is a wonderful way for children and adults, together, to learn about community building, respecting everyone's ideas, and resolving conflicts.

Sand Trays
by Susan Hopkins

Sand trays are boxes or tubs large enough to be used to create miniature scenes, but small enough to be fairly portable. The sides should be high enough to hold the sand and miniature figures without spilling. On the bottom is painted a blue lake. The sand is soft to the touch, and there is a wide choice of miniature figures available for children to choose. Children create their own scenes and play them out in whatever manner they choose, short of throwing the sand or objects. The adult performs a listening role only, never therapeutic unless professionally qualified. Sand trays are very easy to have in the home and school settings and take minimal supervision once limits are established.

Once there was a little boy whose name was John. He had a devoted mommy and daddy and six older brothers and sisters. They were all outspoken and energetic. According to his mother, John, as the youngest, was often not heard in the midst of this lively family. At school, Cal State Fullerton Children's Center, John was plenty verbal, so we had no concerns about his ability to express himself.

We often used a sand tray in our classroom so that people who wanted to have the nonstressful experience of working with the sand and miniature figures could do so. One day John announced he needed to work in the sand tray. He selected all of the small dolls available for use and placed them into the sand. At first he simply appeared to be moving them around at random. But as he worked with them some order started to appear. They were lined up in special ways and told what to do by John. He explained to me that he was planning

his fifth birthday party. He had the guest list all decided — mostly his family — as well as the menu for the party. He was so pleased with his plans! I asked if his mom knew about his plans and he said he didn't think so. Together we decided to write a list of his ideas for his mom so he wouldn't forget anything.

When his mom came to pick him up from the center that afternoon, John ran to his mailbox to retrieve the list he had dictated to me. His mom, busy lady that she was, couldn't have been more delighted to know John's ideas for his party! John found a way to plan and express his ideas in a way which could be heard, even as the youngest in a large, noisy family.

Portfolios

The purpose of creating a portfolio with a child is to provide affirmation of the importance of his/her work through a means of preserving it. The child may select which items are to be saved. Children often have very definite ideas and can be encouraged to make those choices. They learn to evaluate their work, especially if a perceptive adult has a discussion with them about how they decided what to put into the folder or box. The adult will want to reserve his/her judgment and let the child articulate the reasons for the decision. Artwork, photographs, written/ dictated stories, and drawings are a few of the possible items to be included. Remember to put dates on these important treasures.

Languages

As we know, young children may speak languages other than the one of the dominant culture. They bring these languages to our schools, centers, churches, and other group settings. All children may benefit from the exposure to languages different from the ones they speak if care and respect are shown for the many good ways there are to communicate. However, the child who speaks a nondominant language will need support to continue using that language.

Some children at age four or five stop speaking their first language, understanding that the dominant language is the one of power. The result is that the child's use of his/her first language is arrested at an important stage in language development. There is also the unspoken message that his/her first language is not the *best* one. It is important to encourage parents of children who speak a nondominant language to continue use of that language at home. The family culture is kept in tact through a common language they all speak. Children will learn English in their group settings. The parents of nondominant language speaking children may be asked for help through volunteering to interpret and to spend time with the children in the group setting. Their involvement supports the value of the home language to their child. It is important that we honor all languages the children speak.

Children who speak the dominant language will do well to be exposed to other languages. Bilingual exposure assists them in learning more than one language. The world today is wide open to these future adults who will have access to all of it. Knowing more than one language will be essential to their successful careers as well as in their life satisfaction; they will have the attitudes and skills necessary to be heard.

Becoming Bilingual
Two Stories
by Lucy Stroock

Korean speaking children with parents who are associated with the universities in Cambridge, Massachusetts, have been coming to our program at the Haggarty School for 12 years. In those same years, Haitian Creole speaking children, whose parents immigrated to escape economic and personal dangers, have also been a regular part of our three and four year old group. Almost all the children have been born in the U.S. Their parents speak English with varying degrees of confidence; usually the fathers are more fluent, the mothers more hesitant, but all have been learning English to get on with their lives in this country. After one or two years in preschool, the children have all made significant progress in becoming bilingual.

There is an important difference, however, in their future as bilingual learners: the Korean speaking children are going to continue their education in both languages; the Haitian Creole speaking children will

not become literate in their home language. Often they have been taught to ignore or even deny that they speak a different language at home. Cambridge offers bilingual classes in the primary years for both language groups; however, the parents of the Haitian Creole speaking group whom we have taught do not choose to send their children, while the Korean speaking families do make that choice.

In parent conferences and informal conversations with both groups over the years, I have consistently presented the value for children of continued growth in the language of the home and have expressed my conviction, based on research, that children will be stronger students if they continue to learn in two languages. The Korean speaking parents have received these assurances with relief, glad to have a teacher for their child who agrees with their determination to raise their children in Korean. They are eager for the child to make progress in English at school, but have no intention of giving up the Korean education that is part of their home life. Communication about this topic is clear, and the children seem to understand that the challenge of school is to master another way of speaking. The parents are eager to share aspects of their language with the school, giving us important words and demonstrating their phonetic alphabet. A number of children have attended Korean classes on the weekend, and most go on to the bilingual Korean program in the public schools.

When the topic of their child's language learning is raised, Haitian Creole speaking families have consistently responded by indicating that they speak English with their children and have downplayed or denied the role of Haitian Creole in their children's lives. When it is acknowledged by the family, they make a point of saying that it is limited to home and not a part of the child's school experience. The children's home world is cut off from school as a result, and they are often silenced, especially at times when emotional issues arise. One child was relieved of this distance when she discovered that she could tell me about her Meme, the grandmother who cares for her while her parents work. The name Meme came up in a class discussion of the many names we call our grandparents when another child reported the name for her family's French Canadian grandmother. Now I often hear about Meme when Marie is thinking of home, and we can share the love and caring this person brings to her life. What has saddened me is to realize that we had taken so long to know of this important person. Marie's sister had been in the program the year before and Meme had been unknown to us.

I am using these two examples because they are the ones I know best, but it is easy to see how the issues raised affect other groups who are coming to our schools with a home language which is not English. The Korean speaking families are literate in their home language; they have been educated in Korean themselves and join our English speaking world with confidence because they have already succeeded in the world of schools well enough to be part of the university community. And university communities are one of the places where they can encounter a number of other people who are bilingual and where there is some respect for their achievement.

By contrast, the Haitian Creole speaking families come from a society where the 20% who get an education are educated in French. The Haitian Creole language has remained an oral language in Haiti. Success in Haiti both in class status and economic conditions is measured in French. The negative response towards the bilingual programs in Haitian Creole is based in part on the prejudice against the language which the parents learned before they came to the U.S. In addition, when they arrive here, they are struggling to find security and are very aware of the prejudices around them towards non-English speakers. For them, success is defined by leaving their home language behind, and they are trying to protect their children from the difficulties they have encountered. The children carry the pain and confusion of these circumstances into their earliest education. They do learn to speak English, but they will miss the benefits of being fully and proudly bilingual, with all the intellectual and cultural richness that would bring to their futures.

For further information, see *One Child, Two Languages: A Guide for Preschool Educators of Children Learning English As a Second Language* by Patton O. Tabors. It is a useful study of children learning English in a monolingual preschool setting.

American Sign Language

Sign language is a language nonhearing children learn in order to be able to communicate with others. Children who can hear also enjoy learning it because it involves activity and movement. The coordination skills, as well as the memory skills to remember the signs, are very useful to practice. The concept that there are many good ways to communicate is essential to the idea of *Hearing Everyone's Voice*.

Carlos' Story
by Barbara Wright

He was a language impaired four year old with only about three or four words, expressive (car, mine, bye). He generally communicated nonverbally by screaming. One day as he received speech therapy in the kitchen, one of the assistant teachers started preparing the snack. All of a sudden, Carlos started screaming. He was upset and afraid he would miss snack. The teaching staff realized we needed a plan to help Carlos get some control. We instituted a plan using sign language. As Carlos learned some basic signs, he started to communicate and the screaming behavior decreased. His self confidence increased as well.

Letter Writing

An empowerment tool even young children can use is to express their thoughts and ideas in letters to special people. This manual contains several examples of such empowerment: the four year old children who wrote to the university president to save their special tree and the youngster who wrote to the magazine to request inclusion of photographs of more people of color so they wouldn't look prejudiced.

Journals

Young children enjoy sharing their ideas with adults who are willing to write down their thoughts. The adults can take dictation from children, writing their words in notebooks. Children may draw pictures to go along with the words if they wish. At Cal State Fullerton University Children's

Center, Blue Books are used — the kind their parents use for exams! They are a very convenient size and easy to obtain at the campus bookstore. Of course the children like to have something of their own that they have seen their parents use.

Writing Books

Books can be an extension of journals and they usually focus on one topic, or at least similar ones. They may be made by one person, or by a group of people who have thoughts which relate to one another. Books are sometimes created by a group that wants to send something special to a friend in the hospital; they are an easy way to build community as the children come together jointly to do something for a friend. Rosi Pollard tells how her first graders write their own books at Jefferson Elementary School in Pasadena, California. The children tell Rosi their stories, individually, and Rosi tape records them. They draw pictures as they talk. Later, Rosi transcribes their stories from the tape recordings. They work on one or two pages at a time, eventually accumulating 10 or 12 pages which she puts into a cover, a recycled hard cover from a worn out book. The audio tape is kept in an envelope on the back of the book so the child can read his/her book and listen to the tape.

Karel Kilimnik's class book, which follows later in this manual, is an example of affirming children as we hear their voices on the subject of *helping*. Earlier in this writing, mention was made of that group of inner city Philadelphia first graders who were such marvelous helpers. The topic selection of "Helping" gave real affirmation to the children since helping is something they do well and with great pride. It is interesting to note that the topic was not easily selected by us, the adults. In our initial thinking about including the children in this manual, we were not well focused on what they could really contribute; rather, we were focused on what we, the grownups, thought they should be able to contribute. We asked them questions about topics such as *rules* and got little to nothing in terms of responses. They were not uncooperative, simply not able to articulate on our subject.

Their verbal skills were limited at that time so we reframed our thinking as to what and how they could contribute and — in looking at their contributions — realized that the subject of *helping* was of importance to them. We asked them to draw pictures of how they like to help others for the book. Their pictures were filled with detail and clarity about the topic of helping. And, in some cases, they even took the perspective of someone other than themselves — unusual for children so young. By getting past our own needs for the project, we were able to really include, to really hear from, the children. We were able to work with them in a way in which they could be true contributors. The book itself is included in the section on "Children's Issues."

A return visit to the children six months after the original pictures were drawn resulted in a reunion to accomplish two tasks: to draw pictures for the cover of the book and to tell the grownups what they need to know from the children about writing books. A transcript of our conversation:

> *Karel (teacher): "Do you write books at home?"*
> *Shanay: "I always write books at home about dogs and cats."*
> *Juan/Johnny: "I write a book about patterns. First I made two of them, then more and more and more patterns; pictures of patterns."*
> *Karel: "Where do you get ideas for writing books?"*
> *Shanay: "I get help from my brother. He helps me with spelling. I have the ideas. Ideas from my dreams. I put it together with staples."*
> *Henry: "I'd like to write a book about reptiles — snakes."*
> *Karel: "What do you do first when you write a book?"*
> *Henry: "The title. Then write the words. I'd think about the words. Think of what the snake does. Then pictures."*

Clearly, these youngsters have considerable experience in the processes of creating books. They were able to articulate not only the actual processes of writing a book, but how they think of ideas as well. They were very serious and intent upon their tasks as they worked very hard to help us with this book. They also seemed to enjoy our reunion and the affirmation they received by telling us what to tell the grownups about book writing. We can learn a tremendous amount from children when we ask them questions with respect about something they are good at and know.

Sandra Perkins, from Fullerton Peace Camp, helped one of the children at camp who wanted to write a book. The theme of the camp

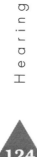

was *Making Our Voices Heard*, and the children had numerous opportunities to speak out on issues of concern to them. Sandra writes:

> In our small group, we discussed various ways in which we could make ourselves heard. Some of those choices were song writing, letters to "decision makers," books, posters, and bumper stickers. Nick chose to write a book. A true artist, his illustrations said so much more than the words on the page. I helped him with the spelling of words, but the pictures were all his.
>
> Nick diligently worked on his book for two days. He would take a break periodically, and then return revived and ready to continue. We would brainstorm and discuss the various issues affecting society. However, what Nick spoke most about was that poor people need money so they can buy food. At the end, he proudly drew the U.S. president shaking his hand and congratulating him on a job well done.

Building Bridges with Families

Sue Bush of Sequoyah School in Pasadena, California, tells that she is always looking for ways to build bridges between school and families. Two ways she builds those bridges are with "The Family Book" and the class newsletter. The Family Book is created when each family sends a page with their child to school which depicts their family. There may be drawings, photographs, writing, and a variety of other ways to show how their family looks and what they like to do. All pages are placed in a loose-leaf notebook, each in a clear plastic envelope. During the year, families add new pages to the book as they record new developments and changes they wish to share.

The monthly newsletter is dictated by the children and then typed up into a readable, reproducible form for families to enjoy. The children select a title for the newsletter through consensus process. Past titles have included: "Cool News" and "Read This Newsletter." Topics discussed in the newsletter focus on learning activities, concerns, and other issues children want to share. The newsletter helps bridge the child's school and family worlds as it communicates what is happening at school with all the families.

Singing and Song Writing with Children

Singing together builds community faster and easier than practically anything. It's fun; it brings people of all ages and abilities and cultures together and binds them through music. It can teach about history; about different ways to think and do things; about traditions; about life — joys and sorrows. Music brings us together to share, to grieve, to learn, and to celebrate and have fun. It is a universal language.

"Aiken Drum" with Three Year Olds
by Cathy Higa

One of our favorite songs is "Aiken Drum." It's the story of "the man who lived in the moon" and whose body is made of different foods for each body part. As beginning song writers, the children love to describe the various parts of his body from foods they know, and to insert the food names into the correct part of the song. After we have sung this song several times, and the children have described various body parts as foods, we try to imagine what Aiken Drum looks like.

When we sing the song, I place a big sheet of paper on the wall. We start with Aiken Drum's head, singing, "His head was made of _____, of _____, of _____. His head was made of _____, and his name was Aiken Drum."

Following is a copy of one of the drawings that our group created. This is what Aiken Drum looks like to the three year olds.

" Aiken Drum "
as described by 3 year olds in Rainbow Room

" Head made of pizza"
by Sydney

"Hair made of spaghetti"
by Heidi

"Hat made of airplane"
by Kyle

" Eyes made of sticks"
by Bradley

"Ears made of cracker"
by Tyler

"Lips made of hotdog"
by Abby

"Coat made of playdough"
by Frankie

Song Writing with Kids
by Lisa Atkinson

For the last 17 years, I have had the privilege to work in classrooms full of children. I visit many schools and I have found that one of the things I enjoy the most is helping them make up songs. "Have you ever really wanted to tell someone how you felt about something important to you?" I will ask. We discuss communication — phone calls, letters, conversation. . . . "How about a song?" I'll ask. Sometimes I'm met with faces that can only be translated as "Oh, I hope she goes away soon." Many more times, I'm delighted by faces that light up at the opportunity to express themselves in a way that has not been offered to them enough. I encourage all of you to sing with children on a daily basis, and then take it one step further: make up your own songs. It gives the children a fantastic sense of ownership. It also helps dissolve the fallacies that you need to:

1. *sound like a recording;*
2. *be a professional;*
3. *have seen it on TV; and*
4. *have a lot of fancy equipment.*

Here are a couple of examples of the stories that have led to some great songs.

My Best Friend

I was writing songs with the kids at the Santa Clara Children's Shelter in Santa Clara, California, when I met five year olds Angela and Bobby Ann. They were so anxious to play my guitar I thought they'd break it in half. As they took turns with the guitar in their laps, I started jotting down the spontaneous lyrics they were creating. None of it seemed to make sense at the time, the words just poured out of the two girls. When I got home, I began to try to put the phrases together like a puzzle. I cried when I understood the simple beauty and truth in what these two abused girls had to share.

MY BEST FRIEND

Words and Music
by Lisa Atkinson
with Angela and Bobby Ann
Age 5
Santa Clara Childrens' Shelter

A friend is a freind for- e - ver. A
friend is a dream come true. Shar- ing a life to- ge - ther. A
friend is a friend like you. Take me for a ride, o -ver the rain - bow
there on the o -ther end. Is a thought meant to share with peo-ple ev ! ry- where
I'm my own best friend. I'm my own best freind.

Is Anybody Listening?

This song was born in a fifth grade classroom in San Jose, California. We were trying to narrow our topics down as more suggestions continued to fly around the room. "Let's write about the environment," said one energetic voice. "No," said another. "I wanna write about the homeless!" "No! I wanna do pollution." As I was asking for a time out to regroup, another dejected voice was heard to say, "Who really cares what we write about, nobody's going to listen to us." The whole room quieted down and looked at me. "That's a powerful statement," I responded. "It'll make a great title." Not only did the kids write a great song, they decided to send it to various environmental organizations. Our song — "Is Anybody Listening?" — was published in four magazines and broadcast nationwide on 200 radio stations. People were listening!

IS ANYBODY LISTENING?

Words and Music by Lisa Atkinson
with Mrs. Bowles' 5th Grade

Is an-y bo-dy lis-ten-ing to the peo-ple on the street? They'll be hungry and cold and a-lone to night when they sleep. If we all took the time to care, may-be they wouldn't all be there. It

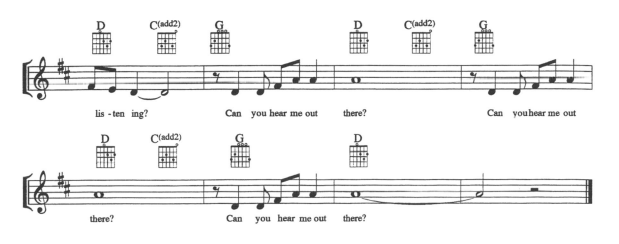

lis - ten ing?   Can you hear me out   there?   Can youhear me out

there?   Can you hear me out   there?

2. Is anybody listening to the earth as she cries?
We're polluting our oceans and poisoning our skies
The forests are empty and longing for trees
The fish and the whales all long for clean seas
We need a solution please
Is anybody listening?

Friendship Songs

Sometimes picking the subject for your song can be the most
difficult part. It's important to choose a topic the kids know a lot about.
A favorite curriculum subject or topic in the school setting is always a
good bet. But, if you're working with kids who aren't in the same class,
I always suggest friends as a topic. Everyone has friends, wants friends,
can have trouble making friends, etc. Here are a few examples of some
of my favorite friendship songs.

The Friendship Song

Friends help friends to be nice
Friends help friends not to fight
Friends help friends to respect each other
Friends help friends to do what's right.

Caring, sharing every day
Friendship is the very best way
I will be a good friend to you
Will you be my friend too
Friendship always sees you through!

This song was written during a song writing workshop with Lisa Atkinson and Ms. Carpenter's kindergarten, Highlands School, San Mateo.

Put Downs Make Me Mad

You've got to build people up
Don't put people down
Make people happy
Don't make'm frown
Nobody likes to feel sad
Put downs make me mad!

You know, nobody likes to feel downhearted
Fighting about how the whole thing started
Ten minutes ago we were both best friends
I wish this argument would end

chorus

Let's talk it out, that's what's needed
You've got to treat other people like you want to be treated

If you're not nice to people and you fight and lie
You can (smack) kiss your friends goodbye

chorus

Let's have a heart to heart
Don't let put downs tear your friendships apart
Oh, yeah!!

This song was written during a songwriting workshop with
Lisa Atkinson and Mrs. Thane's first/second grade,
Highlands School, San Mateo, 1997.

Friends Are Good

Friends are good
They stick up for you
And when you need them they are there.
We laugh alot
And have some fun
And when you're hurt they really care.
You're nice to them
They're nice to you.
You're happy they're around.
And that's the reason I like you
You're the best friend I have found.

And it feels good to know you
And even when we're far apart
I'll still think about you everyday
And you always will remain in my heart.

This song was written during a songwriting workshop with Lisa Atkinson
and Ms. Davis' third grade at McKinley School in San Francisco, 1992.

Community Building

The community of Santa Maria, California, spends a week in community building activities around the theme of peace. The week is called *Peace by Peace: Building a Community of Peacemakers*, and the week looks like this:

MONDAY: *Building a Community of Peacemakers*
   Community Breakfast
   Dedication of the Peace Pole
   Legislative Luncheon
   Greeting of Respect — Drivers are asked to turn on auto lights
      throughout the week

TUESDAY: *Peace in the Home*
   Workshops:
      Anger — Dealing with Mine, Dealing with Yours
      Violence from Unresolved Grief
      How Healing Takes Place in the Family

WEDNESDAY: *Respect the Earth/Respect for People*
   Tree Rescue and Demonstration
   Discussion on Creating Livable Communities

THURSDAY: *Respect for Youth Day*
   Community-Wide Pause for Peace
   Youth Peace Pledge
   Peace Posters
   Student Peace Summit

FRIDAY: *Promoting Peace Through the Media*
   Workshops:
      Promoting Peace Through the Media
      Come and Reflect — Peaceful Thoughts with Peaceful Music

SATURDAY: *Respect for Cultural Diversity/Respect for the Earth*
   Examining Racism
   Butterfly and Hummingbird Gardens
   Sustainable Garden Planting
   Recycling
   Tour of Local Beach

Open House at Discovery Center
Insect Identification
Lead Testing Presentation
Plant Problems
Community Gardens
Tree Care

SUNDAY: *Reflection Day*
Ecumenical Peace Reflection Ceremony
Tolling of Church Bells

Another very specific project which has been developed by Larry Long of Minneapolis, Minnesota, builds community through an oral history gathering with the community elders. The oral history stories are recorded, then Larry transcribes the tapes and organizes the material so that he and a group of elementary school-aged children can create a song, or songs, to tell the stories. Later, a celebration is planned and organized by the community to share the work and songs. The community really comes together as the elders share their lives and community stories and the youngsters create the music to retell the history of their community.

Other community building may happen in less structured ways through activities such as quilt making; group murals; celebrations; neighborhood gatherings such as block parties, concerts, parades; and other opportunities to bring the whole community together. Use any excuse to bring people together to share and enjoy each other!

Integrating Children's Issues and Democratic Practice Strategies to Build Community

To sum up several of these strategies and how they are effectively integrated within a program for children, Lucy Stroock has written the following thoughts about her preschoolers: how the teachers observed their play, assessed the needs expressed, created strategies to support children's trust building, and how they created community.

Weapons Play Revisited:
Building Trust at Haggerty Preschool
Fall, 1997
by Lucy Stroock

It is free choosing time in our small, multi-age preschool class-room, week two of the new school year. Children are painting, rolling play dough, doing puzzles, building the track for the Little Tykes expressway, cooking, and leading their friends around as pet cats. All should be well. But in the climber/large muscle area, a group of rowdy boys are waving a variety of longish, hard objects and making threatening gestures as they climb, jump, and roll among the large, soft blocks.

The new preschool year began with an unusual challenge in 1997. Twenty unknown children, ages 2.9 to 4.5, arrived with only three familiar returnees. As veteran teachers, we brought the confidence of experience to the task and the first days went smoothly. It was primarily the extra attention to bathrooming which told us that these were younger, less experienced children. Very few cried at parting from their parents, and the children were surprisingly ready for our brief group time, eagerly listening to stories and joining in with songs. By the second week, however, we had to acknowledge that we faced an intense outbreak of weapons-focused play.

With no "real" toy guns, swords, etc. in the room, and none allowed from home, the children's ingenuity was demonstrated early on. The reading stick; drum sticks; all the plastic wrenches, pliers, saws; and the long blocks were tried out as we responded by asserting the need for safety and the proper use of these items. Imagination soon led to the dramatic play area and the cucumber, banana, corn, and squash were found to have the favored, suggestive shape. The doctor kit was raided for its plastic syringes and hammers; the rolling pins for play dough turned up in odd places. Duplo blocks were immediately crafted into pistols, and most alarmingly to our adult eyes, the Duplo airplane body overturned with its tail became a hefty machine gun. We protested and redirected to no avail.

The game became one of secretly maneuvering to get the weapons without our suspecting. One child would look up, see us, and immediately begin chewing on the ear of plastic corn in his hand, a big smile on his face. Finally, as all teachers of this age group discover, and children

138

Hearing Everyone's Voice

seem to know instinctively: graham crackers look like guns if you bite off one corner, and an index finger is the pistol of last resort. The soft capes and foam hoses which we offered as alternatives did not satisfy. Weapons need to be hard.

Meanwhile, no real mayhem was occurring. We determined early on that this group was not angry or interested in hurting each other. Nonetheless, the play was alarming to other children who found themselves caught up in its swirl, including those who were brandishing the weapons. All children felt threatened when the pseudo-weapons were waved in their faces. Many avoided the climber area, where active play is encouraged, and so were missing out on the climbing and tumbling opportunities we value for every child. Some parents commented that the play seemed rough, and they were concerned by their children's fascination with weapons. Others were worried about their more shy children's physical and psychological safety.

We determined during conferences with parents that television watching could not account for what we were observing. One father did sheepishly acknowledge that he had been playing some computer games with his son which did involve a lot of doing in of bad guys. And some of the children had been exposed to Power Rangers through contact with older children. The whole pantheon of super heroes were named by the children in the course of their play, but none of the action seemed to mimic the fictional characters. It was the idea of power that seemed to be important as the names of Batman, Spiderman, Superman, and the Power Rangers were invoked. By mid-October, the action had changed some as children got to know the class routines better and made different choices in their play. But we were uncomfortable with the level of need for weapons which a number of the boys still displayed. We were concerned that this play was continuing to interfere with their relationships and limiting the other children's play. In addition, we were worried because several parents, and their children, were beginning to identify a few children as "bad," based on the rowdiness of the play, even though we could confidently assert that there was no physical harm happening, and no one was being victimized.

As we puzzled, observed, and got to know them better, it became clear that for a number of the children there was an undercurrent of anxiety in the way they clung to their weapons and held them up towards each other. These were defensive weapons which the children seemed to feel they needed to protect themselves from their peers. They were not hitting others, but their gestures were looking aggressive and setting off defensive reactions in the children around them. As we began to ask the children to express what they were experiencing, it often emerged that the one who looked most threatening was feeling scared himself. This information came to us sometimes from their words, but, also, often from their faces as we began to take the possibility of fear into account. It became apparent that a lot of what we were seeing was based on misunderstanding, and the children were acting on the old understanding that "a good offense is the best defense."

At this point, a second theme of our fall began to intersect with the ongoing weapons play issue. Since the first week, it had been clear that friendship was important, and difficult, for a significant number of the children. We were startled to discover this emerging so early in the preschool year, but we had to recognize that anxiety about "Who will be my friend?" was undermining a number of the children's pleasure in school. Predictably this story was being played out more clearly among the older girls in the group, but it also involved a number of boys. We found ourselves bemoaning with parents the complexity of friendship, and encouraging them to avoid questions like "Who is your friend?" which convey the assumption that children at this age will have a best friend and that such friendships will be long lasting. We found ourselves constantly trying to repair the damage of a friendship interrupted as one child turned away to pursue a different game with someone new. The message that you can have many friends was not easy to receive, and hearts were being broken daily.

As we grappled with the difficulty of friendship for this group of children, we came to realize that the same issues of trust and control were embedded in the fear we saw in the boys' weapon play and in the pain of not knowing who is one's friend. Preschool age children are labeled in the story of human development as egocentric and impulsive. Teachers refer to this reality as we bemoan and accept our chosen fate. "That's how they are; that's the work we do. We must be able to take them as they are, or we better be in a different profession." The hard truth we recognized this fall is that children in a preschool setting are also confronting this reality. They must find their friends, find a way to trust and feel in control, in the midst of a group of children who, like themselves, are egocentric and impulsive! One might despair. . . .

The daily presence of the children did not allow us the luxury of despair. Several of our usual practices seemed relevant to this predicament. The first is that old chestnut, "Use your words," which we know involves us giving the children the words to use, as often as not. And, in

addition, we have learned that we must insist that the children look at each others' faces as they attempt this feat of communication. We often have to verbalize for them what the other child is feeling or trying to say, because shyness and their limited language skills make it hard for them to be clear with each other. Helping every child to have a voice in the group, and insisting that even the more dominant children must listen to others, is basic to our practice. This year, with so many new children who did not know each other, and whom we did not know, the task has been slow. We must be prepared to reiterate the message many times, and often to the same child. It is not easy, adults struggle with this too, as we know.

Egocentric three and four year olds have an especially hard time. Their voice may have been the only child's voice in the family. Or there may have been a responsive older sister who gives in to all demands, the circumstance for several of our young boys this year. Or they may have wonderful, thoughtful parents who respond to their conversation in reasoned and supportive ways unlikely to be matched by their school mates. For the number of children learning English as their second language, there is an additional challenge. One of the boys is struggling to find the facility with English which he has in Greek. He is frustrated and anxious, missing the comfort of his loving and talkative family, but he is also excited and eager to make contact with his peers. A weapon in hand seems to give him the courage.

Harder even than this task of listening is accepting that the other child has a right to have a different point of view. This lesson is especially slow to take hold among preschoolers. They often prefer to give up and turn to other pursuits when the necessity of paying attention to a fellow's viewpoint is presented. And friendship suffers. The control of the game which they all want is unlikely, and many children are unreconciled. One very young child declares that he wants to be mom, and it is time to go home whenever the game is not going his way. Fortunately, the pleasures of school are sufficient to keep the children coming back while the necessary negotiating skills are being mastered and play becomes more satisfying.

For this year's group of weapons-wielding fellows, fear and anxiety comes from uncertainty about whether their peers were trustworthy. And they have reason for doubt. Most of the group are very inexperienced in the ways of rough-and-tumble play. They have not spent time with brothers or cousins or neighbors with whom they can experiment with the limits. The rules of the game are just being learned. They do not always stop when someone gets hurt or upset. And their impulsiveness can be dangerous, especially with hard objects in their hands.

It is three and a half months into the year now and we can report some progress. What follows are several of the strategies we have found to be helpful. Early on we recognized that the children needed a safe way to confront their anxieties and build trust. The game of Monster, a perennial favorite, gave us a way to help them master their scared feelings in the group. The usual run and chase game on the playground was happening with some children taking the lead as monsters, other fleeing, and another group staying well out of the way. We involved ourselves in the game: taking turns chasing and being chased, growling fiercely at times, and feigning fear at others. This adult presence helped more children trust that the game was safe, and fun! Shy children particularly loved to have their own private game with a teacher. They were delighted to take on the role of monster and cause a grownup to flee.

Meanwhile, we were setting limits and helping the group as a whole recognize that they could not terrorize each other. No one could be chased who did not like it, and no one could be cast as the monster (or "bad guy") without consenting to the role. We regularly stopped the action to check in with the participants and make sure everyone was having fun. Finally the day came when one of the quietest, youngest girls, standing in the midst of the action on the indoor climber, proudly announced that she had "scared Michael," an older and bigger boy. She was beaming and making it clear that she knew and trusted the game and its players. (Reading Where the Wild Things Are and There's a Nightmare in My Closet supplemented this more active approach to the recognition of everyone's normal fearfulness.)

We have worked with the children so that now when a child is hurt or upset the whole group is asked to stop and pay attention. They ask each other "Are you okay?" when they collide or otherwise arrive at painful places. When one is down, the others are asked to help him or her up. These simple expectations allow the children to see themselves and their peers in the role of friend and helper, not so scary and unpredictable as they seemed at first. A moment of success came when one of the more egocentric children was observed spontaneously turning to the child he had just accidentally knocked down and asking, "Are you okay?" One of the side benefits we are learning from this procedure is that the hurt child recovers much more quickly when a friend's hand is being offered.

Another strategy that has helped is our work in problem solving around the idea that everyone must be able to play in the climber area. With an adult present to assure that everyone is comfortable, and insistence that only soft objects can be used there safely, the population of active players has diversified. Turning the climber into a tent and providing flashlights allowed exploration of the shared fear of the dark to become the adventure, and children could experience a new sense of security in the crowded space of the tent. As more children feel confident to assert their right to be in the area, the play has changed and become more often house building and nesting. The super heroes have had to make way or join in, and often now they initiate the gentler activities.

In December, we repeated a strategy from several years back when we were confronted by lots of macho behavior and wanted to support a boy who still came to school hugging his stuffed dog each day. Mark, my co-teacher, brought in his childhood teddy bear and introduced the children to Fuzzy, somewhat less than fuzzy after many years, but still soft, and welcoming of hugs. The children responded warmly to Fuzzy, and to our invitation for them to bring in their own special stuffed animals. In the next weeks, boy after boy brought a soft friend from home to share at school. In a world which so often sends young boys the message that they must be tough, we want them to know that they can acknowledge their gentler nature at school. And we want them to recognize that their peers are also capable of gentleness, and that they all welcome a hug and a soft friend for snuggling. Shar-ing the many   ft friends such as Runa   ling this warm place

Trust is g   resses. We know tha   ne children, but   ; more secure as the   n are getting to kno   bilities for friendship wit   n as the ear of corn is   And we can celebrate   n.

Route Item   12/15/2011 5:14:53 PM

ROUTE ITEM:

TO:

KENDALL COLLEGE LIBRARY
CIRC DESK
ILDS: KEN
Library
Kendall College
Chicago, IL 60642

Patron Category: UBLong
Patron Barcode:
A*24811200053987*

Media Violence Can Undermine Children's Ability to Participate

by Diane Levin
Used with permission from *Remote Control Childhood*

There are several ways that media, media violence, and media-linked toys make it hard for children to develop the attitudes and skills they need to feel empowered to participate in our society.

SECOND-HAND EXPERIENCE

When children watch TV, they are interacting only indirectly with their world. They are having second-hand experience where they passively observe the experiences and ideas of others. What they really need to become problem solvers and active participants in their world is lots of first-hand experience.

IMITATIVE PLAY

When children have time to play, their media-linked toys often channel them into imitating what they saw in the media rather than actively developing their own scripts based on their own needs. This can reduce their opportunities to experience the kind of power that can come from trying out and seeing how their own ideas and actions can affect their world.

VIOLENCE AS THE WAY TO FEEL POWERFUL

Children are shown over and over in media and media-linked toys that violence provides an acceptable, even desirable, way to solve problems and feel powerful. In this situation, instead of experiencing the real power that can come from having a meaningful impact in their environment and the people in it, children only experience the pseudo-power that comes from the media violence they imitate.

DEPENDENCE ON THE MEDIA

As children's ability to feel powerful and effective from their own actions is undermined, their ability to resist the pull of media and media violence also are weakened. A vicious cycle can be set up whereby children NEED media, media violence, and media-related toys to feel strong when what they really need is opportunities to feel strong from their own positive actions. This, in turn, makes them need TV even more.

The media has become a powerful influence and educator in our culture. It has often promoted simplistic solutions to complex issues, solutions which do not take into consideration the multiple perspectives of the participants involved nor the wide variety of possible solutions to any given problem. Television helps develop *either/or* thinking, rarely *both/and* thinking, as it provides experiences in receiving but not interacting with information. In our work with children, it is important that we create as many opportunities as possible to participate in multiple perspective taking and in solving problems — in essence, to interact with one another.

V. Emergent Learning Strategies

Creating learning opportunities for children is a concern for parents and teachers alike. One of the ways teachers of young children think about such planning is through a method variously called *Emergent Curriculum*, *Child-Centered Programming*, and *Teachable Moments*. Teachable Moments are those moments in time in which there is an opportunity to extend someone's understanding and knowledge of a concept, or to provide ways to practice a skill. They are built upon a previously expressed interest or concern from the learner. All of these titles define a way of planning which extend children's knowledge and skills in ways which empower them to develop their own lifelong learning processes.

Such planning can be described in three basic steps which form a spiral because of the ongoing, continuous nature of learning. The three steps are:

1. Observation and listening, to really hear
2. Shared planning for continued learning
3. Implementation of plans, continued observation for next steps

Each of these steps will be further described in the stories which follow, but it may also be useful to expand a bit on them at this point as well. First, observation and listening to describe and, therefore, really "hear" what children have to communicate have been discussed thoroughly in previous sections of this book. In addition, more tips on listening are available in the section on "Adult Obstacles." The second step, shared planning, takes the planning concept beyond the authority (the adult) to share in the process with the learner. Ways to learn more about a topic, concept, or skill — to extend knowledge — may be explored together. Such sharing and collaboration set the model for how to learn, not simply learning the material. The third step, implementation, is the actualization of the plans by the learner with support from the adult. Also involved is continued observation and listening to come around again to hearing what the learner next needs in his/her development. And so the cycle goes: round and round!

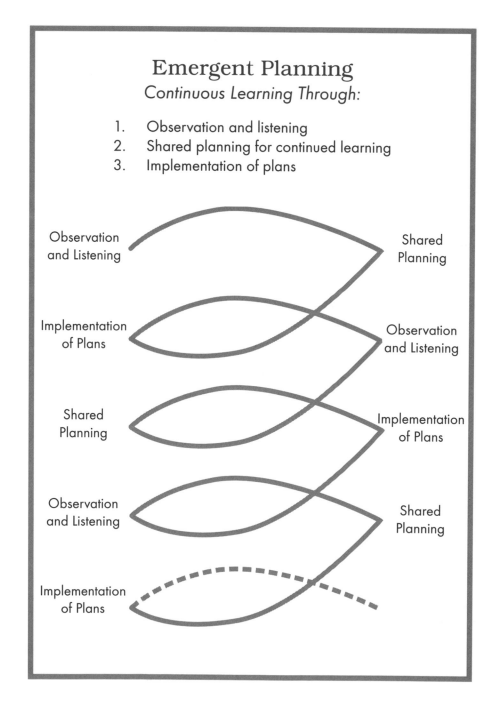

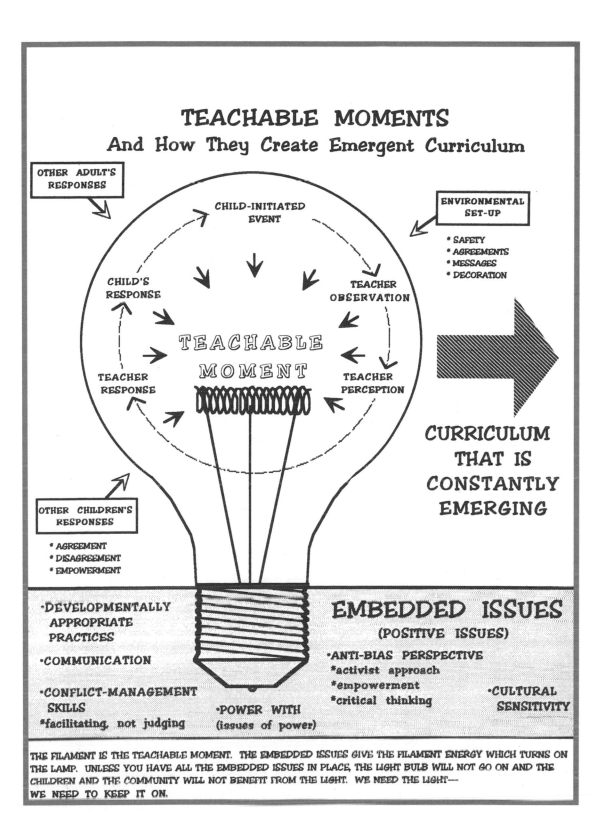

TEACHABLE MOMENTS
And How They Create Emergent Curriculum

OTHER ADULT'S RESPONSES

ENVIRONMENTAL SET-UP

* SAFETY
* AGREEMENTS
* MESSAGES
* DECORATION

CHILD-INITIATED EVENT

CHILD'S RESPONSE

TEACHER OBSERVATION

TEACHABLE MOMENT

TEACHER RESPONSE

TEACHER PERCEPTION

OTHER CHILDREN'S RESPONSES

* AGREEMENT
* DISAGREEMENT
* EMPOWERMENT

CURRICULUM THAT IS CONSTANTLY EMERGING

- DEVELOPMENTALLY APPROPRIATE PRACTICES

- COMMUNICATION

- CONFLICT-MANAGEMENT SKILLS
*facilitating, not judging

- POWER WITH (issues of power)

EMBEDDED ISSUES
(POSITIVE ISSUES)

- ANTI-BIAS PERSPECTIVE
*activist approach
*empowerment
*critical thinking

- CULTURAL SENSITIVITY

THE FILAMENT IS THE TEACHABLE MOMENT. THE EMBEDDED ISSUES GIVE THE FILAMENT ENERGY WHICH TURNS ON THE LAMP. UNLESS YOU HAVE ALL THE EMBEDDED ISSUES IN PLACE, THE LIGHT BULB WILL NOT GO ON AND THE CHILDREN AND THE COMMUNITY WILL NOT BENEFIT FROM THE LIGHT. WE NEED THE LIGHT—WE NEED TO KEEP IT ON.

Step 1. Observation and Listening, to Really Hear

The Mockingbird Song
New words for an old song by Ben Silver

This terrific rewrite of a standard lullaby was written for Gabriel Silver, born November, 1996. When Gabriel was a few weeks old, his visiting grandmother started singing "Hush Little Baby" to him, and Ben noticed that Gabriel responded really strongly to the beautiful music. Ben wanted to keep singing it but he didn't like the words, so he changed them to fit his own message to his son.

Yes, little baby, you'll be heard,
Papa's gonna listen to every word;

And if those words don't get you by,
Papa's gonna be there when you cry.

And when that crying is all done,
Papa's gonna take you to have some fun;

And if that fun should make you smile,
Papa's gonna laugh with you awhile.

And if by chance you should get blue,
Papa's gonna hold you 'til you get through;

And if you need to scream and shout,
Papa's gonna be there while you work it out.

And as you make your dreams come true,
Papa's gonna encourage you;

And if you get a great idea,
Papa's gonna really want to hear.

It ain't about no mockingbird,
Children should be seen — and heard!

Now You See It . . .
by Kathy "Omie" Olmstead

Kathy Olmstead is a teacher at Cal State Fullerton Children's Center with the infants, ages six to fourteen months. She uses her keen observation skills and experience with the development of babies to support these little ones in their needs as they first separate from their families.

Jeremy had been crying since his mother had dropped him off in the Infant Room about ten minutes before. He had never been separated from his mother in the 11 months since he was born and he was both frightened and angry. Caregivers had offered him opportunities to be picked up but he wiggled away from them and crawled away to sob in a corner of the room that had a soft mattress and pillows. One of the caregivers who had been watching him went over quietly carrying a large square of sheer white material three feet by three feet. She didn't look at him or speak to him. She just sat down near him and gently covered her own head and shoulders with the piece of material.

She sat very still. Jeremy could see her through the cloth. Then she softly began to sing the song "Bingo." Jeremy stopped crying and watched her carefully. When her song was done, he patted the cloth and it slipped slightly. He pulled at it and, when it came off, revealing the caregiver, she smiled and said, "Peek-a-Boo, Jeremy." He smiled, so she covered herself again and, after a moment, he pulled it off again. They played this game together a few more times and then Jeremy pulled the cloth over his head. The caregiver let him keep it there, knowing he was seeing the world around him in an intriguing new hazy way. When he pulled the cloth off and looked expectantly at her, she answered his unspoken request and said, "Peek-a-Boo."

Being left in a strange place for an unspecified length of time with people you don't know is unappealing to most people, no matter what age. We are unsure of the rules, of how the stranger will react to what we might do, and unable to predict what will happen from moment to moment. We feel powerless.

Everybody needs to feel powerful in appropriate ways, even babies. When Jeremy played "Peek-a-Boo" with the caregiver, he had the power to decide a number of things. *He could choose to play or not.* He waited until *he* was ready to approach the caregiver. She let him take the cloth off of her when *he* wanted to. As it became obvious that he wanted the game to continue, she covered herself and let *him* uncover her. *When he was ready,* he covered himself and she verbalized the "Peek-a-Boo" for him.

She offered Jeremy the opportunity to play the game, originally, but he made up the rules as they played together. Jeremy couldn't make his mother reappear right away, but he could explore making the caregiver "disappear" and then reappear.

Pretty powerful stuff for an 11 month old!

Step 2. Shared Planning for Continuous Learning

"Piecing the Quilt"
by LuAnne Venham

I was at Fullerton Peace Camp during the first week of August, 1995. I brought my sewing machine into the arbor area of the Arboretum on Thursday to piece together the children's peace quilt.

The year before I had taken the pieces home after our week of Peace Camp and made a quilt which was now hanging in the Arbor. This year I wanted the children to see the whole process and have the quilt on display Friday for our closing family celebration. What I did not realize at the time was that it was going to present an opportunity for negotiation and problem solving, in a very hands-on fashion, for some of the first, second, and third graders.

The muslin squares that the children had painted were 12x12 inches. There were 24 squares which I laid out on the floor in six rows of four. I began to sew. One child was very interested in the sewing. I showed her how I would sew pieces with the right sides together so when I opened them up, the rough edges wouldn't show. I sewed the first two pieces together and laid them back in the spot to show her where I would add the next piece.

At this point, five or six children had gathered and began saying things like "I want mine next to his." I told them that they could move the

squares in any way they wanted, but it had to be in the six rows of four, and I could not take out any of the sewing I had already done.

I continued on with the first row. Each time I finished a square, I would lay it back in place so the children could see it come together. Each time I did this, I noticed some of the pieces had been moved. I tried very hard to let the children do the moving, placing, and replacing of the pieces on their own. I facilitated as I went about my work of sewing piece by piece. I asked questions like "What do you need?" or "What would happen if . . . ?" For the most part, the children did this on their own. By the time all 24 pieces were sewn together, everyone had had a voice, and each child was happy with the placement of each piece.

I showed the children how I first put the sheet face down on the floor, then rolled out the fiber fill, and on top our pieced together squares. I folded the edges of the sheet to make a binding and finally used a needle with yarn to knot the corner of each square to hold the layers of the quilt together.

On Friday, the quilt was on display for the parents to see what the children had painted as their images of peace. What they could not see was all the negotiation, the listening to each other's ideas, and the problem solving that went into the placement of each and every square.

As the quilt is on display at Peace Camp and around the country in Advocacy Centers, it is admired for the art work. When I see this quilt, I think of the skills that the children were building that day and I hope that they felt empowered to continue on with this type of "peace work."

It Was Just a Fish — But What an Experience!
by Janice Sheffield

At the California State University Fullerton Children's Center, the Sunshine Room algae eater died in the aquarium. Jan, the teacher in that classroom of four year olds, got a net, took the fish out of the tank, and put it into a small container. The children gathered at the table so everyone could see that the black fish (algae eater) was dead. Jan explained that when a fish dies, other fish nearby will eat it. The body of the dead fish has nutrients in it to help the other fish stay strong.

Nothing is wasted. The dead fish no longer needs its body. The black fish had been eaten on his underside by the others; therefore, no heart, stomach, liver — only bones and an empty body cavity. The fish had even nibbled on his fins. The children got up close looks and could touch if they wished. Actually, from the top, it still looked like the black fish.

Outside, a burial hole was made in the turtle pen. It's in an out-of-the-way place where no one walks and the turtles do not dig. Other small pets have also been buried in this area over the years.

Jan placed the small algae eater into the hole and then asked if anyone would like to put a pinch of dirt on the fish. Almost all the Sunshine children wanted to have a turn. The children waited very quietly and patiently for their turns. They were serious and respectful. Some of the younger children came by to watch; Jan asked them if they would like to put a pinch of dirt on the fish too. They were pleased to be included, and certainly wanted turns. The whole time there was very little talking among the children, and what little there was simply explained what was happening to include the newcomers on the scene. A few of the children also spoke of pets they had when they were "little" which had died. They had some warm memories and one could hear a bit of sadness in their voices. They seemed to feel better as they shared their stories with others.

Karina, a four year old, asked if she could play her "horn" — she put her thumb and pointer finger in a circle up to her lips. Jan told her it certainly would be all right to play her horn. Karina asked several times while waiting, and Jan encouraged her to play; but she just stood there and looked at the fish. At the very end, when all the dirt had been used up to fill the hole, Karina quietly played "Taps" all the way through on her horn. Everyone was quiet and listened until the song was over.

Sharing such a moving experience with young children is unforgettable! Their compassion and concern, shown by their quiet attention, was obvious. For many, this may have been a first experience with death. And what a healthy one! It provided opportunities for the children to see the fish, to participate at all levels of burying the fish, to talk about their own experiences, and to be able to be sad. They had the support of each other and a teacher well practiced in listening, observing, and providing ways for the children to process the experience in their own best ways.

Step 3. Implementation of Plans

Emerging Conflict Resolution Skills
by Sharon Davisson

A critical ingredient in the success of the Stepping Stones Preschool program is that the children are together for at least two years. This significant block of time together sets the stage for meaningful relationships to develop. It also provides adequate time to develop conflict resolution skills. During the nursery year, as conflicts arise, the teachers reflect what they see, "I see that two children want this one toy; let me hold the toy while we try to work this out." Or, "I see that when you took the truck out of Sammy's hands, he began to cry." We also give direct instructions on words that might help the child, "You can say, 'Sammy, may I have a turn with the truck?'" We also affirm that the children have choices, "Sammy, you may say 'yes,' or you may say 'no.'" The children begin to understand that the adults are not going to jump in and solve the problems, but rather will help the children learn how to negotiate, brainstorm, and problem solve. We then begin turning the conflicts over to the children. In the nursery class, this usually begins occurring during the third month. We may say to two children tugging over a toy, "I see that we have a problem here, it looks as though two children want one toy. Johnny, do you have an idea on how to solve the problem? Sammy, do you?"

During the second year (and once in a while during the nursery year), a conflict may occur that causes distress in a number of children. When this happens, we deal with the crisis in the regular way, but later (usually during circle time) we process what happened. The children then do some brainstorming while one of the teachers draws illustrations of the problems and suggested solutions. At this point, the children begin the process of establishing their own rules of safety. We call the process "Making a Safe Place" and the chart may grow throughout the year. The current chart for the nursery class includes illustrations for "no hitting," "no punching," "no throwing toys." It also includes child suggested safety hints such as "go up the stairs safely," "talk," and "hugs!"

We often have a designated spot for conflict resolution. A favorite in the play yard is the *Talking Table* where the children with the problem and any other children who wish to help sit and offer ideas. Indoors, the children naturally go to the circle room.

The second year we introduce another tool for problem solving — the *Talking Stick*. Before we bring it into the classroom, we present a puppet story. The story has two little animals that repeatedly argue and tug on a toy until it breaks (we use a rolled up piece of paper that breaks easily). After the third attempt to play together without success, they go for help to Miss Mouse, who introduces the Talking Stick. After using the stick, they are able to take turns and happily sing a little song about "Use a Word."

The next step is introducing the Talking Stick. We do this by telling another story at circle time. The story incorporates the concept that the Talking Stick helps bring peace, that the child who is holding the stick may speak and the rest of us must listen. Each child has a right to hold the stick and speak. We then bring in a stick and let the children decorate it. The final addition is a pouch we attach that holds small stones that we have each held and "put our love into." The children love this formal process and spontaneously use the Talking Stick throughout the rest of the year.

The children become so fascinated with the brainstorming aspects, the challenge and the satisfaction of working on problems, that they usually come to the point of getting very eager to problem solve. Conflicts become opportunities! We do not wish to have a conflict-free environment but rather a safe environment. Conflicts offer the children great opportunities to use their emerging thinking skills and empathy. We sometimes are unable to resolve a problem but learn to accept that, in life, problems sometimes do not have solutions.

By December or January of the second year, it is common to see children spontaneously going into the conflict resolution process on their own. We often hear the children shouting, "We did it!" or "We figured it out!" Sometimes it takes a simple reminder from the teacher such as "Do you have a problem?" or "Are you listening?" for the children to shift into the problem-solving process. The confidence, enthusiasm, and independence evidenced by these children is truly heart warming.

Constructing Knowledge
Using Shared Authority to Hear the Children

As stated earlier, children build their knowledge upon previous learnings. Because new understandings are constructed upon previous ones, we strive to give children new experiences which build logically on what they have already learned. It may be challenging to us, the adults, to decide upon the next best step. But, if we are willing to let the children help tell us the next step, or when we have not chosen the appropriate next step, we can trust that together we'll be able to work out what's needed. Children tell us what they need — we just have to be open to putting our own ideas aside and listening to them.

Looking at our title, *Hearing Everyone's Voice*, it is interesting to consider the topic of shared authority when it comes to listening to the children and letting them guide us in planning how to meet their needs. There is always the paradox for us, the adults — we want to listen to the children but, "Aren't we supposed to know what's best?" What if our ideas of "best" differ from the children's? One of the important ways to think about this question is in terms of both/and. How can we support the needs of the children as well as bring in our experience and knowledge? This question will challenge us in all our relationships and in planning for best practices. How we make these decisions to share authority with children is the basis of our work in *Hearing Everyone's Voice*.

In planning these experiences for learning, we are also very careful to use our knowledge of development to bring our expectations of the children in line with their growth. We generally do not have the same expectations of a two year old and a four year old. We are not referring to intelligence; we are referring to the development of coordination, focusing ability, attention span, and how children's thinking affects the way they understand things. These developmental areas of growth progress in unique ways for individuals and create opportunities for the grownups in children's lives to listen and observe them carefully to best determine what the next steps in knowledge construction could be for them. Hence the importance of "The Teachable Moment" and emergent strategies. These ways of planning for children's needs blend what they are telling us together with our knowledge of them.

How Children's Thinking Progresses

Diane Levin has developed this chart in her book, *Teaching Young Children in Violent Times: Building a Peaceable Classroom*, which has been adapted and used with permission for this section on "Emergent Strategies."

Children's thinking progresses:

From	To
Focusing on one thing at a time	Bringing in and coordinating many aspects of a situation
Egocentrism and taking their own point of view	Being able to consider more than one point of view
Thinking in rigid and dichotomous categories	Seeing that more than one attribute defines a category and that attributes can fit along a continuum
Focusing on the concrete and visible aspects of situations and ideas	Being able to imagine what cannot be seen and to think abstractly
Failing to make logical connections between causes and effects	Making logical causal connections between events
Static thinking — as in a slide show — from one slide to the next	Dynamic thinking, where transformations occur as in the frames of a movie.

"Change occurs as children have many opportunities to try out their ideas, see how they work, and then modify them based on what happened." (pages 24-25)

Hearing Everyone's Voice

Observation of Children's Concerns
Linking to Build Emergent Learning Strategies and Nurturing Communities

Play for Empowerment
by Susan Hopkins

Those of us who have dedicated our lives to making the world a better place for children know how important it is that we support children in their efforts to comprehend the experiences which touch their lives — to help them make sense of their world. Children are exposed to some very complex issues including violence and family problems — either first hand, through the media, or at school and in the community. These are powerful influences and it is important that children be given opportunities to work through them in supportive, nonjudgmental environments. This is our job; this is our responsibility; this is our commitment to children!

How are opportunities provided for children to make sense of the world as they see it? It is our role to: first, create carefully planned environments; second, observe and listen thoughtfully to be able to pick up on children's concerns; and, third, integrate children's issues into their learning, the knowledge they are constructing.

The very first step is to set up an environment in which children can trust and take charge of their play: areas for dramatic play, blocks, creative expression; fluid materials such as water, paint, sand trays, and so on. Children need time to fully develop their play, opportunities to make choices, and experiences in taking initiative to develop their skills in creating new ideas. All in all, we're talking about empowerment: about setting up environments for children in which they have some control and responsibility.

Second, set about making time to observe and listen to children in order to develop awareness and understanding of their issues, concerns, and interests. Look and listen — really listen to what they are saying with a focus on their concerns. Watch as they bring props into the play, as they select materials, as they set up their own play environments to work out themes. As an observer, please do not intrude or ban certain types of play unless a safety or respect issue is involved. If it's necessary to intrude, then a discussion with the children is needed so they understand the reasons for the decision and can participate in suggesting compromise ideas. Observe the themes children work out in their play such as power, safety, inclusion/exclusion. Notice the roles children take: the patterns in their interactions such as submission to others, becoming the victim, peacemaker, or controller. And, of course, be aware of the feelings being expressed and worked through: fears, anger, and so many others.

Careful observing and listening will lead the adults into planning how to meet the children's need to understand the issues which affect their lives. The third step in the process is to help children integrate their concerns into their play. For example, after the "civil unrest" in Los Angeles several years ago, the four year olds at Cal State Fullerton Children's Center were taking small blocks into the dramatic play area to create police radios. They were empowering themselves to call for help in a scary situation such as they had seen on television. We brought out the fire fighting clothes and tools, helped children make radios if they wished, and encouraged lots of verbal interaction about fears, roles, and what to do.

As the theme evolved over several days, the play became more sophisticated and a hospital was set up by the children for the victims. The adults were constantly watching and listening to be able to more fully support the children with materials, discussion, and encouragement. Different roles were tried, problems were solved, and feelings were shared.

Group discussion evolved along with the dramatic play and started with what the children had seen on television, how they felt about it, and moved into clarification from the teacher when there was confusion. Questions included:

Teacher: What have you been watching on TV?
Child: The news, riots, fires, stealing . . .

Teacher: Why were people taking things?
Child: Because they were angry . . .

Teacher: Is it okay to take things when you are angry?
Child: No, it's not okay . . .

Teacher: Why were the people angry?
Child: They were angry at the police . . .

Teacher: Why?
Child: Because they hurt someone . . .

Teacher: Do you remember the name of the man they hurt?
Child: Ummmmmm . . .

Teacher: His name is Rodney King. Do you know what happened to him? Why the police hurt him?
Child: (Blank stares . . .)

Teacher: He was driving too fast and tried to run away from the police when they stopped him.
Child: Why was he running away?
Teacher: Probably because he was scared.

Teacher: The police were angry about him running away so they hurt him. What do you think about that?
Child: It's not okay; they shouldn't hurt him . . .

Teacher: What could they do instead?
Child: They could talk to him on the radio . . .

Teacher: Do you think all police officers hurt people?
Child: No, police are to help people . . .

Teacher: Most police help people keep safe by arresting the ones who steal things and set fires. It's their job to keep people from getting hurt.

The children worked on these issues for weeks, gradually moving on to other concerns as they felt more comfortable about the "civil unrest" and its impact on their lives. Such events in our society do give us unique opportunities to work with children to develop some of the skills and qualities needed to be effective members of a democracy. Children are aware of the world around them, as it directly affects them. It's important that adults include them and help them resolve their concerns in ways which are appropriate for their level of development. Inclusiveness is basic to democratic practice and therefore it is our role to determine how the children are feeling and what their concerns may be relating to a significant event. It's important not to ignore them or make them feel that they cannot participate when critical events occur.

Integrating children's issues into their play may involve themes around safety and fears, as discussed above, as well as themes such as power, fairness, and many others. For example, issues of power can be incorporated as we interact with children when shared authority is modeled with them, as leadership is encouraged in forms which help others (rather than having "power over" them), and as our "power" is used to work together to accomplish tasks. Fairness and inclusion/exclusion issues are opportunities for discussion and problem solving. The "why" a person may be excluded is critical and the needs of all participants must be considered.

Looking at children's issues and concerns brings a deeper commitment on our part to our work. We must be willing to challenge our own issues of power, authority, and control, our own biases, and really be ready to grow. The children we're working with these days are experiencing complexities in their lives which are incredible. Most of us growing up years ago were not exposed to the world these children witness. It is our responsibility to give them the tools and support needed so they can not only cope, but really are empowered to live and work successfully in this world.

Charting the Connection: Making Decisions About Strategies Through Observation of Children's Concerns

As we become more and more careful listeners of children, we are better able to discern their concerns and issues. Children are trying to make sense of the world; they may do it awkwardly, but their efforts can be understood and respected.

The following chart looks at some typical behaviors we can observe in children, states a concern the child may be working through, and then suggests some possible strategies to support the child's growth in working through the concern. These strategies have been discussed previously in this work and are used to promote democratic practice.

Observation	Child's Concern	Democratic Strategies
Observation of child backing away from child who might hit him	fears/safety	◆ Meeting to create safety rules using: • shared power • decision making
Hearing child say "You can't play"	inclusion/exclusion	◆ Group discussion and decisions on when it's okay to say "You can't play"
Observation of two children fighting	getting needs met	◆ Problem solving skill building
Karate chopping Power Rangers	feeling powerful	◆ "Power Helpers"
Child not looking at the adult while creating a picture	adult will tell me what to draw	◆ Adult waits to be invited by child
Sand tray work: buries figures in the sand and then brings them out again	gain understanding of mom coming back	◆ Adult reflects on child's words

Songs and Social Health
by Sarah Pirtle

When a group of children is clicking, when we are singing together happily, or writing a song about something that matters to the class, or talking and discovering, there is a feeling of drinking from a deep well. I see this well as an innate place of peace and interconnection that we can dip into together. We go to this well to heal the trauma we all carry from the epidemic of violence in our world. We bring children to this well to help them grow into adults, not hurt vengeful unskilled children in adult bodies, but adults, who by definition of what it really means to be an adult, are nonviolent peace builders.

I want to explore this sense of how I experience music bringing us to this place of connection. I think of songs and story games as a way to set up a pattern of cooperative interactions among children. When I enter a classroom with songs "in my back pocket," I feel like an herbalist walking in with a basket of herbs. One of the ways that herbs and flower essences help a human body return to health is by modeling for the cells in the body what healthy functioning looks like. They assist the cells in entraining to those patterns of fuller functioning. Songs in their own way help children entrain to mutual respect, clear communication, creative collaboration and joy, hallmarks of a healthy community.

For instance, when partners sing the song "Cloud Hands," the song invites them to affirm each other's ideas for movement through mirroring. The pairs interact while they are moving slowly and gently like clouds. Children take turns leading and following each other's movements:

> *Wave your hands like clouds in the sky.*
> *Wave your hands like clouds in the sky.*
> *Wave your hands like clouds in the sky.*
> *Look each other in the eye.*
> *Now the other one leads.*

I wrote this song by visualizing what it would look like for children to play a mirroring game so that it was fun for both people. I tried to find words and images that set up a pattern of interaction which would lead to a positive experience. Children face each other, moving slowly and safely, often laughing, keeping in sync through cloud hand movements.

It was in 1980 that I first happened upon this way of creating new songs by visualizing what was needed. I was engaged in a songwriting project for an early childhood center in Deerfield, Massachusetts, at the same time that I was volunteering at Traprock Peace Center in the very same town. At Traprock we were helping to launch the Nuclear Freeze Campaign to halt production of weapons. We had to visualize the potential dangers and the potential possibilities for change. At the same time, I tried to see into the nub of the problem of violence and warfare. I carried the words of the poet Rumi in my head as a touchstone:

You cry peace peace
but inside you there is a loaded gun.

I learned that if you dismantled the trigger of a nuclear weapon, even if the large warhead still stood, it could no longer do harm. What were the triggers that people carried? How could they be dismantled? How could we lovingly go inside ourselves and find our own "loaded guns" and create enough safety that the guns could be released and replaced by true security? I used to walk down the street and imagine I was living in a world without weapons. What did it feel like? My tense shoulders would relax. I had time to breathe deeply and enjoy the daffodils. I wanted to participate in both levels of peace work at once, the inner and the outer.

In that same period, I was doing independent study in graduate school to create a peace education degree. I liked to hear about Jean Piaget's discoveries that children develop an understanding of mathematical relationships by interacting with materials. What did that mean for moral development, I would muse. How can we give children opportunities to interact and make meanings about how to get along? I thought that songs could do that and wanted to try out my hypothesis.

At the early childhood center, I watched three and four year old children play fighting like puppies. As I watched fun turn to hurt, I reflected on what the children really wanted. The rough and tumble was a way to connect and touch and be close. Maybe a game could set up clear boundaries within which they could be safe and be explorers of friendly interaction. I wrote an activity called "Creeping Mouse" where our hands were mice that lived behind the tall mountains of our backs. We sat kneeling in a circle and brought our hands out to meet the other mice while we chanted, "Creep, creep, creeping mouse." Then the mice were invited gently to touch and greet the fingers of their classmates. Children touched hands until the call of an eagle sent all of us scurrying back into hiding. We played the sequence — creeping out, touching, then running away — over and over again. Not once did a child hurt the hands of another. The boundary of the game held us in the agreements of care and respect while we laughed together.

What has fascinated me over the years — doing "Creeping Mouse" and other song games — is the way that we as teachers can deeply trust the wisdom of a group. One child calls out their needs and the group responds. Or one child is a mouthpiece conveying where the whole group needs help. Piaget said that children's growth depends upon their relationship to the life force central to us all. Robert Kegan in the *Evolving Self: Problem and Process in Human Development* (Harvard University Press, 1982) illuminates this aspect of Piaget's work. Kegan writes:

> *Piaget's model derives from a model of open-systems evolutionary biology. . . . (Piaget's conception) places us in a single energy system of all living things. Its primary attention, then, is not to shifts and changes in an internal equilibrium, but to an equilibrium in the world, between the progressively individuated self and the bigger life field, an interaction sculpted by both and constitutive of reality itself. Central to Piaget's framework — and often ignored even by those who count themselves as Piagetian — is this activity, equilibration. Whether in the study of the mollusk or the human child, Piaget's principle loyalty was to the ongoing conversation between the individuating organism and the world, a process of adaptation shaped by the tension between the assimilation of new experience to the old "grammar" and the accommodation of the old grammar to new experience.*
> (pages 43-44)

Interactive music takes up the child's input and flows like a tide, responsive to what emerges. What if the child's old "grammar" is the experience of being mistreated? How does the child make meaning of the process of getting along with other children? How do we convincingly invite the child into a world of safety and help him/her to assimilate to this new experience?

In 1996, a teacher asked me to work with her three to five year old class and let me know that one girl named Carly needed special support. From Carly's angry self protective lashing out, she surmised that Carly did not have a foundation of safety in her life. As I walked in with the "herbal basket of songs" under my arm, I thought of the game of "Creeping Mouse." In the past 16 years, I'd never seen a child hurt anyone else during the game. I felt that the activity would be a place to experience safety and trust in a concrete way.

On my second visit with the group, I introduced "Creeping Mouse." As the game began and the "mice" waved to each other, even before the idea of touch was introduced, Carly made her hands into claws and began to growl. I tried different ways of guiding and interacting to

Hearing Everyone's Voice

make the game safer. I suggested children could let us know if they didn't want their hands touched so that touch was an option. She continued to growl and two boys began to growl as well. I had to switch the game. As I responded to her signals, I realized I needed to join her world.

"Let's make up a song about growling," I said.

I searched for a way to enter into the making of a song that would speak to them. "Is there an animal that's growling in the song?" I asked. I wanted to see if the image of a tiger or bear might be active in the imagination of the children growling. They made no verbal response. They didn't want to pretend to be animals. They continued growling. By this I learned it was the growling itself that was of interest. I visualized a full expression of growling and I visualized what its opposite would be. Here's the song that came out:

> Sometimes I feel like growling. (We make our hands like claws
>   and move our hands vigorously in a circle leaving plenty of
>   room so that no person is near our claw hands.)
> And sometimes I run away. (We hide our hands behind our
>   backs.)
> And sometimes I go to my own little house. (One hand forms the
>   roof of a house, palm up, right by our stomachs. Two fingers
>   from the other hand stand on this platform like a little person.
>   The fingers jump up and down.)
> And here's where I'm going to stay. Um!

Carly's teacher reported that for the next two months she asked to sing the song every day.

Later the song evolved to the "Anger Chant." I use it to introduce a discussion about all the different things that can help us when we're angry. I've added a message of how to get support when you are upset:

> Sometimes I feel like growling.
> And sometimes I hide away.
> And sometimes I want you to hold me (wrap your arms around
>   yourself)
> And hear what I want to say.
> 'Til my anger's slowing down. I got my feet back on the ground
>   (tap legs).

After hearing the song, we make "anger plans." We discuss whether we'd like to scribble an anger drawing, be by ourselves, or come get a hug when we're upset.

In 1984, I was working on the Traprock staff as the coordinator of peace education. Putting together a pilot project, I asked elementary schools in our area if I could come in to try out a series of peace education activities. I wanted to write a new song that would carry a message about conflict resolution. When Charles Walker, founder of Peace Brigades International, led a workshop at Traprock that winter, I asked him what he thought was at the kernel of his work. Charles responded that the key concept he conveys when he works with young people is "There's always something you can do." That became the seed for the song which follows.

When I sit down with children to help them with a conflict or sit down with another adult to handle our own conflict, sometimes the words of that song tap me on the shoulder and give me courage and confidence. I hope that songs can be a beacon pointing to how social health and healing are possible. This feels like a lifetime journey — learning about the dismantling of weapons inner and outer while rebuilding connections between people and inside self. I hope to find many new songs — like herbs hovering in the air in invisible gardens waiting to be brought into our world.

There Is Always Something You Can Do

©1984 Words and music by Sarah Pirtle
Discovery Center Music, BMI

Verse 1

There is always something you can do, do, do
when you're getting in a stew, stew, stew.
You can go out for a walk.
You can try to sit and talk.
There's always something you can do.

Bridge 1

Whether in a school or family argument,
when you feel you'd reallly like to throw a fit.
Don't be trapped by fights and fists and angry threats,
reach for this very ordinary plan.

Verse 2

There is always something you can do, do, do
yes, it's difficult but true, true, true.
See it from each other's eyes.
Find a way to compromise.
There's always something you can do.

Bridge 2

You can use your smarts and not your fist, fist, fist,
you can give that problem a new twist, twist, twist.
You can see it 'round about and upside down,
give yourself the time to find a way.

Verse 3

There is always something you can do, do, do
when you're getting in a stew, stew, stew.
When you want to yell and scream,
find the words for what you mean.
There's always something you can do.

VI. Strategies for Taking Action

The discussion of building democratic community now brings us to the advocacy role needed to live in a democracy — the role of speaking out and taking action. Self esteem and a strong sense of identity help us advocate because we know who we are and what we believe for ourselves. We also trust ourselves to put forth our best; and we take responsibility. We have the skill to make good choices and decisions as we solve problems. We enjoy the challenges diversity of ideas brings and we are eager to give of ourselves to make our communities better places for all of us.

Sometimes it's easy to feel helpless and hopeless when considering the challenges we all face. Our daily lives, the concerns and problems of our neighborhoods and communities, as well as the world at large, tend to overwhelm us if we are not empowered to take action. Children can be empowered with the attitudes and skills necessary to enhance their abilities to do what they can to make a difference. When we adults make it a habit to encourage children to respectfully speak out about their concerns, and when we listen to all children, then children expect to have their voices heard. They become adults who feel empowered to speak out and take responsible action. By practicing the empowerment skills appropriate to their development, young children learn how powerful they can be to help create change.

The following song was written by a mom using the words her daughter said to her in the face of discouragement. It's written from the perspective of her daughter.

Just Get Started

by Joanne Olshansky Hammil
© 1991 JHO Music

I'm sittin' in the middle of my bed
I think I'm kind of depressed
'Cause my Mom said I have to clean up my room
And — it's a total mess.

I don't know where to start
And I wanna go out and play
This job's too big for a kid like me
And it's wrecking my whole day.

Oh I'm not a Superhero
I can't make a miracle appear
If I close my eyes tight and wish real hard —
The same darn mess is here.

Well, my Mom came in my room
She said, "Just get started — you'll get through today"
I gave her the meanest look I know
And said, "Easy for you to say."

Well, sure, I can pick up my underwear
And put the clean ones back in the drawer
I can throw these Legos back in the box
But don't ask for much more.

'Cause I'm not some Superhero
I can't make a miracle appear
If I close my eyes tight and wish real hard —
The mess is still right here.

Oh I can kick this ball in the closet
And I can pull these sticky things apart
And . . . hey, ya' know, when I look around
I've actually made a start!

Well, I worked for a really long time
Put on a tape to get in a better mood
And after a half an hour! —
I took a break, went to get some food.

Mom was sittin' in her favorite chair
Starin' at her coffee, looking kind of sad
I said, "Hey Mom, what's the matter?"
She said, "Oh, I'm feeling bad . . .

"You see, this morning when I read the paper
And thought of the problems in our way
I got so overwhelmed about this world
We're living in today.

"'Cause there's pollution and holes in the ozone
And more toxic waste every hour
I don't know how to make it better
I'm just one person with only so much power."

I said, "Mom, it's hard to solve all this
Just sittin' in your chair
But maybe you could just get started
Take it from me — I've been there."

'Cause you're not a Superhero
You can't make a miracle come true
But you can take these bottles back to the store,
write a letter to the newspaper . . .

<u>Start</u> makin' it better — me and you.

◆ ◆ ◆

"Just Get Started" can be heard on *The World's Gonna Listen!*
available as Cassette, CD, and Songbook from
JHO Music, 70 Capitol Street, Watertown, MA 02472 • (800) 557-7010

Just Get Started

Words and Music by
Joanne Olshansky Hammil

Hearing Everyone's Voice

Just Get Started

175

Just Get Started

Just Get Started

Just Get Started

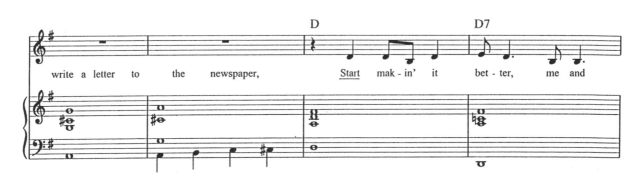

Guidelines to Empowerment

The following guidelines to taking action emphasize the importance of developing expectations for young children which are appropriate to their own growth and development. Their involvement will be most significant to them if the concerns being addressed by the action are of special interest to them. That does not mean that the grownups do all the planning and organizing — children can do a lot. They may come up with ideas which we, in all our adult wisdom, never would have created. Giving children the authority to create solutions to their concerns, with adult support, is critical towards empowering them to ultimately become the problem solvers our communities and nation will need when they are grownups.

We, as adults, cannot abdicate our responsibility for taking action ourselves. It's not up to the children to clean up the mess created long before they were born. And it is critical that we adults model such advocacy for the children in our own lives and activities. Children can and should play a part in our advocacy work, but we must always take the responsibility to be certain their actions are safe and appropriate to the situation.

Guidelines for Helping Children Learn to Take Action
Used by Permission from Diane Levin, *Remote Control Childhood* (page 115)

◆ Make sure children know it is the job of adults to make the world a safe place for children, although they can contribute. They should not think that their own sense of safety and well-being is dependent on their own actions.

◆ As children plan actions to take, do not expect them to plan the most effective possible actions from the adult point of view. They cannot fully think through the logic of their ideas. As long as safety is assured, children need to try them out to see how they work.

◆ Choose topics for action where children are likely to experience some kind of direct effect of their actions. For instance, it is often more meaningful for children to do something around issues that directly affect their lives or where they get a direct response.

◆ Choose topics for action with which you are comfortable sharing your power and control with the children. While your input is vital to the children's successful actions, the children will probably come up with action plans that are different from the ones you would use if it were up to you.

Action Steps
Adapted and Used by Permission from Diane Levin, *Remote Control Childhood* (Chapter 8)

1. Help children "take action" on matters in their own lives that they really care about.

2. Give children many opportunities to problem solve and take responsible actions on issues related to their home/school environment, relationships which affect them personally, and then, in the larger community, on concerns such as the environment, media violence, and toys.

3. As children become more aware of concerns such as toys which promote violence, for instance, they can also become "activists" who help others understand the concerns and problems. They can take action on a wider scope by, for example, collecting signatures on a petition they help write and take to the toy store which sells the offensive product. They can articulate their concerns through letters, songs, and other creative actions for change.

4. Provide opportunities for children to talk to other children about what they have learned in the process of problem solving around an important issue. They can share the problem, what they have learned, what they are doing differently now, and what others can do.

5. Help children learn that they can take action to promote change in the wider community around issues of the environment, community needs, media violence, and toys.

Each of the five Action Steps as suggested by Diane Levin will be further defined and explained through stories and songs.

1. Help children "take action" on matters in their own lives that they really care about.

"I Really Can Change Things!"
by Robin Song

When my oldest daughter was eight years old and my youngest was six, there was a conference at San Francisco State University that I wanted to attend. As usual, I had called to see if there was child care available and was told, "Yes, there will be child care available for the entire weekend of the conference." With that information, I went to negotiate going to the conference with the girls. Usually when I took the girls to an event, the child care would be poor to moderate so the girls were skeptical about attending. I encouraged them to try it before making a judgment.

On the first day of the conference, we arrived to find the child care was completely planned for babies. There were no toys for older children, no snacks that were appealing to older children, and no activities planned for older children. Needless to say, my daughters were outraged at the lack of planning. We talked to the planners who said they would try to find some things for child care that the girls would enjoy, but it was a poor attempt. The girls felt left out and did not want to attend the following day.

That evening, we discussed the situation and I asked them if they wanted to write a letter to the organizers and let them know how they felt about the situation. They were excited about having an opportunity to voice their frustration to the women in charge. Nancy, the eight year old, went to her room and busily worked at writing a letter, asking Jane, the six year old, what she wanted to add. When the letter was complete, Nancy proudly read it to me and asked if they could go with me the next day and give the letter to the organizers.

The next day, the chair of the event accepted the letter from Nancy and at the morning gathering of the entire conference read the letter from Nancy and Jane. They made a public apology to the children who attended and vowed that in future planning they would concentrate more money, time, and thought on the child care portion of the event.

Needless to say, Nancy and Jane were happy about the outcome. On the way home in the car, Nancy told me in amazement, "Gee Mommy, I really can change things!" It was a very empowering moment for those young girls.

2. Give children many opportunities to problem solve and take responsible actions on issues related to their home/school environment, relationships which affect them personally, and then, in the larger community, on concerns such as the environment, media violence, and toys.

Demonstration Against Discrimination by the Four Year Olds
by Susan Hopkins with Janice Sheffield

I'll never forget the day I was working diligently in my office at the California State University Fullerton Children's Center, when I heard loud chanting coming from the classroom of the four year olds. What was going on? I wandered down the hall to satisfy my curiosity. There they were, about ten four year olds, standing at the table as their teacher was writing their words on tag board cards. They were chanting the words "change them" as the teacher was writing out the cards. I watched a few moments. Then the children moved together to create a line holding their signs, still chanting "change them."

They weren't satisfied with their signs and came back to the teacher to ask if she had anything to put on the signs to help the children hold them more easily. The children were invited to look through the supply cupboard where they discovered large wooden tongue depressors. These would work, once taped onto the signs, they decided. Once back in line to chant "change them," I noted the children went from activity center to activity center.

They were focusing their protest on the new signs posted at each center which stated pictorially that some children could not play there that day. The signs were developed as an experiment to discriminate by physical characteristics such as hair color or wearing tie shoes. Obviously, the children did not like these new rules, hence the "change them" protest.

The teacher stood back and watched the chanting and protest for a few moments. The children decided to march up and down the hall, chanting. The teacher suggested that they could protest in the hall for three minutes, but then it seemed time to have a class meeting. The children agreed and came back to the room eagerly. The teacher started the discussion about the "change them" signs and their meaning. The children said they didn't like the new signs put up in the activity centers and wanted them changed. When asked why the new signs, which stated that some children couldn't play there, needed to be changed, the children firmly announced that it wasn't "fair." They had a discussion about what is fair and what isn't. They also discussed rules and who gets to make them.

The children in this classroom have always played a significant role in developing the code of behavior. There had not been arbitrary rules which appear from nowhere — except this one time. The children knew it wasn't fair. The teacher had carefully worked with them all year to develop:

- ◆ their skills in verbalizing their needs and feelings;
- ◆ the confidence to stand up for themselves; and
- ◆ the ability to become problem solvers.

Certainly her hard work had paid off — not necessarily in the way she envisioned (a protest march!), but these four year olds clearly knew how to use their voices to protest injustice. These children were empowered and they knew it. The new rule signs were brought down and never went up again!

3. As children become more aware of the issues which promote violence, they can also become "activists" who help others understand the concerns and problems. They can take action on a wider scope by, for example, collecting signatures on a petition they help write and take to the toy store which sells the offensive product. They can articulate their concerns through letters, songs, and other creative actions for change.

In "Tell the World," Joanne Hammil sings about the need to get out there and become "activists" from the perspective of a young person. The message clearly defines the importance of "speaking out."

Tell the World

by Joanne Olshansky Hammil
© 1989 JHO Music

chorus: I like to sing (I like to sing) I like to shout (I like to shout)
I like to tell the world what I'm thinking about
'Cause I'm growin' up and I know I think just fine;
I like to tell the world exactly what's on my mind.

1.
Well, if I could talk to my parents straight, here is what I'd say . . .
Why don't you stop being so darn busy — and play with me today!

2.
And if I could talk to my teacher straight, here is what I'd say . . .
Please don't yell at us kids — we're trying our best each day!

chorus

3.
Well, if I could talk to my brother straight, here is what I'd say . . .
I hate when you're mean to me and tease me — does it always have to be this way??

4.
And if I could talk to the president straight, here is what I'd say . . .
Why don't you take all your nuclear missiles — and throw them all away!

chorus

5.
And if I could talk to my family straight, here is what I'd say . . .
Even when I'm really mad at you — I love you any way!

◆ ◆ ◆

"Tell the World" can be heard on *Pizza Boogie*,
a collection of 17 original songs by Joanne Olshansky Hammil,
available as Cassette, CD, and Songbook from
JHO Music, 70 Capitol Street, Watertown, MA 02472 • (800) 557-7010

Tell the World

Words and Music by
Joanne Olshansky Hammil

I like to sing! (I like to sing.) I like to shout! (I like to shout.) I like to tell the world what I'm think-in' a—bout, 'cause I'm grow—in' up and I know I think just fine (grow-in' up and I think just fine); I'd like to tell the world ex-act-tly what's on my mind.

⊕ to Coda

1. Well if I could talk to my par — ents straight ___ here is what I'd ___ say ___

185

4. Provide opportunities for children to talk to other children about what they have learned in the process of problem solving around an important issue. They can share the problem, what they have learned, what they are doing differently now, and what others can do.

This story, by Diane Levin, has been used with permission from *Remote Control Childhood* (Chapter 8).

One day a child walked into his kindergarten classroom and held up a toy action figure (based on a popular TV program and movie) which was missing a leg. He indignantly told his friends how he had gotten it the week before for his birthday; it had been his favorite present. The second time he played with it, the leg fell off. He didn't think it was fair!

The other children all heatedly jumped in to describe their own experiences with toys that broke. The teacher saw the children had a lot of intense feelings about their broken toys. She suggested that they bring in their broken toys the next day to talk about at a class meeting.

At the meeting, the children talked at length about their broken toys — how and why each toy broke, how they felt when it broke, their sense of unfairness about it breaking, how the toy could have been made so it didn't break.

Then the teacher asked the children for their ideas about what they could do about their broken toys. The children enthusiastically came up with some interesting ideas:

◆ "Have a funeral and bury them."
◆ "Don't get toys like those that broke any more."
◆ "Be gentle and don't fight with toys."
◆ "Make a 'toy hospital' in the classroom where the toys can go to get fixed."
◆ "Take the broken toys to the toy store where they came from, so the 'owner of the store' knows which toys break too easily."
◆ "Write a letter to the 'toy factories' to say they shouldn't make toys that look so good but break so easy."

The teacher helped the children decide to make a toy hospital in the construction area (where the children could work on fixing their toys) and "write" letters to the toy companies (with the teacher's help).

For children to become responsible and contributing members of society, they need to learn how to participate actively in their communities. They also need to believe that what they do can really make a difference to what happens. Children learn these lessons best when they have many opportunities to take action and see the concrete impact their actions have on their immediate environment. As they do this, the foundations are laid for knowing appropriate ways to take action on things they really care about and for having a voice that they believe will be heard in their wider community. The scenario above illustrates the kind of process that helps children build the foundation they need to become active participants in society. It is a process where children learn to:

◆ identify and understand problems they really care about and want to change;

◆ formulate possible solutions to the problems;

◆ have a repertoire of action ideas and skills they can use to work toward those solutions.

5. **Help children learn that they can take action to promote change in the wider community around issues of the environment, community needs, media violence, and toys.**

Showing Solidarity
by Robin Song

The time was the early '80s. I was co-directing a children's camp at a West Coast Music Festival. The age group I was responsible for was the eight and up group. We had many activities and concerts planned for the children — puppetry, dance, a workshop on disability awareness, a Holly Near concert just for the children, arts and crafts, and much more.

The kitchen staff at the festival were mostly women of color, and they were receiving less pay than the rest of the festival staff. They

decided to go on strike during one of the days of the festival. Several of the women who were striking had children at the camp who seemed concerned about what was happening. I sat with the children and we talked about what was happening, and how it was an example of the unfairness that people of color experience in the world. The children were full of questions during the discussion so we took their lead and responded as appropriately as possible to the questions they were asking.

We had scheduled a very special mime workshop during the time that the women were going to "go on strike." I asked the children if they wanted to attend the workshop or go to the demonstration in support of the women striking. They all agreed to go to the demonstration.

As the group of about 12 children and myself walked toward the striking women and their supporters (approximately 50 people), we took up the chant that the women were chanting and sat with the women. After an hour of chanting and listening to speeches, the children and I got up to return to camp. We told the women that we supported them in their action and then began to walk back to camp. The women in one huge group stood up in unison and cheered the children. They thanked them for coming to show their solidarity for their cause. The women's cheering in unison was a strong affirmation for the children. Discussion on the walk back focused on how good it felt to stand up for their mothers and to be able to take action. The children truly felt a sense of their own power and hopefully experienced what it means to stand up for what you believe.

It seems most appropriate to end our chapter on "Taking Action" with a song about the importance of courage. Without courage, none of us would be able to face the hard things in our lives. Children need lots of encouragement — that's what we can do to help them feel courageous. Encourage them!

It takes courage to speak out and take action. Joanne Hammil again captures the perspective of a child who has worked through some issues around courage.

Every Little Act of Courage
by Joanne Olshansky Hammil
© 1996 JHO Music

chorus: Every little act of courage
Every little act of courage
Every little act of courage
Gives us dignity!

1.

Pam's a bully at our school, everybody thinks she's cool
She tells us who to hate and what to wear;
One day she said "No one talk to Jen," but Jen was sorta kinda my friend
I sat with Jen at lunch – I didn't care . . .

2.

My Dad never learned to read, he's embarrassed – he's 33,
But he wanted to vote on election day;
I walked with him to the voting booth, I held his hand and he told them the truth,
They read the questions to Dad and he had his say!

3.

Joey hardly spoke all year, he had a stutter – it was hard to hear
He'd turn all red and look like he might cry;
Teacher told him he could do it, we would all help him get through it
The whole class smiled when he said he'd try . . .

4.

My father always hits my mom, she's really scared – he's very strong
When they fight I just wanna run;
One night It got so bad, she was crying and he was still mad
I ran to my friend's house and called 911.

5.

We each have our own fears, sometimes they last for years,
It's so hard to change and take a stand;
But every little step y' take moves us all to a better place
And together our steps say – "Yes, we can!!"

◆　◆　◆

JHO Music, 70 Capitol Street, Watertown, MA 02472 • (800) 557-7010

Every Little Act of Courage

words & music by Joanne Hammil
©1996 JHO Music

Hearing Everyone's Voice

VII. Children's Issues: In Their Own Voices and Images

Children have issues and concerns upon which they are working to understand in their efforts to make sense of the world. What are some of these concerns children worry about? How can we support them in expressing these concerns and in taking appropriate action around them? How can we help them work through these issues in ways which are culturally relevant and promote social justice and democratic practice?

The sections on strategies in this book gives many ideas as to ways we may support children in expressing and managing their concerns. A few of those strategies have been used to hear from the children for this book, and have been reproduced in this section on "Children's Issues." We have grouped the principles for democratic practice in ways to more easily connect with some of the concerns which children have expressed to us. In hearing the children, we have used careful listening, in nonjudgmental ways, to support them as they have shared their thoughts with us. Following are several categories with stories, songs, a poster, and even a book to express how children are working through some of their concerns.

Children's Concerns
Children's Concerns Around Trust

Children are thinking a lot about safety and trust. Grownups can ask themselves these questions as they consider ways to build trust.

◆ How do we build trust with children and adults?
◆ What are the issues of safety and how do they relate to trust?
◆ What about taking risks? Every time we trust, aren't we taking a risk?

◆ How do we create an environment for children and grown-ups which is safe enough that people can take the risks of speaking out?

Toothbrushes
by Susan Hopkins

Visiting the Kentucky Flat Head Start program near Nevada City, California, is a special treat. Eighteen children work and play in a one room schoolhouse built in 1903. It's cozy, busy, and very welcoming. On a recent visit, I sat down on the floor to watch two four year old boys "play trucks." They had a handmade wooden garage and were busy maneuvering vehicles in and out and all around in the process of getting them all repaired. The boys didn't know me, and looked at me out of the corners of their eyes. I smiled and said nothing. After a couple of minutes, they informed me briefly about the vehicles, their problems, and plans for repair. I acknowledged the information with seriousness and respect by asking a clarifying question which I knew they could respond to easily. A simple dialogue evolved, with the children taking the lead. After a few moments, one of the boys looked up at me and said, "Would you like to see my toothbrush?" "Of course," I responded with genuine interest. We looked at the tray of toothbrushes and the child explained carefully to me all about how he brushes his teeth. I felt honored to be included in this very special and personal routine. This child clearly was expressing acceptance and trust of me by involving me in an important aspect of his life. Such trust and inclusion creates a bond; it touches one's heart and brings us together in special ways.

Pat Landry, from the Native American Head Start in Boston, sent us this story written by a child to work through her dream. In such sharing of her worries about death, she also expresses her trust of the teacher who heard the story.

My Nightmare Story
As told to Pat Landry

My robot died and I don't want my robot to die.
The robot's baby is a baby and the baby won't die because the
dinosaur doesn't know where the baby's at.
By Natteal (five years old)

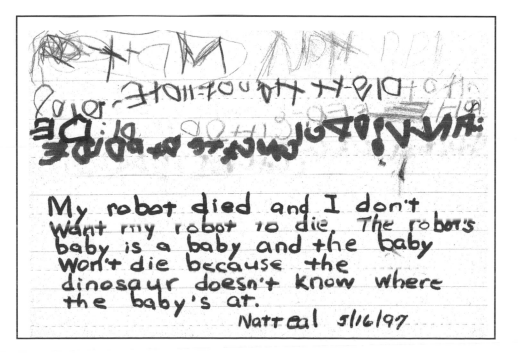

My

Nightmare Story
as told to Pat Landry
May 15, 1997

My robot died and I don't
want my robot to die. The robot's
baby is a baby and the baby
won't die because the
dinosaur doesn't know where
the baby's at.
Natteal 5/16/97

Children's Concerns
About Fairness, Same and Different, and Inclusion

"Everybody Needs to Be Different"
Cameron's Story
As told to Susan Hopkins

Cameron, who was seven and a half when we talked, created a poster to protest wearing school uniforms. It made the front page of the local newspaper, so I interviewed Cameron about how he decided to make his protest poster. The poster and his thoughts:

FIRST QUESTION: *"How did you get the idea to make the poster for 'No Uniforms'?"*

Cameron: "Well, we sat down on the rug and the teacher told us that some schools are thinking about wearing uniforms. We listened for 45 minutes. Then the teacher asked if we wanted to wear uniforms — everyone yelled 'No.' She asked why we didn't want to, and kids said things like:
'We can't be free.'
'We can't wear what we want.'
'We can't do anything fun.'
'We can't get dirty.'
'We can't have colors.'
'Everybody needs to be different.'"

SECOND QUESTION: *"Who did you give the poster to after you made it?"*

Cameron: "I shared it at school and they put it on the piano. Then they put it on the wall."

THIRD QUESTION: *"Do you think you'll have to wear uniforms?"*

Cameron: "Some schools have to wear uniforms. But probably not at Orangethorpe School. Mr. Backus refuses. I think the School Board will probably say 'No'".

The following drawing and text appear within a box:

Vote no on Uniforms!

uniforms Stink!

DanMc

CamH.

Hi, my name is Cameron, and I say, "No uniforms!" I mean it's the 90's! American kids don't need and deserve to wear them. Anyway it's a free country. Kids can't be free if they have to wear them. By Cameron
P.S. Vote no. Please! Kids count on it.

On Conformity

More thoughts come from Alfie Kohn, author, this time on conformity and its relationship to promoting critical thinking and responsibility.

If we want students to grow into critical thinkers and ethical people, then we have to aim higher than mere conformity. Children, after all, learn how to make good decisions by making decisions, not by following directions. If we want them to take responsibility for their behavior, then we have to give them responsibilities; we have to join them in asking, "What kind of school do we want to create?" (from "The Trouble with School Uniforms," Boston Globe, October 2, 1996)

Melody, age 13, writes from her heart about her choice to be herself. She mentions the courage it takes to confront her peers, and is proud of her decision.

Solo
by Melody Mitchell

My whole life, I've been put down because I did what I believed was the right thing for me to do with my life. I have always been determined to be myself: to look, act, and do what I feel is right although others may put me down for it. Most kids like to pair off into groups called cliques where they can be a part of something. A clique is sort of like a herd of horses. The mares (kids) will try to impress the stallion (lead kid). The kids in a clique will try to impress their leader by giving him or her things or doing things that they wouldn't normally want to do so that they may fit in. Because of this, the things that most kids think are cool are the things that the leaders of a clique considers cool.

I have chosen to not be like a kid in a clique, but to be myself. When I made this choice, I gave up a lot, including popularity. I was teased a lot, too.

I could have never done it if I hadn't been raised in a democratic family. I was treated as an equal. I helped make rules and other important decisions in the family. This gave me both self esteem and decision making skills which have helped me in life and will help me in the real world.

Although it's hard to have no clique, if I had to choose again, I would make the same choices I have made now. Although there are downs, by being different I can be myself.

Children's Concerns
Around Shared Authority, Including Decision Making, Problem Solving, and Choices

Decision making encompasses issues of "shared authority" and provides opportunities to really practice what can be called "Both/And Thinking." We often think our choices must be made from the perspective of "Either/Or Thinking." Cindy Santa Cruz writes about her struggle with both/and thinking: the children need to be safe *and* creative. She works together with them to be able to do both.

Safety and Creativity: Let's Have Both!
by Cindy Santa Cruz

The four year old children at Silver Springs Head Start in Grass Valley, California, were creating some marvelous structures out of blocks. As one of the structures grew in design, it also grew in size. It got taller and taller. It became apparent that the next step for the children would be to climb it. They started taking turns climbing, then things started to get a little crazy. I did not want to stop the creativity, but this looked dangerous. So, we sat down together to hear how this great structure was definitely an amazing creation, yet it made me, the teacher who has to keep everyone safe, very nervous. I explained that I did not want them to get hurt. I asked the children to decide how to make the block area safe again.

They spoke right up and said that they did not want to get hurt or to hurt their friends. We decided to talk about some safe rules for the block area. I told them I would get some paper and write down what they said if everyone agreed. We could put their rules up on the wall to remind them of what they said. These rules are still up in the room. They mean much more to all of us because we used democratic process, that of hearing what everyone had to say, to set the guidelines for our class.

The rules as stated by the children read:

- ◆ *Build it low.*
- ◆ *Do not climb on the blocks.*
- ◆ *Stop when the teacher says stop.*
- ◆ *Keep your eyes open — look where you are going.*
- ◆ *Don't throw blocks.*
- ◆ *Don't push the blocks over.*
- ◆ *Build it as tall as you.*

Rules
by Joanne Hammil

This song was written by Joanne Hammil as she was inspired by the questions her own children asked. They were expressing their concerns about being heard in the creation of the rules which they were expected to obey. Issues of power, cooperation, and problem solving all emerge in the lyrics created by the children's questions.

Rules

Words and Music by
Joanne Olshansky Hammil

a 2 part round

Hearing Everyone's Voice

Rules

by Joanne Olshansky Hammil
© 1988 JHO Music

2-part round:

How can I follow all the rules that you make
If I don't get to make some too?

If you let me make some I won't have to break some
To show that I'm important like you!

◆　◆　◆

"Rules" can be heard on *Pizza Boogie,*
a collection of 17 original songs by Joanne Olshansky Hammil,
available as Cassette, CD, and Songbook from
JHO Music, 70 Capitol Street, Watertown, MA 02472 • (800) 557-7010

Children's Concepts of Friendship

Following are transcripts from interviews with children of various ages on the very important topic of friendships. Specific details about interviewing children are contained in the Strategies section on "Interviewing Children."

In talking to the younger children, we phrased our questions very concretely and specifically. We started with the question "Who do you like to play with?" and moved into "Why?"

The four year olds at the Head Start program at Silver Springs High School in Grass Valley, California, were interviewed using the questions as suggested above. Their teacher, Cindy Santa Cruz, did most of the interviewing, which is quoted below.

Teacher: *"Tiffany, who are your friends?"*
Tiffany: *"Sarah, Amanda, Jennifer."*
Teacher: *"Why?"*
Tiffany: *"I play with them 'cuz I play with the toys. They like to play with toys, too."*
Teacher: *"Alex, who do you like to play with?"*
Alex: *"I like to play with Seth — he likes me. He sings a song about 'I love you.'" Then Alex sings his song: "We're best friends with great big hugs that say 'I love you.'"*
Teacher: *"Amanda, we're talking about friends."*
Amanda: *"I like to play with them. We play games and housekeeping and playdough and books and the marble game."*
Teacher: *"Who are your friends?"*
Amanda: *"J. D. and Sarah and Seth and Jacob and Jennifer and Tiffany."*
Teacher: *"Seth, how do you make friends?"*
Seth: *"A long time ago I came here and saw the school and the playground. I liked my other school better — it had a bigger playground. Now I like this school 'cuz I have friends."*
Teacher: *"Who is your friend?"*
Seth: *"Sarah. When we first met we became friends."*
Teacher: *"How did you make friends?"*
Seth: *"To make friends she told me her name."*

Teacher: "Why do you like Sarah?"
Seth: "I like Sarah 'cuz she made me happy. We like to do things together."

With older children, we found we could simply ask them to tell us about "friendships," or a wealth of other topics. We discussed friendships with the nine year olds at the Peace Camp in Chico, California, and the transcripts follow.

Jennifer: "I think friendships should never end, even when you are in college. Never let down a friend. If they are really upset, like someone dies in their family, you should never leave them alone. Then they'll feel like no one cares. If no one cares, you should still be nice, even when no one else is. If people make fun of you for your friends, you should never make fun of people even if your friends say someone is really ugly."

Christian: "I think that friendship is love. You should spread the joy to each and everyone beside you. I make friends by talking to them. I ask them how they feel when they're new at school. I think whether they can be a good friend to me. If they cooperate with me and show respect, they could be a good friend."

Valerie, who wanted to be interviewed: (I make friends) "by talking to them and telling them I am their friend and helping them on their problem." (I know they like me) "because they talk to me, they are nice to me, and they help me." (I help them) "on homework and calling them to see if they are coming to school." (And in Spanish) "Llamandolos y hablando con ellos para que sean mis amigos. Y eso es lo que hago. Adios amigos y amigas."

Manuel and Diego: "Friendship is about two friends who never say bad words and they never fight. And they respect each other." (If there were a conflict) "we'd make a game that one goes first who won that game. Or choose a number — who got close to the number. Or call another friend to ask which one to choose."

(A teacher commented that both boys speak Spanish. The interviewer expressed an interest in the boys speaking two languages. And they said) "If you speak two languages, you can make more friends. Like if your friend likes the Spanish, you could show him how to speak Spanish. If you don't know how to speak very well, the English, he could show you. Friends that know two languages and one language: the person that knows two languages has to help the other friend that knows one language. We have a lot to say BECAUSE WE'RE BEST FRIENDS."

Kera and Hannah: "We're best friends. We met each other and we started to get along better and better. And we think the same things. Like if we get in a fight we try to work it out in good ways. We talk it over — you hear and we find out what happened. There might be a misunderstanding." (Friendship is) "people like each other like they get along together and like each other's ideas. We agree with each other without getting into fights. We play a lot. We love to make nicknames like 'Jucky Mucky' and 'Surg Feed the Rush.'"

Clarabel: "Friendship is something you enjoy with a friend. Friends understand what you tell them and don't tell others. Like a secret. Friendships are something in your future that you could keep in your heart. And that person understands when you have a problem like with your parents — you can tell them anything. And you could even talk about something like your cousin has a problem with drugs. Your friend understands and keeps your secret in her heart."

Drew: (To make friends) "go up to them and say 'Hi.'" And see what they say. If they give you a nice 'Hi' back, they might be your friend. If you think they'd be right for you, be nice to them every time — not just once."

Mario, who made a new friend the day before at Peace Camp: "Friendship is like happiness and wonderful. You can have fun. And you have a lot of friends like Drew — I know him yesterday. We made things like signs together. We made glasses (Goofy Goggles) five minutes ago. We made them kinda the same since we're friends. We don't argue. I would let him do his idea to play. I don't want to argue — just be his friend. Friendship is like you're free to play and we could play and do activities and just have fun together."

Jesus and Angel: "We're best friends."
(How did you get to be best friends?)

Angel: "When I just got here in Rosedale School and I didn't know Jesus and I talked to my cousin and then I talked to Jesus."
Jesus: "I talked to Angel and we played soccer with his brother."
Angel: "In a couple of weeks I invited Jesus to play soccer with me and my dad at the university. Then Jesus' mom went to my house and told my mom she could make carpools and she could pick them up. I asked my dad to go to the university to play soccer with Jesus again."

Jimmy: "A friendship is a lot better than being rich. And a friendship is a powerful thing. Friendships are very powerful because they are better than just friends. Friends are always there when you need them if they are good friends. Sometimes friends will help you succeed in life. Everybody needs a friend in life."

A Child's Story About Anger and Frustration

A teacher of third graders in Central Bucks County, Pennsylvania, shared this letter written by a youngster who was expressing his frustration over a disappointing school trip by beating the trunk of a tree back at the school. After some discussion, the teacher suggested to Matt that he write a letter to the tree to express his thoughts instead of beating on it. The teacher was delighted by Matt's letter, which shows much reflection in his written expression. The spelling has not been corrected.

Dear Greeny Green,
I'm sorry when I hit you with my papers. I will not hit a tree ever again. I will even help protect trees as I get older. Hear are four resons why I should not hit trees. They are: animals live in them, they clean our air for us to breathe, they provide shade, and they are beutiful to look at. Oops, I almost forgot I hit you for no reson. I just had to use up some energy because I just came back from a boring feild trip at a musem.
Your Freind,
Matt

Contributed by Kate Sweeney of Yardley, Pennsylvania

Children Talk About Courage

The question asked of the children, who have written these stories, was to tell us about a time when they showed courage or bravery. The stories pull together their feelings and fears. Learning to speak out takes lots and lots of courage, especially when your ideas are not the easiest or most popular.

Bailie's Story About Courage

I wanted to do something for my school, so I tried out for cheerleading. It was a last resort; I'd tried out for sports but didn't make the team for tennis or volleyball. When I went for tryouts the other person who tried out with me could do cartwheels, but I couldn't. I didn't make the cheerleading squad. I was so disappointed in myself since I didn't make cheerleading or any of the sports teams.

It took a lot of courage to try out for cheerleading and now I'm disappointed. But I still want to do something for my school, so now I'm going to try theater. I like to sing in the chorus and I've been in musicals before. Maybe theater is how I can help my school.

Bailie is 12 years old.

Amanda's Story About Courage

When I was at swimming lessons last year our teacher wanted us to go off the high dive. I was nervous — I thought I'd break my arm. My stepmom was standing by and suggested that I not look down. Then I did it, and did it again. If you just do it and get it over with, then you'll have the courage to keep trying.

Amanda is 11 years old.

Nick's Story About Courage

This one kid was beating up my best friend. I said, "Stop beating up my friend." He was six and I was seven, but he

was bigger. "You're not allowed to beat up my friend — want me to go tell the teacher?"

He said, "I won't stop."

I said, "Then I'll go get the teacher." He got scared and then he stopped. He ran away. He knew he'd get in trouble and spend the whole recess on the bench. There's a rule: "You can't beat up people."

He was my very, very, very best friend. I couldn't let him beat him up. My teacher said it's okay for me to talk to other kids about not beating them up.

Nick is 7 years old.

Sarah's Story About Courage

I hadn't seen my dad in two years — when I had to leave him it took courage to leave. I miss him.

I got courage to leave through my dreams. I see him in my dreams. I call him on the phone a lot. He helped me with my courage to leave by talking with me. We talked about what I could do like calling him to talk. I hope we can see him next summer.

Sarah is 10 years old.

Courage: An essential component needed to "Speak Out"!

The Song "Courage"
by Bob Blue

"Courage" is based on a true story a proud parent told to Bob. The course Alyson was taking in middle school was called "Facing History and Ourselves." She applied what she learned about the Holocaust to her own life. Alyson sang the song on Bob's tape *Starting Small.*

A small thing once happened at school
That brought up a question for me,
And somehow it brought me to see
The price that I pay to be cool.

Diane is a girl that I know.
She's strange, like she doesn't belong.
I don't mean to say that that's wrong.
We don't like to be with her, though.

And so, when we all made a plan
To have this big party at Sue's,
Most kids in the school got the news,
But no one invited Diane.

The thing about Taft Junior High
Is secrets don't last very long.
I acted like nothing was wrong
When I saw Diane start to cry.

I know you may think that I'm cruel.
It doesn't make me very proud.
I just went along with the crowd.
It's sad, but you have to in school.

You can't pick the friends you prefer.
You fit in as well as you can.
I couldn't be friends with Diane,
'Cause then they would treat me like her.

In one class at Taft Junior High,
We study what people have done
With gas chamber, bomber, and gun
In Auschwitz, Japan, and My Lai.

I don't understand all I learn.
Sometimes I just sit there and cry.
The whole world stood idly by
To watch as the innocent burn.

Like robots obeying some rule.
Atrocities done by the mob.
All innocent, doing their job.
And what was it for? Was it cool?

The world was aware of this Hell,
But how many cried out in shame?
What heroes, and who was to blame?
A story that no one dared tell.

I promise to do what I can
To not let it happen again.
To care for all women and men.
I'll start by inviting Diane.

Courage

Words and music by Bob Blue

A small thing once hap-pened at school that brought up a ques-tion for me.
Di-ane is a girl that I know. She's strange, like she does-n't be-long.

And some-how it brought me to see the price that I pay to be cool.
I don't mean to say that that's wrong. We don't like to be with her, though.

Di

And so, when we all made a plan to have this big par-ty at Sue's, most kids in the school got the news, but no-one in-vit-ed Di-ane.

Last verse ending

I'll start by in-vit-ing Di-ane.

A Book by the Children: *Helping Children*

The first graders from Mary McLeod Bethune School in Philadelphia created a book to share their ideas about the subject of helping. The details of the creation of the book have been described in other sections of this work. It is enough to say here that the children were clearly very involved in both the subject and in their creative expression.

Helping Children

By the First Graders
at
Mary McLeod Bethune School
Karel Kilimnik's Class
May, 1997

Lee fell I ran as fast as I can then Keith fell and I helped them up.

Henry

Ball Wall

I like to help peuap *people*
and I like to lunshto The *listen*
feuyr. Alran *teacher*

Allan ♡n Room 11

I help naKia when she fell
no The grond.
Tamiah

Tamiah May 28, 1997

I can help people
with thir math so they can
get the anser right.
Sekea Dow

Sekea Dow

I Help Tamiah whith her painting Punting Nakia

Nakia Williams

I LoUd you

I love

I tell n Malik help
me up.

Kalief

Kalief

I like
xau
Kalief

The box fall and I help him up.
Keith

Keith May 28 1997

I'm helping Malik measure The KNEX rods. Hamza

Hamza muhammad

Every body was in the Wrong lihes
I fixed it up. Joseph F.

Joseph Ford

Tahnaya

I hple Danièle with
her rasing. reading

Tahnaya ♡

Shanaylet
Tahnaya lot me hold her
Penlio.
pencil

[Shanay Shvone]   [enero]

like

I Lot Whand let

Shanay Lat me

hold   pencil

holt   hre penLio

Juan

Juan Torres

Helping Children   Shanay S. H.

Thoughts On Compassion

Ruth Pelham writes columns for The Children's Music Network journal *Pass It On!* In the Fall 1997 issue, she wrote about compassion and children, ways we can work with them through music to promote caring about others. Ruth's example of how she uses the song "We Shall Overcome" may be a bit of a stretch for those of us working with the very youngest children. Nevertheless, the idea of teaching children compassion by coming together in meaningful experiences, such as singing a powerful song which unites them through the common energy of the group, is important and relevant to our work with even the very youngest. Ruth shares her thoughts from *PIO!* with us.

Compassion is a way of being whose practice is rooted in an attitude of love, respect, and caring for what is outside the boundaries of self and one's immediate communities. Responding with a compassionate heart affirms our willingness to look out for each other's welfare and act responsibly for our common good.

Many of us in The Children's Music Network teach compassion to children as a way of breaking down stereotypes, promoting tolerance, and building bridges of peace and friendship. Teaching children to be compassionate opens their hearts and minds to other people's circumstances, and also broadens their acceptance of their own limitations and frailties. As children learn how to be compassionate, they gain access to the kinder, gentler parts of themselves and grow to value those parts as a source of personal power and creativity.

An example of a song that many of us sing with children to teach compassion is the profound yet simple song "We Shall Overcome," the anthem of the Civil Rights movement whose yearnings for equality and justice have worked their way into the consciousness of people all around the world. When we sing "We Shall Overcome" with children, we take them through a rite of passage that opens their eyes to the evils of racism, and opens their hearts to the healing power of people working together to fight against oppression.

When children sing "We shall Overcome," they are drawn in by the drama and beauty of the melody and the profound meaning of the words, which they can understand even on the most elemental level. As they sing with conviction and passion, they generate inside themselves a sense of unity with the other children who are singing, and also with the

people who lived and struggled during the Civil Rights era. For the children to experience a sense of unity with people who have lived during a different time in history, the children must use their imaginations to journey outside the boundaries of self and time. The compassion that children learn and experience by singing "We Shall Overcome" hopefully becomes integrated within them to be called upon in the future on behalf of other oppressed groups of people.

When children sing "We Shall Overcome" in a group, and other songs whose words or sentiments they fervently believe in and feel, they not only experience the exquisite power of their individual voices and convictions but are also enveloped by the radiant energy of the group, the we. The energy of the group is so big and abundant that it can hold the combined love, power, hope, commitment, inspiration, and strength of all the individuals. As the children simultaneously experience individual separateness and unity with others, the seeds of compassion flourish and grow. The children's boundaries of self metamorphose and merge into one community singing out for the common good.

Teaching children compassion is urgent in these times when the forces that propel violence, poverty, drugs, racism, greed, and environmental degradation assault the sacredness of our human connections and cause us to believe that we are each other's enemies. As enemies, we need to fortify the boundaries of self and personal community, and lock out what we believe will harm us. We must mind our own business, stay on our side of the block, mix only with our own kind, and not talk to strangers.

It is by teaching children how to be compassionate that they will have the skills and desire to open their hearts and minds to other people whose color, religion, traditions, age, sexual orientation, abilities, or economic status are different from their own. By learning and using the tools of compassion in their lives right now, children will be more prepared to live responsibly with others as friends and not as enemies in the increasingly diverse and complex world of tomorrow.

Songs that are meaningful and important to us nest in a special place in our minds and stay with us throughout our lives to be called upon for inspiration, affirmation, grounding, and comfort when needed. Singing the songs and recalling our powerful memories and experiences associated with them can catapult us out of our apathy and fear, and renew our hope, courage, and commitment. As we open our own hearts to lovingly embrace the children of the world with our music and our lives, let us give thanks to each other for our gifts of song and for looking out for each other with compassion in these hard times.

VIII. Adult Issues: Obstacles to Overcome on the Way to Achieving Democratic Practices

As grownups who are doing our best to promote democratic practice with children and with each other, there are many obstacles in our paths. We carry our own personal baggage – our histories. We carry our unique personalities and styles. We carry our fears and biases. We carry our needs for control.

We all have continuous personal work to do to understand ourselves so that our own issues will not dominate and prevent us from being able to really hear the messages from others. To listen with respect and a deep commitment to understand provides an environment of safety and trust.

First of all, *Hearing Everyone's Voice* is communication! Communication is complex: it is speaking, writing, and singing. It is dancing, acting, and moving. It is being open with facial expressions and body language. And it's listening! Genuine communication can affirm; it can build trust; it can bring people closer to each other in relationships. Communication shares with others when we are really hearing what people are communicating. It's the hearing of the feelings behind the words and the body language.

Obstacles to Hearing Everyone's Voice

Sometimes we do and say things which keep other people from sharing and being open with us. It is important for us to be aware of the ways that we block other people from expressing what they feel. We call this blocking "roadblocks." Roadblocks come in a variety of shapes and sizes. Many of them are things that we do with our bodies, like not looking at a person, crossing our arms across our chests, pointing our fingers. Our facial expressions can also roadblock someone's feelings, if we scowl, yawn, laugh at someone, or make faces. And tone of voice can also be a roadblock.

Roadblocks to Opening Communication

GIVING ADVICE

Suggestions of solutions communicate to other people that you are superior and they are inferior. It communicates lack of confidence in their ability to work things out for themselves. It also encourages dependency and lack of ability to think for oneself. This is true even when people ask for advice. It is most helpful to support the person in discovering his/her own best solutions through resources such as problem solving and experimenting.

Logical arguments may follow giving advice. People seldom like to be shown they are wrong. Often they will defend their position to the bitter end and will end up learning nothing. Defensiveness, resentment, and feelings of inadequacy are often the results.

Interpreting, telling people what their problem is communicates that you have things all figured out. This is threatening, frustrating, and insulting and may bring about feelings of embarrassment, resentment, and anger. If it is so easy for you to figure out, why couldn't they?

Moralizing (shoulds, shouldn'ts, oughts, musts) makes people feel that their judgment is not to be trusted. Instead, they always accept what others say as right rather than evaluating for themselves.

JUDGING

Judging makes others feel inadequate, inferior, stupid, and bad. People need support, not our judgments. Commenting specifically, especially *describing,* on the kinds of things people do well is more helpful than judgments. Descriptions are more likely to be nonjudgmental than general praise.

Praising often embarrasses people and makes them uncomfortable. They also know that if they can be judged positively, they can be judged negatively as well.

RELATING FEELINGS

Reassuring and sympathizing tells people you want them to stop feeling the way they do. This makes them feel unaccepted. People often reassure and sympathize when they, themselves, are uncomfortable with the feelings of another person. If the feelings do make you uncomfortable, make a mental note to consider why they do and perhaps you can gain some personal insight.

Distracting and humoring communicates to people that you are not interested, or are uncomfortable with, reject, or don't respect their feelings. Kidding about an important feeling does not open communication and provide support. Problems put off are seldom problems solved. People want to be heard and understood respectfully.

These roadblocks are not roadblocks if nobody has a problem or feeling they are trying to express. They do become roadblocks when a person is hurting, and we respond to him/her in these ways. It's a long, hard process to learn when not to respond with a roadblock. Nobody says it is easy. But, if we can all learn to cut down on the amount of blocking we do, we will find that our children, as well as our family and friends, will feel like talking to us more often about the important things in their lives. If we can learn to listen to feelings without roadblocking, we help people to feel more accepted and understood. We'll be better able to *hear everyone's voice.*

Listen
Author unknown

When I ask you to listen to me
and you start giving me advice,
you have not done what I asked.

When I ask you to listen to me
and you begin to tell me why I shouldn't feel that way,
you are trampling on my feelings.

When I ask you to listen to me
and you feel you have to do something to solve my problem,
you have failed me, strange as that may seem.

Listen!
All I asked was that you listen,
not talk to or do — just hear me.

Advice is cheap;
twenty cents will get you both Dear Abby and Billy Graham
in the same newspaper.

I can do that for myself;
I'm not helpless;
maybe discouraged and faltering, but not helpless.

But when you accept as a simple fact that I do feel what I feel,
no matter how irrational,
then I can quit trying to convince you and get about the
business of understanding what's behind the irrational feeling.
When that's clear, the answers are obvious and I don't need advice.

Irrational feelings make sense when we understand what's behind them.

Perhaps that's why prayer works, sometimes, for some people —
because God is mute,
and He/She doesn't give advice or try to fix things.
"They" just listen and let you work it out for yourself.

So please listen and just hear me.

And if you want to talk,
wait a minute for your turn — and I'll listen to you.

Listening

Adapted from the "Chinese Ideogram 'To Listen'"
Exercise written by Bob Barns of Sierra Foothills
Alternatives to Violence Program (AVP), Nevada City, CA

The following description is used by The Sierra Foothills Alternatives to Violence Project with the Chinese Ideogram on page 234.

232

Only 7% of our feelings come out in words. Over a third of our feelings come out in how we use those words: our tone of voice, the pitch (higher or lower), the volume, the pauses, the timing of the utterance. And over half (55%) of our feelings are shown in body language: our posture, our expressions, our whole-body tenseness or relaxation. So if we want to really know what another person is trying to get across to us, we need to do more than just use our ears.

The Chinese have known this for a long time. When we look at their ideogram (picture writing) for the word "to listen," we find there are several parts to it: Heart, Ear, You, Eyes, and Undivided Attention. When we truly listen, we use ALL of us.

◆ When we listen, we use our ears. We use our ears to hear the words, all of the words. We listen for the meanings behind the words: the rhythms, the inflections, the choices of words and phrases. We listen to hear "where words come from," to quote a Native American chief of 200 years ago.

◆ We listen with our eyes to see the language of the body: body posture, changes in position and facial expressions especially around the eyes.

◆ We listen with our heart. We listen with an open heart, with compassion, we listen accepting every bit of what is being communicated to us, making no judgments about what is said or where it comes from. Ask yourself, "What is this person's SOUL telling me?" As St. Benedict said, "Listen! Listen with the ear of your heart!"

◆ And we listen with undivided attention. We listen with our complete presence, totally right here, right now. We keep completely focused on the speaker and the message.

To truly listen to someone is one of the rarest and most valuable gifts we can give. There is very little else we can really do for a friend: we can't make decisions for them, we can't solve their problems for them, we can't alter the past or bring a particular future to them. But we can give them the gift of truly being present for them — the gift of giving ourselves to them without reservation.

AVP is a 22 year old all-volunteer network of local groups working in prisons and communities in 21 countries around the world. AVP's multi-day experiential-process workshops follow the sequence of affirming ourselves and one another, building communication skills, creating community, and using role plays to practice conflict resolution skills. The purpose is to show participants they already have within them the resources to resolve conflicts nonviolently.

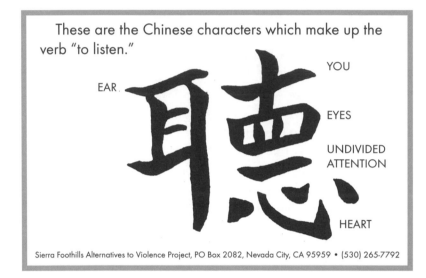

These are the Chinese characters which make up the verb "to listen."

EAR

YOU

EYES

UNDIVIDED ATTENTION

HEART

Sierra Foothills Alternatives to Violence Project, PO Box 2082, Nevada City, CA 95959 • (530) 265-7792

Trust and Helping

Helping can be more complex than merely offering. It is appropriate for us to examine our desire to help others, or not, as the case may be. Why and when do we choose to help, or choose not to? When is it appropriate to speak up? How do we offer help respectfully? And what about accepting help? Sometimes accepting help from another can be a gift given to the helper.

Recently, a gentleman who moves around on a scooter due to MS planned to sit all night in a bus station after a conference rather than pay the expensive taxi fare to get home in the middle of the night. When his friends heard about this plan, a collection was taken up to cover the taxi fare. At first, he refused the offering; he values his independence! But it was explained to him, with love and sensitivity to his need for independence, that the gift to him was also a gift to the givers.

Then he accepted. The respect for his needs was clearly articulated, as were the concerns of his friends. He gave them the gift of not worrying about his sitting up all night in the bus station. He was able to value the concerns of his friends over his own need to maintain his independence in this situation. He listened and heard. He was the real giver!

Thoughts About Helping
from Mary Perkins

Mary Perkins, a retired primary school teacher, is now devoting her time to helping people in her community. She enables physically challenged people to maintain their independence by helping them with running errands and grocery shopping. She volunteers at Head Start and she goes to church where she says, "I am not on any committee now but I greet and help serve the hungry." Mary has a solid sense of values which include "doing the right thing," service to her community, and helping people when they need it.

Mary shared a story about helping others. She is well known in her community, but as an African-American woman she knows that if she approaches someone who doesn't know her in an effort to be helpful, her action could be misunderstood. She told of sitting in a mall parking lot for a full five minutes watching an elderly woman trying to cross to get to her car.

"This elderly woman came out of a store, and was trying to get to her car in the parking lot with her package. The woman was unsteady and the cars simply wouldn't stop." Finally Mary decided to risk offering assistance. She knew the woman might be frightened, so very carefully offered her help by stating, *"I've watched you trying to cross the street, but the cars won't stop. I'm not here to harm you, but will help you cross if you want me to."* The woman expressed her gratitude as Mary stopped the cars and then took the woman with her package safely across.

Helping others may not be as simple as it appears. There are complexities both in offering help, as Mary knows, and in accepting help. We've been taught to fear strangers. We've been taught to fear those different from us. It's hard to trust in these times of frequent violence, and we should be cautious. Not everyone is well-meaning. Additionally, not everyone wants to be helped. Being independent is something we value; loss of that independence feels devastating. Treating people with respect can go a long way in guiding us to know when help is wanted. Being aware of safety can help us protect ourselves. Trust with caution must guide us in these times.

The Adult Journey

The narratives and stories that follow tell of experiences which focus on the sensitivity needed to hear each other's voices. They tell of the struggles needed to share our humanness and vulnerabilities. They address power and domination at the adult personal level, and they consider the complexities of these issues. All are given as gifts to be shared with those who are on the journey, struggling with these concerns for personal growth.

Obstacles to Taking Responsibility

It's difficult to learn to take responsibility for our own choices and decisions. How do consequences and accountability relate to our perspectives on taking responsibility? How does responsibility connect with power and control? How do we feel about taking the responsibility to speak out when we have ideas to share, perhaps when it is easier to keep quiet? What happens when we are faced with overwhelming responsibility?

Don't Blame Me
by Ann Johnson

Ann's song uses humor to address the issues of responsibility in the face of overwhelming concerns. She illustrates the apathy and the violence into which we are all tempted to escape. Her poetic work reminds us whose world it is and whose job it is to take responsibility for it.

I woke up feeling blue,
Like being stuck in glue,
I read the morning news,
Then I knew just what to do.

Hearing Everyone's Voice

I'll blame the government, the Communists,
Those scheming environmentalists,
Capitalism, Socialism,
The guy who writes the news.
But, DON'T BLAME ME!

Let's blame the feminist, the pharmacist,
The scientist, the abortionist,
The liberals, conservatives,
The Catholics and the Jews.
But, DON'T BLAME ME!

Chorus:
It's the parents of that kid with rainbow hair.
The apathist who does not even care.
The terrorist who says it's only fair.
The inner city bum without a prayer.

Let's blame the immigrants, the media,
The FBI, the CIA,
My parents, no my shoes,
The weather, it's the schools.
But, DON'T BLAME ME!

Let's blame the welfare state, the president,
The hippies and the yuppies,
It's the planets and the stars,
It's the aliens from Mars.
But, DON'T BLAME ME!

Chorus:
It's the parents of that kid with rainbow hair.
The apathist who does not even care.
The terrorist who says it's only fair.
The inner city bum without a prayer.

I'm feeling so much better now.
I'm gonna lick this thing somehow.
Grab a gun and grab a horse.
Victory at any cost.
The world is just a pool of cess.
My life is such an awful mess.
But, DON'T BLAME ME!

Struggling with Our Biases

What are the ways in which we honor differences and find common ground with other people? How do we select and make our friends? How do we include those who are different from ourselves in our lives? Do we speak out about inclusion, and about the omissions which can so easily be overlooked? Do we stay alert and respond appropriately to comments and actions which offend certain cultures and traditions? Is inclusion of "the other" constantly in our thinking as we go about our daily lives of work, committees, learning, and community involvement?

Not long ago, several folks were eating in a very small town, home style, restaurant in Tennessee. These people were mostly visiting from big cities in the north and were used to being anonymous when they are out in public. They spoke in loud voices, possibly habit from having to contend with city noise. And they commented negatively about southern food. They said they didn't like grits and beans dripping with butter. The restaurant was small, and their comments could be heard throughout. It's hard not to wonder what the local folks who heard these comments were thinking about these strangers who were so insensitive to their culture. We often feel unaccepted when we go into strange places; perhaps it would help to look more closely at our own behavior in different settings. Perhaps our discomfort is causing us to reject a culture which is different from our own. What can we do to better understand and appreciate the many cultures which impact our lives?

Inclusion involves developing awareness of the value of many different cultures, perspectives, ideas, ways of living our lives, and much, much more. Inclusion is often perceived as difficult, challenging, and even threatening. It's hard enough to communicate and get along with people who are very similar to us; and those we don't understand can possibly prove even more challenging!

Communication plays a big role in how our perspectives of same and different are shared. We all try not to be misunderstood, but even with the people most similar to us it happens frequently. Although we speak the same language, our words have many meanings to all of us. But it is especially difficult when people come from different backgrounds. There is also the whole business of nonverbal communication: gestures, body language, facial expressions all are interpreted from our own unique experiences and cultures. It's really amazing that we ever understand each other.

Finding Our Voices: Speaking Out for the Omissions

What are the ways we acknowledge our shared humanity and nurture all children and families to fulfill their potential? It's a big question, but as people who work with young children and their families know, it is the critical one to consider thoughtfully and keep in mind at all times.

The question goes beyond meeting basic needs. Looking at the special contributions of everyone and acknowledging what each one brings to us provides value to all. It means speaking to every child and parent in ways which affirm who they are. It means finding the common likenesses and talking about them with children, teachers, families. It means getting excited about our differences and unique ways of doing things. It means valuing everyone's contributions. It means including everyone, especially when it's hard. It means taking a long, hard look at ourselves and what causes us to throw up our defenses . . . what causes us to deny the rights of another. What are the ways we as human beings first, and parents and teachers second, can work with ourselves and support one another to provide inclusive environments for children which go beyond mere tolerance?

One of the more difficult aspects of this work we do with children is to be aware of the omissions. We're pretty good at making every child feel basically welcome, but how do we acknowledge the aspects of that child's life which make us uncomfortable? When we talk about homes, do we include the child's home which may be in a shelter or an old school bus? When we talk about families, how do we include the child in foster care? Do we talk about families in which there are two moms or two dads? Are we prepared to accept the child no matter under what circumstances he/she may come to us? Are we prepared to look past acceptance and find ways to promote each child's specialness so that the contributions and unique qualities which he/she brings to the family or group are acclaimed and enhanced? Are we prepared to take notice of, to speak up, and to find our voices when the omissions go unnoticed? Are we really willing to take a long, hard look at ourselves to search out our own biases so that we are aware of whose family, whose history, we could easily ignore? Are we willing to listen to perspectives which are different from our own and to value them, even when we do not agree?

It's the omissions which are so hard. We try our best to be inclusive; but only when we all search within ourselves, trust friends and colleagues to support us, and seek guidance from those who have been on the journey longer than we have will we be able to grow toward a more inclusive culture which seeks to omit no one, and seeks to acknowledge our shared humanity. Only then can we begin to expect people to be able to reach their full potential.

Letting Go of Power and Control
Adult Issues Around Power and Domination
Written and Edited by the
CAEYC Non-Violence Project Team

About five years ago, several early childhood educators decided it was time to focus serious attention on developing a teacher training program on "nonviolence in the lives of children." These professionals had been in the field for many years, were accomplished and respected in their work, and taught adults at this stage in their professional lives.

The development of the training project itself was immensely challenging. Questions evolved, such as: What should be the focus? Which needs of teachers should be given priority? What skills did teachers need the most? What about the roots of violence — societal issues? How might we frame all the components? It was like trying to get a hold on an elephant — the whole thing kept escaping us.

Surprisingly, the development of the training project turned out to be the easier part of it all. We did get a handle on it. But our very own group of professionals was having its own interpersonal challenges as we created the training. As in all groups, we had a variety of personalities — some dominant, some submissive, some merely quiet. The dominant ones talked a lot; the others listened a lot. It wasn't a very good process for democratic work!

Ultimately, as usually happens, unhappiness started to prevail as frustration at not being heard continued. One of the group members, a mental health professional, was available to give us the support to start looking at ourselves and how we were working together. We all did some serious thinking and discussion about our process and what we value about each other as well as how we wanted to work with each other. Another professional helped us immensely during a three-day "consensus-building process" workshop to set goals. In the course of the three days, the leader always made sure that every participant in the group did speak to every idea presented. Having a facilitator really helped us to appreciate the process of including everyone, a requirement of the collaborative work.

By this time, we were actually doing some of the training we had developed. At the first two trainings, one member of our group clearly dominated most of the sessions. She valued being spontaneous, which included using as much time as she felt she needed, and covering any point or topics that occurred to her. While there is a great value to such skill, it caused difficulty when the other trainers in the group couldn't present their topics, previously decided on and assigned, because one person had exceeded the time limit and/or covered subjects for which others had prepared. We were starting to develop serious conflict within our group of trainers. Fortunately, it was at this time in the training project development that we were joined by the mental health professional, and four months later the facilitator on consensus building, both of whom became contributing partners in our work.

We were at a serious divide in our group functioning. One individual felt strongly that her style was important to the training and that she should not be asked to change her unique style to accommodate the module as a whole. The other trainers felt strongly that each trainer should have the security of a reasonably structured and agreed upon schedule so that material would be covered in timely, carefully planned sessions by the presenters who had prepared to it. We struggled with each other, thoughtfully weighing our needs and those of the project, carefully listening to each other, and lovingly accepting each person's gifts. In the end, much to the sadness of all, the trainer who wanted to work with little structure or time limits decided that this project did not accommodate her style. With regret, we realized that some problems are not resolvable to everyone's satisfaction but that we must keep in mind the rights and well being of all.

What did we learn from this process which actually took several years?

Three members of the group chose to share their thoughts on our process, what they learned, and their overall perspective.

Comments from L.M.

First of all, I learned that it's okay to go our separate ways. I also learned that it's more productive to speak up and openly discuss issues with the group members than to acquiesce and allow resentments to build. The longer avoidance continues, the stronger the underlying negative feelings become until a volatile situation develops and eruption is inevitable. Also, it's unfair to the participant who is unaware that a conflict exists and, therefore, has no opportunity to work with others toward a resolution before the situation has grown. We all need to express our own views and feelings, listen to and respect each other's views and feelings, and accept our feelings of disequilibrium during the process. We must be willing to give up individual control (letting go) to work together as a creative group.

Comments from M.S.

I learned as a member of this team that we really did need help clarifying our problem. We had carefully, and we assumed collaboratively, worked out a schedule for the workshop and were shocked and surprised when one of the team threw in a time consuming new activity! One real shock was that one of our topics was on the difference between cooperation, coordination, and collaboration. I was really overwhelmed with sadness when I realized that this team member did not fully understand and/or buy into modeling what we were teaching.

The project took on a life of its own and grew away from one of its founders — much as some couples grow apart and don't have enough in common to maintain communication. In our case, we developed a fundamentally different value system.

Comments from L.M.

I was one of the quiet ones because when I spoke I felt devalued, that my comments were not important. When my part of the writing was

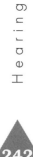

turned in, it seemed to me that it was criticized with no constructive criticism or guidelines given. I felt very discouraged. After the change, I found my voice because no one person dominated and the group now listened to everyone. We worked collaboratively on our writings.

Sharing Authority

What are children currently learning from us about relationships and power and authority structures? What are we modeling for children? How are we hearing everyone's thoughts and ideas, even when they conflict with ours? What are the issues around authority for us as adults who are responsible for the welfare of children?

Modeling Cooperative Learning
by Susan Hopkins

I still find it remarkable to realize how much children learn, or maybe absorb, from the other people in their lives — especially the adults. We tend to think that unless we are actually "teaching" children that they are not learning. We forget that they are constantly absorbing the stimuli around them.

The four year olds at Cal State Fullerton Children's Center taught me — again (!) — that I must always be watchful of what I am "teaching." My co-teacher and I used the few minutes of time between breakfast cleanup and the morning meeting time, while the children had free choice of center activities, to finalize the day's plans and set up materials. We talked and set up together while the children used materials at the art center and others. The children could hear our discussions, solving of problems, and general cooperative style. I hadn't really thought much about what the children might be learning from us as we prepared for our day with them. But one day we overheard them talking at the table using our same words and methods of cooperation as they worked together on a joint art activity. During this time of the day, no specific projects were put forth — children had open access to materials to use in their own best ways. So the cooperative project was of their own invention. What a pleasure to hear them interacting with

each other in ways of respect as they shared their ideas and created together.

Sharing Control

Control and domination are significant issues for most people. Even young children are often trying to figure out how to get "power." We like to be in control, in charge; but when does domination become a concern? There are questions to consider of inclusiveness and responsibility to all those involved which are serious and must be addressed by us if we really are to implement the principles of democratic practice. How are we sharing control with others in meaningful ways? Are we really willing to hear everyone's voice? What methods do we use to speak and listen in ways which invite others to participate? Two stories follow about how adults worked through some of these issues and their reactions to the processes.

Voting vs. Consensus
by Ann Johnson

At a committee meeting of the Education Committee for our local Head Start, there was a vote taken about an issue which could concern all members personally — financial support for continuing education classes. Although it was actually a complex issue, little discussion occurred because there was not enough information for people to understand it. After the quick discussion, the vote was taken. There was one dissenting voice — that of the bus driver. After she was overruled, we moved on to the next order of business, feeling we had finished the other since we had voted on it. The bus driver interrupted and asked if we didn't want to know why she had voted against the suggestion on the previous issue. Usually no one asks that question, so we were surprised, but we really did want to hear her thoughts. Interestingly enough, her thoughts provoked an in-depth discussion and convinced us all to change our minds!

At that point, one of the teachers commented that perhaps voting on issues was not the best method to hear everyone's ideas. Certainly

it had not proven very helpful in this situation. People asked what other ways she could suggest. Consensus decision making was presented as a method to be considered. The consensus process involves hearing everyone's ideas before making a decision. It may take longer than voting, but it includes everyone and is therefore usually a very thoughtful, inclusive process. Decisions come from a sense of the group as verbalized by the leader, and therefore are supported by all. The committee decided to try using consensus decision making.

Grownups at The Peace Table

Underlying problems can wreck havoc in our lives when we least expect. Sometimes, we're not even aware that there is a problem, or we may be trying to solve a different problem from the one which is really getting in our way. How can we best learn to define and articulate which problem needs solving? How can we learn to ask the "right" questions?

Adults, as well as children, struggle with communication and solving problems together. At a two-day training for adults who lead Children's Peace Camp in Chico, California, two of the coordinators were attempting to demonstrate a role play of problem solving at the Peace Table.   They had selected a children's problem to work through. However, they kept getting stuck and couldn't move through the problem-solving framework. It was decided to return to the process the next day. After an evening to reflect, the teachers came back and asked if we could do a Peace Table to work through a problem they were having with each other. They could hardly wait to express how angry they were with each other. As it turned out, they were frustrated with each other because of a misunderstanding which had prevented a group of teachers from attending the Peace Camp training. They shared their feelings of frustration, their perceptions of what they thought had happened, and what had actually happened. They expressed their needs for better communication, created a plan, and really cleared the air so that Peace Camp could happen without all the underlying tension. At the end, there was a collective cheer from the entire group for the courage and openness which had been shared and modeled.

Taking the Risks of Letting the Children Make Choices

Being able to make choices gives us power! Young children can learn to make choices very early in their lives if we provide appropriate opportunities for them to do so. How can we give them practice to learn to make the best choices possible? Children need a focus in choice-making to help guide them. Wide open choices will overwhelm them and may create negative behavior if children make choices which the adult did not anticipate. In contrast, carefully framed choices presented within the appropriate perimeters will create opportunities for success in choosing. A simple example: When asking young children to wash their hands before lunch, the choice is not whether or not to wash hands but, "Do you want to wash your hands now or in five minutes?" This choice gives children the power to decide if they want to stop playing now or in a few minutes.

Children also need to be able to make mistakes and to be able to learn from them, to take responsibility for them. Adults who can promote appropriate choice-making and risk-taking give children real opportunities to learn these skills. How can we best support these needs of children? Sometimes it is difficult for adults to let children take the risks of making their own choices; sometimes adults don't realize the importance of letting children practice making choices. Following is a story about a young mother and her struggles in giving her daughter the independence appropriate for a child growing up in a culture different from her mother's.

Carmen's Story
as told to Susan Hopkins

In 1993, Carmen and her three young children first came to Peace Camp at Fullerton, California. Recently she reminded me of that initial experience when Crystal was six, Derek was three, and Michael was four. Crystal was doing an art activity which involved gluing objects onto paper, collage style. Carmen told Crystal where to put the objects on her paper. The teacher, upon observing Carmen, explained to her that Crystal needed to be able to make the choices in her own creative style. Carmen explained to the teacher that the way Crystal was doing it didn't "look good." Again, the teacher talked to Carmen about the need for Crystal to make her own best choices and to do it her very own way. Finally, when Carmen continued to "help" Crystal, the teacher moved Carmen, sitting in her chair, away from her daughter. Carmen still remembers being removed from within reach of her daughter and laughs about it now.

Later that day, Carmen and I had lunch together. We chatted casually about how Peace Camp was going for her and the kids. Carmen explained that it was a very different experience than she had expected. She had thought it would be more "campy": tents, hot dogs, and so on. Then she told me about the experience with Crystal and the art project. She was clearly giving it serious thought. We talked about choices and how important it is to give children lots of opportunities to make choices in carefully monitored situations. Peace Camp is one of the best times for children to practice choice-making. Carmen told me about her own childhood which had been carefully controlled by her family. She was not permitted to make choices, so had not thought until then about how important it is for children growing up in a democracy to learn to make effective choices. However, the more she thought about the need for her children to be able to be independent grownups, the more interested she became in exploring some of the methods we use to help children gain in confidence through doing things for themselves. Carmen continued to come to Peace Camp that summer to learn all she could. She also came at least one day of the week other summers and contributed extensively to our knowledge of plants and plant uses.

Carmen talked to me again about the cultural obstacles she has encountered in trying to raise her children in different ways than her family. Her family is very traditional in the roles they consider for the children, and girls especially are expected to be quite submissive. We talked once more about what she wants for her children, and she is fully committed to supporting their growing independence as best she can. I feel confident of her strength in holding onto her ideals to give her children the very best possible start in life.

Taking the Risks of Honestly Sharing with Children

"Mom, It Must Have Been Hard for You"
by Robin Song

My daughter was nine years old. For weeks, we had been hearing reports about the San Francisco police raids on gay and lesbian bars and the many men and women who had been badly beaten by those who, presumably, were there to protect us. A call had gone out to the community to meet at Castro and Market for a rally to organize some action to stop the abuse.

My daughters and I went to the rally to support what was happening. I had been "out" as a lesbian for three years and my children and I had been involved in many political and cultural activities in the lesbian/gay community. As the many speakers talked on, I noted that my daughter was listening very intently to what was being said. There was much anger and the speeches were filled with emotion. The rally ended and we made our way to the car and began our trip home to the East Bay. As we drove home, my daughter asked, "Why would anyone want to hurt lesbians and gays?" Why indeed!

I tried to put it in perspective of her own life. I said, "Think about how most people live. They live in houses, have jobs, drive cars, have several children. They get up every morning, eat, go to work, and basically live the same thing over and over again. They are very similar, and it is hard for them to think about things that are very different from themselves. If someone like a lesbian woman or gay man enters into their lives, it makes them think about things differently and that often scares people. It may mean they have to change how they think. Sometimes when people are scared and frightened, they want to get rid of the thing that frightens them. I think the police are frightened and they just don't want to deal with changes in the way they would have to think about things. So they get angry and beat up the people who frighten them."

My daughter sat there in the front seat of the car, lights flashed by as we crossed the bridge. She was quiet for a long time after I had finished speaking. Finally she turned to me and said, "Mom, it must have been very hard for you." It took me a moment to understand exactly what she meant, and then it hit me. My daughter, with all the amazing depth of compassion and understanding that the human heart

can hold, realized that I had been one of those people in the picture I had painted and had broken away from that narrow thinking against great odds, to live a life that was truly mine.

Not only was her comment a great blessing to me, but I also realized that young children can and do understand complex issues that seem to overwhelm many adults. Children also have the capacity to feel great compassion and are able to support those they love in genuine, mature interactions.

This daughter is now a mother herself and is in the child care field. Many have been and will be blessed by her gentle, understanding way.

More Than Five Worries
by Julie Carrara
(illustrated by Jason Carrara)

A recent rainy afternoon found my six year old son Jason and me browsing the shelves of a local Nevada City, California, import store. Great fun to explore, the shop is overflowing with unique and interesting musical instruments, toys, art, and clothing from around the world. With a crumpled dollar bill wadded in his fist, Jason chose his purchase carefully and proudly exited the store wearing it around his neck — a small, brightly colored cloth pouch containing Guatemalan "Worry Dolls." As legend has it, the children of Guatemala tell a worry to each doll at bedtime before placing them in the sack for the night. In the morning, their worries have disappeared. My son's woven pouch came with these instructions along with five tiny dolls, each the size of a fingernail.

Upon leaving the store, Jason looked up at me and said in a concerned tone of voice, "Mom, what should I do if I have more than five worries?" It was an honest question and the words were momentous to me. And, weeks later, I found that they were with me still — like the dollar bill held steadfastly in his small closed fist, I kept his question as a talisman of the very real world in which our children live today. And my determination to make the world a better place for children was left further strengthened.

It is significant to note that my son comes from what is considered to be a traditional family setting — two loving and supportive parents, a nice stable middle class home in a safe rural small town environment — unlike so many children in far less fortunate circumstances. Nevertheless, it is not easy to be a child of six anywhere in the world today. It is not without more than five worries.

Ducking out of the rain, we took refuge under the awning of a nearby building. Huddled together, I took out the dolls and placed them in the palm of his outstretched hand. He named his worries one by one, big and small, all of them important. Some dolls he told twice. I confessed that I, too, had more than five worries. Could I borrow his dolls? I worried that I hadn't defrosted anything for dinner that night. He worried his brother might break his favorite toy. I worried about my grandmother's upcoming back operation. He worried his father might die if he kept smoking. The tiny dolls stared vacantly back at us as together we voiced the words to our fears amidst a wintry downpour.

Yet a tangible warmth hung between us. Through our sharing and listening to each other, a very real connection was unfolding. I knew he felt glad to be heard, as I did myself. And it wasn't just listening to each other; it was listening to ourselves as well. The listening was an affirmation that left us feeling both confident and hopeful, empowered to find our own solutions and make change in our lives. I smiled to myself for having found the real magic of the Worry Dolls. I reached over to tuck the dolls back into their pouch and tell Jason of my discovery — but it was too late. He had carefully put them back into their pouch, and with the drawstring pulled taut, the dolls once again swung loosely against his chest, their mystery held safely within. Jason had been given a voice, and had chosen to believe in himself. He reached for my hand, urging me to my feet. The sun for a moment shining, the world sharply in focus, together we headed for home.

Obstacles from Our Own Childhoods

Jay Mankita, songwriter, looks at the subject of compassion from the perspective of the parent who learns about the meaning of love as he explores his own feelings about being punished as a child. He writes this explanation to go along with his song, "Another Name for Love."

I awoke from a dream wherein a woman sang a beautiful song to me in Spanish. I didn't understand the words except for the last line which I somehow knew to mean *Is this another name for love?* In my attempts to recreate this song in my own language, I needed to find a meaning for this haunting phrase. As a songwriter, I often take liberties with the facts of a story, while remaining true to the feelings involved. Although I don't have children of my own, feelings like helplessness and rage, as well as the desire for healing and compassion, are universal to the human spirit. I think it's a successful song because, like myself, others have found themselves reflected in it as well. My greatest gift has come several times when told by a friend or audience member that they've stopped hitting their child because of this song.

Another Name for Love

A young boy walks into the house, tracking mud all over the floor
His father loves him very much, but he's warned him several times
*   before*
The boy says I don't understand. His father scowls and lifts his
*   hand*
Though he doesn't want to hit him he has got to learn right now
He's beaten till he's cried enough then told that they still love him
*   anyhow*
And he cries as he asks the question of
Is this another name for love?

His father lifts him from his knee and hits him one more time on the
*   face*
He doesn't want to hurt his son but he's got to know his place

The boy runs up and locks the door; he can't stand it anymore
This time they've done something they'll regret
But as he is planning his revenge, he falls asleep in order to forget
And as he does, he asks the question of
Is this another name for love?
Is this another name for love?

Years go past and he grows fast; he's learned so many things
    while he's grown
He moves away and then one day he finds he has a family of his own
He's always trying to be fair, his children think he doesn't care
Though he doesn't want to hit them it's the only way he knows
But every time they run upstairs he remembers all the doors he
    used to close
And as he does he asks the question of
Is this another name for love?
Is this another name for love?

He just wants to do what's right, But he still cries every night
Is this another name for love?
Is this another name for love?

His young boy walks into the house, tracking mud all over the floor
He loves his son so very much, but he's warned him several times
    before
Then as he raises up his hand
He stops — and starts to understand
I've thought of something easier, he gently tells his son
And as they both clean up that floor he is grateful for the gift that
    he has won
And as he cries he asks the question of
Is this another name for love?
THIS IS another name for love.

Family Traditions
by J. Chris Olander

Chris wrote "Family Traditions" in response to his own painful
childhood and adolescence growing up in the Sacramento, California,

suburbs. He writes that he was too much influenced by mass-media advertising, peer pressure, and adults who didn't discuss concerns in respectful ways. Both parents and school teachers did not have the time or power to be sensitive, listen to children, or explain social pressures and manipulation that extract a child's self worth, dignity, and honor.

After high school and seeing myself and most of my friends become victims of misinformation from peers, mass media, and government institutions and systems, I took the responsibility to gain an education for myself in an effort to see more clearly and to become a poet and teacher in the schools. I wanted to give children the opportunity I didn't have to express feelings and ideas in a trusting and accepting environment that encourages honesty in words in order to learn from each other and examine truths and fallacies we all acquire while growing up. This poem is from my own experience.

1.
What sparked him was traditional
blind power forcing rigid
authoritarian creeds
proclaiming the patriarch's
"A Man's World!"

"Son, males are aggressive
be tough
don't cry or hug those boys!"
"Eighteen and still a virgin?"
"We Build Men!"
"You all come on, ride out
to Marlboro country
where a man belongs!"

And he rides on —

"I hereby sentence you to one year
imprisonment for the
brutal beating of the plaintiff!"

"It's your responsibility to marry me
you're the father!"
"Any male that's shamefaced, spineless
is a queer, a coward, and
doesn't deserve to be called a man!"
"I'm sorry — but the malignant lung
will have to come out or he'll die!"

What got him
was a bullseye in responsibility
a .30 caliber hollow point
blasting skin bone brain to gore!
"A man's world"
Oblivion!

2.
What burned her was the lie
an unsurmountable assemblage
of congressional housewifery
a concentrated congestion of
the easy way out!

"Mr. Clean's nine week floor polish!"
"Our spotless glassware
impresses the neighbors
dear!"
"The only laundry soap with three cleaning agents
and deodorizer!"
"The natural make-up
fashioned look!"
And it rolls on —
"How many times have I told you
wipe your feet!"
"Our neighbors own
a set of crystal
dear!"
"Dammit
put your dirty clothes where they belong!"
"You don't appreciate
what I do for you!"

What got her
was rejection to recapitulate
responsibility's understanding
in becoming what could be:
the easy way out
insanity!

The next contribution, as shared by Tony Pellicano, presents his view of growing up in an immigrant family and community some 60 years ago. He discusses his view of the "ghetto" from his perspective of immigrants: from people who choose to come to this country, who embrace the freedoms they perceive democracy will give to them, and who may be absorbed by the dominant culture with relative ease.

"High Expectations"
by A. J. "Tony" Pellicano

In offering this passage to HEARING EVERYONE'S VOICE, I felt rather compelled to add my own personal experiences about culture, having lived them as a youngster, and within the parameters of my own belief, conquered them to enjoy with satisfaction, the life I have lived and am still living today. If it but helps just one person to conquer the obstacle enamored by the word "ghetto," I would feel totally compensated for the time it took to put it into words.

There is a very distinguishable dichotomy to the word "ghetto" that needs to be explained before accepting it as a reason for one's failure and inability to cope with the societal mechanisms necessary to succeed in today's world. Accordingly, Webster tells us that the true meaning of ghetto is a foundry where cannons were cast. The word also was used to describe a particular area set aside for a Jewish community to subsist within the confines of Venice, Italy, where cannons were made. It would seem that the latter meaning of the word transcended to America with the European immigration at the turn of the century and attached itself to the areas where people of like ethnicities grouped.

These communities offered unity while the inhabitants entrenched themselves in the newly established democratic way of life. In its truest sense the ghetto eventually pandered to people (new citizens of America) who were in need of economic security, and so prevailed until

they were able to raise themselves to higher levels on America's escutcheon. Many of America's finest minds and personages have had their starts in so-called ghettos such as Little Italy, The Bowery, Chinatown, Lower East Side, just to name a few, that exist around New York City. It is very difficult for me to accept the idea of ghettos as slums and "dens of iniquity." Oftentimes when reading biographies of successful people, the word "ghetto" can be found mentioned in discussing their earlier lives.

I perceive that to perpetuate the thought that being raised in an immigrant ghetto gives one cause to believe that there is no future for its inhabitants is a negative self-fulfilling prophecy, and is the wrong message to send, both to adults living there, for whatever the reason, but especially to the children growing up in an area that has already etched a place in their developing minds. It seems to me that my parents and family faced many of the same conditions which prevail today because there are still areas that cater to the lower end of the economic scale. However, my parents used those pallid conditions to establish a firm drive to better themselves, rather than to fall prey to the prophecy.

In thinking about it, my family, along with many of our neighbors, worked unceasingly in community to refute the prophecy. We worked together and played together, sharing and recognizing our diversity as well as tolerating other cultures, because our needs were similar. For most, the goals were identical in that we put education in front of the family's needs so that the children would have a better chance to make it in the new democracy and carry on with their progress. These are the personal values and understanding we learned from living the immigrant ghetto life. No, I just cannot buy living and being raised in a ghetto as a cause for failure.

Born and raised by immigrant parents, I feel that I survived the negative prophecy because my parents taught me the importance of values and independence that have stood me in good stead throughout my life. One needs to recognize and accept the valuable lessons that ghetto life can teach — values that in reality cannot be bought for any amount of money and can only be attained by challenging them. I was born a depression baby in the '20s so I started out my life learning how to make the most of what I had. Communication and realization were my ever present companions; but mostly my goals in life were chiseled in stone, and as I grew, married, and progressed on life's stage, I look back at my start in the ghetto and realize more than ever how important that part of my life really was. While there are rocks in everyone's road of

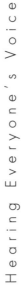

life, I have never encountered one that I could not circumvent because problem solving was part of my ghetto life.

My parents moved to California at the start of World War II and it was then that appreciation of what we learned as a family helped us to grow into a middle class family — and, ultimately, home owners — with an eye on our future. It was many years, 40 to be close, before I was able to go back on a vacation. The associations that I had made in that early homestead were still valid as several people were still around, although living so much better. I really was not surprised to find that the ghetto that I came from had given rise to doctors, lawyers, politicians, school teachers, engineers, and even a cousin of mine who is a Wall Street broker. A few made the military their career; but even more interesting was that ethnicity, color, religion, and sex appeared to present no bar to those now successful lives. I again took stock, packed up my own degrees, and returned home to California in retirement, and my own expanding family.

When I decided to do this short biography about "immigrant" ghetto life, I was only too happy to put it into words so as to share the feeling that ghetto life was not permanently demeaning to me or my friends. The ghetto itself is really not the cause for one's failure to cope with life. What is important to realize is that promising futures await people if they persevere in getting the education needed to build lives of productivity. Having families who promote values which stress the importance of education, goal setting, and perseverance help children succeed. Someone (I don't remember who) once quoted me an adage that I have always remembered, "Success belongs to those who persevere." Never has any written word that I have ever read had more meaning. If you really want something, then go and get it!

IX. Resources

The following lists of organizations, children's and adult books, video and audio tapes have been developed to supplement and enhance the work of democratic practice.

Organizations

Action Alliance for Children: (510) 444-7136
Children's Advocate newspaper is published bimonthly and addresses a wide variety of issues relating to children.

Alternatives to Violence (AVP): Contact: Rick Krouskop,
2057 Pepper Ridge Drive, Shreveport, LA 71115
Training program for adults used in prisons.

Chico (California) Peace and Justice Center: (530) 893-9078
Monthly newsletter on issues of peace and justice.

Children's Creative Response to Conflict (CCRC): (914) 353-1796
Workshops and newsletter on conflict resolution skills.

Children's Defense Fund: (202) 628-8787
Monthly news magazine carries updates on federal legislation relating to issues affecting children. Advocacy steps are suggested and statistics outlined.

Children's Music Network: (847) 733-8003
Progressive music for children of all ages; quarterly journal includes songs with lyrics and musical notation, as well as lots of activities for music education.

Clear Vision Dolls: (909) 592-4299
    A source for Persona Dolls.

Concerned Educators Allied for a Safe Environment (CEASE):
    (617) 864-0999
    Newsletter for early childhood educators on issues relating to
    peace education, social justice, and the environment.
    Wampanoag Curriculum — Available from CEASE.

Donnelly/Colt: (860) 455-9621
    Progressive Resources Catalogue, including buttons, bumper
    stickers, posters, etc.

Growing Communities for Peace: (651) 433-4303
    Quarterly newsletter, *Peacemaker's News,* shares peacemaking
    skills and other practical strategies for teachers and parents.

National Association for the Education of Young Children (NAEYC):
    (800) 424-2460
    *Developmentally Appropriate Practice in Early Childhood
    Programs,* Revised Edition.

Northeast Foundation for Children: (800) 360-6332
    Pubishes free newsletter, *Responsive Classroom,* three times a year.

The Peace Resource Center of San Diego (California): (619) 265-0730
    Monthly newsletter on a wide variety of peace issues, including
    war toys and media.

People of Every Stripe — catalogue: (503) 282-0612
    A source for Persona Dolls.

Prevent Handgun Violence Against Kids: (415) 331-3337
    Workshops and seminars, as well as local organizing ideas.

Resource Center for Nonviolence, Santa Cruz, California:
    (831) 423-1626
    Bookstore and resource center for peace and justice.
    Peace Education: A Bibliography Focusing on Young Children,
    written and edited by Rosmarie Greiner.

Rethinking Schools: (414) 964-9646. Publications promoting equity
and justice.
Quarterly newsletter packed with information on issues around
social justice concerns such as bilingual education, unions,
progressive education, and other topics.

Southern Poverty Law Center: (888) 414-7752
Fax requests (205) 264-3121
Teaching Tolerance is a quarterly resource magazine for materials
to suppor anti-bias education. *Starting Small* video and book are
specific to the needs of early childhood educators.

Stand for Children: (800) 663-4032

Teachers Resisting Unhealthy Children's Entertainment (TRUCE):
PO Box 441261, West Somerville, MA 02144
Presents annually a list of toys which promote healthy, creative
play, as well as some current toys to avoid.

War Resisters League: (212) 228-0450
Youth Peace program promotes nonviolence among children and
youth.

Wellesley College Center for Research on Women: (781) 283-2500
Research on gender issues; developed *The Bullying Curriculum*.

Women's International League for Peace and Freedom (WILPF):
(215) 563-7110
Contact Susan Hopkins about WILPF Children's Peace Camps:
(530) 274-1862.

Zero to Three: (202) 638-1144
Resources to help meet the needs of infants and toddlers, including
a bimonthly journal.

Musicians

Lisa Atkinson — Songwriter and Musician
317 West 41st Avenue, San Mateo, CA 94403
Marcia Berman — Singer; Songwriter; Educator
13045 Mindanao Way, #1, Marina Del Rey, CA 90292
Bob Blue — Musician; Songwriter; Storyteller
170 East Hadley Road, #82, Amherst, MA 01002
Jacki Breger — Musician; Teacher; Singer; Recording Artist
918 18th Street, Santa Monica, CA 90403
Victor Cockburn — Artist-Educator; Troubadour
126 Payson Road, Chestnut Hill, MA 02167-3272
Fundi — Director, Vukani Mawethu Choir
PO Box 98, Oakland, CA 94604
Joanne Hammil — Musician; Songwriter
70 Capitol Street, Watertown, MA 02472
Tom Hunter — Minstrel; Educator
2524 Victor, Bellingham, WA 98225
Ann Johnson — Parent; Concerned Citizen; Head Start Supervisor;
Songwriter — 13232 Devin Lane, Grass Valley, CA 95949
Bonnie Lockhart — Musician; Songwriter; Teacher
1032 Winsor Avenue, Oakland, CA 94610
Jay Mankita — Musician; Songwriter
PO Box 142, Malden, NY 12453
Ruth Pelham — Musician; Songwriter; Founder/Director of The Music/
Mobile — PO Box 6024, Albany, NY 12206
Alisa Peres — Performer; Music Educator
2631 Woolsey Street, Berkeley, CA 94705
Sarah Pirtle — Children's Musician and Songwriter; Director of The
Discovery Center — 63 Main Street, Shelburne Falls, MA 01370
Patricia Shih — Singer; Songwriter
PO Box 1554, Huntington, NY 11743
Ben Silver — Musician; Songwriter
210 West 77th Street, #2A, New York, NY 10024

Children's Books for Early Childhood

These stories have been categorized according to the seven democratic principles as defined throughout this book. The categories overlap and the stories may be used to illustrate several ideas and concepts together.

Self Identity within Community

Welcoming Babies, by Margy Burns Knight. Gardiner, ME: Tilbury House, 1994.
There are as many ways to welcome babies to the world as there are cultures. We sing, kiss, bless, name, announce, celebrate, give gifts, and honor the births of our youngest ones with dignity and joy. Warm, gentle pictures enhance the simple text of this story which brings together many ways of welcoming.

All The Colors of the Earth, by Sheila Hamanaka. New York: Morrow Junior Books, 1994.

All The Colors We Are: The Story of How We Get Our Skin Color, by Katie Kissinger. St. Paul, MN: Redleaf Press, 1994.

Two Mrs. Gibsons, by Toyomi Igus. San Francisco, CA: Children's Book Press, 1996.

Safety and Trust

Grandpa's Town, by Takaaki Nomura. Brooklyn, NY: Kane/Miller Book Publishers, 1991.
Told in both Japanese and English, this story of a young Japanese boy, worried that his grandfather is lonely, accompanies him to the public bath. Their walk through the town is an expedition filled with meeting friends, visiting, and sharing the best of Grandpa's community.

Kimi and the Watermelon, by Miriam Smith. New York: Puffin Books, 1983.

On Mother's Lap, by Ann Herbert Scott. New York: Clarion Books, 1972.

Storm in the Night, by Mary Stolz. Publisher: Harper Trophy, 1988.

Tell Me A Story, Mama, by Angela Johnson. New York: Orchard Books, 1989.

The Relatives Came, by Cynthia Rylant. New York: Aladdin Books, 1993.

Responsibility and Dependability

The Story of Ruby Bridges, by Robert Coles. New York: Scholastic, Inc., 1995.
  For months, six year old Ruby Bridges must confront the hostility of segregationists when she becomes the first African-American girl to integrate an elementary school in New Orleans in 1960. Robert Coles presents a moving portrayal that captures a young girl's amazing courage and faith.
Very Last First Time, by Jan Andrews. New York: Atheneum, 1985.
Working Cotton, by Sherley Anne Williams. New York: Harcourt Brace Jovanovich, 1992.

Cherishing Diversity and Inclusion

Everybody Cooks Rice, by Norah Dooley. Minneapolis, MN: Carolrhoda, Inc., 1991.
  A child is sent to find a younger brother at dinner time and is introduced to a variety of cultures through encountering the many different ways rice is prepared at the different households she visited. Recipes for preparing rice from several cultures are included.
Bein' with You This Way, by W. Nikola-Lisa. New York: Lee & Low Books, Inc., 1994.
Daddy's Roommate, by Michael Willhoite. Boston, MA: Alyson Publications, 1990.
Gathering the Sun: An Alphabet in Spanish and English, by Alma Flor Ada. New York: Lothrop, Lee & Shepard Books, 1997.
How My Family Lives in America, by Susan Kuklin. New York: Bradbury Press, 1992.
Ragsdale, by Artie Ann Bates. Boston, MA: Houghton Mifflin Company, 1995.
Somos Un Arco Iris — We Are A Rainbow, by Nancy Maria Grande Tabor. Watertown, MA: Charlesbridge, 1995.
White Sox Only, by Evelyn Coleman. Morton Grove, IL: Albert Whitman & Company, 1996.

Shared Authority

The Streets are Free, by Kurusa. New York: Annick Press Ltd., 1995.
Based on the true story of the children of a barrio in Caracas, Venezuela, who wanted a place to play, the story depicts how the children met, decided how to approach "City Hall," and what they did when confronted with discouragement. It is a story of building community and speaking out.

The Day Gogo Went to Vote: South Africa, April, 1994, by Elinor Batezat Sisulu. Boston, MA: Little, Brown and Company, 1996.

The Table Where Rich People Sit, by Byrd Baylor. New York: Atheneum Books, 1994.

Hey, Little Ant, by Phillip and Hannah Hoose. Berkeley, CA: Tricycle Press, 1998.

Problem Solving and Choices

The Knight and the Dragon, by Tomie De Paola. New York: G. P. Putnam's Sons, 1980.
A knight who has never fought a dragon and an equally inexperienced dragon prepare to meet each other in battle. The ultimate result is a delightful cooperative enterprise.

Best Day of the Week, by Nancy Carlsson-Paige. Minneapolis, MN: Redleaf Press, 1998.

Galimoto, by Karen Lynn Williams. New York: Mulberry Books, 1990.

Rebel, by Allan Baillie. New York: Ticknor & Fields Books for Young Readers, 1994.

Roxaboxen, by Barbara Cooney. New York: Puffin Books, 1991.

Shoes Like Miss Alice's, by Angela Johnson. New York: Orchard Books, 1995.

Sharing and Helping

Something from Nothing: Adapted from a Jewish Folktale, by Phoebe Gilman. New York: Scholastic Inc., 1992.
In this retelling of a traditional Jewish folk tale, Joseph's baby blanket is transformed into ever smaller items as he grows until there is nothing left — but then Joseph has an idea to save the blanket forever in his memory.

Ben's Trumpet, by Rachel Isadora. New York: Mulberry Books, 1979.

Follow The Drinking Gourd, by Jeanette Winter. New York: Alfred A. Knopf, 1988.

Smoky Night, by Eve Bunting. New York: Harcourt Brace & Company, 1994.

Books for Adults

The following list of adult resources have been selected and categorized according to the topics suggested in the introduction to this manual as useful for the reader to consider:

- ◆ Inspiration and Confidence
- ◆ Theoretical Background
- ◆ Program and Strategies for Children
- ◆ And one more we have added: Training for Adults

The categorization of these resources have been created only to give very general guidance as to topics. Clearly they will overlap extensively.

Inspiration and Confidence

Belenky, Mary Field, et al. *Women's Ways of Knowing: The Development of Self, Voice, and Mind.* Basic Books of Harper Collins, 1986.

Coles, Robert. *The Moral Intelligence of Children: How to Raise a Moral Child.* New York: Random House, 1997.

Freire, Paulo. *Pedagogy of the Oppressed.* New York: Continuum Publishing Company, 1996.

Goodwillie, Susan (editor). *Voices From the Future: Our Children Tell Us About Violence in America.* New York: Crown Publishers, 1993.

Hoose, Phil. *It's Our World, Too! Stories of Young People Who Are Making A Difference.* Boston, MA: Little, Brown and Company, 1993.

Kohn, Alfie. *Beyond Discipline: From Compliance to Community.* Boston, MA: Houghton Mifflin Company, 1993.

Kohn, Alfie. *No Contest: The Case Against Competition.* Boston, MA: Houghton Mifflin Company, 1986.

Paley, Vivian Gussin. *You Can't Say You Can't Play.* Cambridge, MA: Harvard University Press, 1992.

Zinn, Howard. *You Can't be Neutral on a Moving Train: A Personal History of Our Times.* Boston, MA: Beacon Press, 1994.

Theoretical Background

Bredekamp, Sue, and Copple, Carol. *Developmentally Appropriate Practice in Early Childhood Programs.* Washington, DC: National Association for the Education of Young Children, 1997.

California Department of Education. *Toward a State of Esteem: The Final Report of the California Task Force to Promote Self-Esteem and Personal and Social Responsibility.* Sacramento, CA: California Department of Education, 1990.

Chang, Hedy Nai-Lin. *Affirming Children's Roots: Cultural and Linguistic Diversity in Early Care and Education.* San Francisco, CA: California Tomorrow, 1996.

Delpit, Lisa. *Other People's Children: Cultural Conflict in the Classroom.* New York: The New Press, 1995.

Dines, Gail, and Humez, Jean M. (editors). *Gender, Race and Class in Media.* Thousand Oaks, CA: Sage Publications, 1995.

Garbarino, James, et al. *Children In Danger: Coping With The Consequences of Community Violence.* San Francisco, CA: Jossey-Bass, 1992.

Garbarino, James. *Raising Children in a Socially Toxic Environment.* San Francisco, CA: Jossey-Bass, 1995.

Gilligan, James. *Violence: Reflections on a National Epidemic.* New York: Vintage Books, Random House, 1996.

Hooks, bell. *Killing Rage: Ending Racism.* New York: Henry Holt and Company, 1995.

Kivel, Paul. *Uprooting Racism: How White People Can Work for Racial Justice.* Gabriola Island, BC: New Society Publishers, 1996.

Kohl, Herbert. *Should We Burn Babar?* New York: New Press, 1995.

Prothrow-Stith, Deborah. *Deadly Consequences: How Violence Is Destroying Our Teenage Population and a Plan to Begin Solving the Problem.* New York: Harper Perennial, 1991.

Shor, Ira. *Empowering Education: Critical Teaching for Social Change.* Chicago, IL: University of Chicago Press, 1992.

Tatum, Beverly Daniel. *Assimilation Blues: Black Families in a White Community.* Northhampton, MA: First Hazel-Maxwell Publishing Co., 1987.

Walsh, David. *Selling Out America's Children: How America Puts Profits Before Values — And What Parents Can Do.* Minneapolis, MN: Fairview Press, 1995.

Program and Strategies for Children

Bisson, Julie. *Celebrate! An Anti-Bias Guide to Enjoying Holidays in Early Childhood Programs.* St. Paul, MN: Redleaf Press, 1997.

Blue, Bob. *Mister Blue Songbook.* AccuWrite, 810 Kater Street, Philadelphia, PA 19147, 1997.

Brody, Ed, et al. *Spinning Tales Weaving Hope: Stories of Peace, Justice, and the Environment.* Gabriola Island, BC: New Society Publishers, 1992.

Campbell, Duane E. *Choosing Democracy: A Practical Guide to Multicultural Education.* Upper Saddle River, NJ: Merrill (an imprint of Prentice Hall), 1996.

Carlsson-Paige, Nancy, and Levin, Diane. *Before Push Comes to Shove: Building Conflict Resolution Skills with Children.* Minneapolis, MN: Redleaf Press, 1998.

Charney, Ruth Sidney. *Habits of Goodness: Case Studies in the Social Curriculum.* Northeast Foundation for Children, 71 Montague City Road, Greenfield, MA 01301, 1997.

Charney, Ruth Sidney. *Teaching Children to Care: Management in the Responsive Classroom.* Northeast Foundation for Children, 71 Montague City Road, Greenfield, MA 01301, 1991.

Child Development Project. *Ways We Want Our Class To Be: Class Meetings That Build Commitment to Kindness and Learning.* Developmental Studies Center, Oakland, CA, (800) 666-7270, 1996.

Crary, Elizabeth. *Kids Can Cooperate: A Practical Guide to Teaching Problem Solving.* Seattle, WA: Parenting Press, 1984.

DeBenedetti, Ellen J. *Conflict Resolution and Diversity: A Manual of Participatory Activities.* EduPRESS, PO Box 1777, Pittsburgh, PA 15230, 1993.

Derman-Sparks, Louise, and the ABC Task Force. *Anti-Bias Curriculum: Tools for Empowering Young Children.* Washington, DC: National Association for the Education of Young Children, 1989.

DeVries, Rheta, and Zan, Betty. *Moral Classrooms, Moral Children: Creating a Contructivist Atmosphere in Early Education.* Columbia University, NY: Teachers College Press, 1994.

Drew, Naomi. *Learning the Skills of Peacemaking.* Rolling Hills Estates, CA: 1987.

Faber, Adele, and Mazlish, Elaine. *How to Talk So Kids Will Listen and Listen So Kids Will Talk.* New York: Avon Books, 1980.

Gibbs, Jeanne. *Tribes: A New Way of Learning Together.* Santa Rosa, CA: Center Source Publications, 1994.

Hammil, Joanne Olshansky. *The Pizza Boogie Song Book.* JHO Music, 70 Capitol Street, Watertown, MA 02472, 1990.

Hammil, Joanne Olshansky. *The World's Gonna Listen! Song Book.* JHO Music, 70 Capitol Street, Watertown, MA 02472, 1995.

Hatch, Virginia, et al. *Human Rights for Children: A Curriculum for Teaching Human Rights to Children Ages 3-12.* Alameda, CA: Hunter House, 1992.

Hopkins, Susan, and Winters, Jeffry (editors). *Discover the World: Empowering Children to Value Themselves, Others, and the Earth.* Gabriola Island, BC: New Society Publishers, 1990.

Janke, Rebecca Ann, and Peterson, Julie Penshorn. *Peacemakers' ABCs for Young Children: A Guide for Teaching Conflict Resolution with a Peace Table.* Growing Communities for Peace, 16542 Orwell Road North, Marine on St. Croix, MN 55047-9754, 1995.

Levin, Diane E. *Remote Control Childhood? Combating the Hazards of Media Culture.* Washington, DC: National Association for the Education of Young Children, 1998.

Levin, Diane E. *Teaching Young Children in Violent Times: Building a Peaceable Classroom.* Cambridge, MA: Educators for Social Responsibility, 1994.

Lewis, Barbara A. *The Kids' Guide to Social Action: How to Solve the Social Problems You Choose.* Minneapolis, MN: Free Spirit Publishing, 1991.

Oyler, Celia. *Making Room for Students: Sharing Teacher Authority in Room 104.* New York: Teachers College, Columbia University, 1996.

Pirtle, Sarah. *Discovery Time for Cooperation and Conflict Resolution.* Children's Creative Response to Conflict, PO Box 271, Nyack, NY 10960, 1998. Available directly from Sarah Pirtle, The Discovery Center, 63 Main Street, Shelburne Falls, MA 01370.

Pirtle, Sarah. *Linking Up: Using Music, Movement and Language Arts to Build Caring, Cooperation and Communication for Ages 3 to 8.* Cambridge, MA: Educators for Social Responsibility, 1998. Available directly from Sarah Pirtle, The Discovery Center, 63 Main Street, Shelburne Falls, MA 01370.

Porter, Holley, and Jones, Garfield. *Tribal Rhythms: Creating the Village.* Boston, MA: Cooperative Artists Institute, 1995.

Prutzman, Priscilla. *The Friendly Classroom for a Small Planet.* Gabriola Island, BC: New Society Publishers, 1988.

Rogovin, Paula. *Classroom Interviews: A World of Learning.* Portsmouth, NH: Heinemann (division of Reed Elsevier), 1998.

Schniedewind, Nancy, and Davidson, Ellen. *Open Minds to Equality: A Source Book of Learning Activities to Promote Race, Sex, Class, and Age Equity.* Boston, MA: Allyn and Bacon, 1983.

Schneidewind, Nancy, and Davidson, Ellen. *Cooperative Learning, Cooperative Lives: A Source Book of Learning Activities for Building a Peaceful World.* Dubuque, IA: William C. Brown Company, 1987.

Singer, Dorothy G. *Playing for Their Lives: Helping Troubled Children Through Play Therapy.* New York: The Free Press, 1993.

Wolfgang, Charles, and Wolfgang, Mary. *The Three Faces of Discipline for Early Childhood: Empowering Teachers and Students.* Boston, MA: Allyn and Bacon, 1995.

Training for Adults

Arnold, Rick, Burke, Bev, James, Carl, Martin, D'Arcy, and Thomas, Barb. *Educating for a Change.* Toronto, Ontario: Between the Lines, 1991.

Cantor, Ralph, Kivel, Paul, Creighton, Allan, and the Oakland Men's Project. *Days of Respect: Organizing a School-wide Violence Prevention Program.* Alameda, CA: Hunter House, 1997.

Carawan, Guy and Candie (editors). *Sing for Freedom: The Story of the Civil Rights Movement Through Its Songs.* Bethlehem, PA: Sing Out Corporation, 1990.

Derman-Sparks, Louise, and Brunson Phillips, Carol. *Teaching/Learning Anti-Racism: A Developmental Approach.* New York: Teachers College Press, Columbia University, 1997.

Jones, Elizabeth, and Nimmo, John. *Emergent Curriulum.* Washington, DC: National Association for the Education of Young Children, 1994.

Kaner, Sam. *Facilitator's Guide to Participatory Decision-Making.*
Gabriola Island, BC: New Society Publishers, 1996.

Kivel, Paul, and Creighton, Allan, with the Oakland Men's Project.
*Making the Peace: A 15-Session Violence Prevention Curriculum
for Young People.* Alameda, CA: Hunter House, 1997.

Macbeth, Fiona, and Fine, Nic. *Playing with Fire: Creative Conflict
Resolution for Young Adults.* Gabriola Island, BC: New Society
Publishers, 1995.

McKay, Matthew, Davis, Martha, and Fanning, Patrick. *Messages:
The Communication Skills Book.* Oakland, CA: New Harbinger
Publications, 1983.

Video Tapes for Adults

A Prayer for Children, read by Marian Wright Edelman
Available from:
The Children's Defense Fund
25 E Street NW
Washington, DC 20001
(202) 628-8787
Showing Time: 3 minutes

Teaching Students to Be Peacemakers, by David W. and Roger T. Johnson
Available from:
Interaction Book Company
7208 Cornelia Drive
Edina, MN 55435
(612) 831-9500
Showing Time: 8 minutes

It's In Every One Of Us
A visit with the human species depicting nobility, grace, and compassion.
Available from:
New Era Media
425 Alabama Street
PO Box 410685-W
San Francisco, CA 94141
(415) 863-3555
Showing Time: 5 minutes

Paulo Freire at Highlander 12/5/87
A look at Paulo Freire and Myles Horton participating in an adult learning environment on community organizing.
> Available from:
>> Highlander Research Center
>> 1959 Highlander Way
>> New Market, TN 37820
>> (423) 933-3443
> Showing Time: 102 minutes

Violence Prevention Kit – Video
"Violence Is for People Who Don't Think"
A look at common scenarios which are potentially violent, and thought-provoking questions which help people think before they act.
> Available from:
>> Harvard Health Care Foundation
>> 185 Dartmouth Street
>> Boston, MA 02116-3502
> Showing Time: 20 minutes

The Color of Fear, a film by Lee Mun Wah
This film documents the pain and agony of eight men struggling to overcome racism.
> Available from:
>> Stir-Fry Productions
>> 470 Third Street
>> Oakland, CA 94607
>> (800) 370-STIR
> Showing Time: 90 minutes

The Killing Screens: Media and the Culture of Violence
> Available from:
>> Media Education Foundation
>> 26 Center Street
>> Northampton, MA 01060
>> (413) 586-4170
> Showing Time: 37 minutes

Sadako and the Thousand Cranes
"I will write peace on your wings and you will fly all over the world."
A video for young people about courage after the bombing of Hiroshima.
    Available from:
        The Video Project
        5332 College Avenue, Suite 101
        Oakland, CA 94618
        (800) 4-PLANET
    Showing Time: 30 minutes

The Shadow Of Hate: A History of Intolerance in America and
A Time for Justice: America's Civil Rights Movement
    Available from:
        Teaching Tolerance
        Southern Poverty Law Center
        400 Washington Avenue
        Montgomery, AL 36104
        (888) 414-7752
    Showing Time: 40 minutes

*Prejudice: Answering Children's Questions, An ABC Special
Presentation, with Peter Jennings*
    Available from:
        MPI Home Video
        16101 South 108th Avenue
        Orland Park, IL 60467
        (800) 323-0442
    Showing Time: 75 minutes

Understanding and Resolving Conflicts
Scenarios involving various alternatives to conflict management,
including problem solving and communication skills.
    Available from:
        United Learning
        6633 West Howard Street
        Niles, IL 60714
        (800) 424-0362
    Showing Time: 22 minutes

Maya Angelou: Look at Me and See Yourself
Inspiration from Maya Angelou on diversity, empowerment, and the unique gifts of all people in facing challenges: "You are a rainbow in the clouds."
> Available from:
> > The Children's Defense Fund
> > 25 E Street NW
> > Washington, DC 20001
> > (202) 628-8787
> Showing Time: 35 minutes

Howard Zinn: Overcoming Violence: Looking at History, Teaching Today, Transforming Tomorrow — NAEYC, 11/22/96
A panel presentation including Howard Zinn and three early childhood teachers who share their thoughts and strategies on history and social change within the context of early childhood education.
> Available from:
> > Radio Free Maine
> > Roger Leisner
> > PO Box 2705
> > Augusta, ME 04338
> > (207) 622-6629
> Showing Time: 120 minutes

Blue Eyed: A Guide to Use in Organizations
Jane Elliott's unique approach to diversity training. Workshop guide included.
> Available from:
> > California Newsreel
> > 149 Ninth Street
> > San Francisco, CA 94103
> > (415) 621-6196
> Showing Time: 93 minutes

Freedom On My Mind
Tells the inspiring story of the Mississippi freedom movement in the
early 1960s when a handful of idealistic young activists believed they
could change history — and did.
    Available from:
        California Newsreel
        149 Ninth Street, #420
        San Francisco, CA 94103
        (415) 621-6196
    Showing Time: 110 minutes

Starting Small: Teaching Children Tolerance
    Available from:
        Teaching Tolerance
        400 Washington Avenue
        Montgomery, AL 36104
        (888) 414-7752
    Showing Time: 58 minutes

It's Elementary: Talking About Gay Issues In School
    Available from:
        Women's Educational Media
        2180 Bryant Street, Suite 203
        San Francisco, CA 94110
        (415) 641-4616
    Showing Time: 78 minutes

What Matters: The Music and Teaching of Bob Blue
    Available from:
        Bob Blue Video
        8 Arlington Street
        Portland, ME 04101
    Showing Time: 45 minutes

X. Appendix

Principles of Child Development and Learning

Excerpted by permission from S. Bredekamp and C. Copple (editors), *Developmentally Appropriate Practice in Early Childhood Programs,* Revised Edition (Washington, DC: National Association for the Education of Young Children, 1997), 16-22.

1. Domains of children's development (physical, social, emotional, cognitive) are closely related. Development in one domain influences and is influenced by development in other domains.

2. Development occurs in a relatively orderly sequence, with later abilities, skills, and knowledge building on those already acquired.

3. Development proceeds at varying rates from child to child as well as unevenly within different areas of each child's functioning.

4. Early experiences have both cumulative and delayed effects on individual children's development. Optimal periods exist for certain types of development and learning.

5. Development proceeds in predictable directions toward greater complexity, organization, and internalization.

6. Development and learning occur in and are influenced by multiple social and cultural contexts.

7. Children are active learners, drawing on direct physical and social experience as well as culturally transmitted knowledge to construct their own understanding of the world around them.

8. Development and learning result from interaction of biological maturation and the environment, which includes both the physical and social worlds that children live in.

9. Play is an important vehicle for children's social, emotional, and cognitive development, as well as a reflection of their development.

10. Development advances when children have opportunities to practice newly acquired skills, as well as when they experience a challenge just beyond the level of their present mastery.

11. Children demonstrate different modes of knowing and learning and different ways of representing what they know.

12. Children develop and learn in the context of a community where they are safe and valued, their physical needs are met, and they feel psychologically secure.

Guidelines for Decisions About Developmentally Appropriate Practice

Adapted by permission from S. Bredekamp & C. Copple (editors), *Developmentally Appropriate Practice in Early Childhood Programs*, Revised Edition (Washington, DC: National Association for the Education of Young Children, 1997), 9-15.

1. Create a caring community of learners.
   Developmentally appropriate practices occur within a context that supports the development of relationships between adults and children, among children, among teachers, and between teachers and families.

2. Teach to enhance development and learning.
   Early childhood teachers strive to achieve an optimal balance between children's self initiated learning and adult guidance or support.

3. Construct appropriate curriculum.
   The content of the early childhood curriculum is determined by many factors, including the subject matter of the disciplines, social or cultural values, parent input, and the age and experience of the learners.

4. Assess children's learning and development.
   Assessment of individual children's development and learning is essential for planning and implementing appropriate curriculum.

5. Establish reciprocal relationships with families.
   Developmentally appropriate practices derive from deep knowledge of individual children and the context within which they develop and learn. The younger the child, the more necessary it is for professionals to acquire this knowledge through relationships with children's families.

Program Descriptions

CSUF Children's Center
Fullerton, California
by Betsy Gibbs

OUR MISSION

CSUF Children's Center's mission is to enable parents of young children to attend Cal State University Fullerton by providing safe, affordable, and convenient child care in a setting where children experience responsive relationships and enjoy learning about themselves, others, and the world.

OUR PHILOSOPHY

The cornerstone of this program is a deep-felt conviction that high self esteem is the most important goal for children, as well as for parents and staff. It underlies all decisions, systems policies, and planning, and generates a feeling of respect by and for each individual. To build high self esteem in children, we help them know that they are lovable, special, competent, and capable and show them that we trust them to take responsibility for their behavior. Adult-child communication is the most significant factor in developing these feelings, so staff training in the area of communication skills is emphasized. Through skillful communication we create an atmosphere in which feelings and ideas are expressed openly and heard respectfully, from the youngest to the oldest participant. This forms the foundation of the interactions of adults and children, adults and adults, and children and children; it is central to the parent education plan and the curriculum.

OUR GOALS FOR CHILDREN
> We provide an environment which encourages children to:
> - ◆ grow in all areas: socially, emotionally, cognitively, and physically
> - ◆ develop a positive sense of self
> - ◆ be aware of, accept, and express one's own feelings in an atmosphere of respect
> - ◆ listen to and respect the feelings of others
> - ◆ be open to new experiences and willing to try new things
> - ◆ develop problem-solving and decision-making skills
> - ◆ become creative
> - ◆ gain knowledge and respect for the natural world
> - ◆ take responsibility for one's own behavior
> - ◆ accept and enjoy diversity
> - ◆ participate in self care with increasing independence

CURRICULUM
> The Children's Center staff bases curriculum on the interests of the children. Activities are offered which give frequent opportunities to experience choice, challenge, and success to help build feelings of competence and confidence. The activities encompass expressive arts, literature and language, cooking, science, physical development, and their community. Families' cultural identity is interwoven into the program activities, materials, and environment. Challenges, choices, recognition of feelings and culture, respect and pure enjoyment of being are a part of the program for infants, toddlers, preschoolers, parents, and staff.

Stepping Stones Preschool
Nevada City, California
by Sharon Davisson

DESCRIPTION OF SCHOOL AND FAMILIES

Imagine driving seven miles on a twisty country road, through lush cedar, pine, and oak, ascending to an elevation of 3,000 feet. Turn onto a rough gravel road and continue until you reach a gambrel-roofed home with a large play yard attached. You have arrived at Stepping Stones Preschool.

Stepping Stones is licensed for 14 children, but chooses to limit enrollment to nine or ten. Parents drive from the gold country towns of Nevada City and Grass Valley, sometimes traveling 40 miles round trip to bring their children to this small, rural school. Many of the parents are professionals: teachers, physicians, therapists, lawyers. Several of the parents are in the arts or in the building trades. These communities have an unusually homogeneous population with very little ethnic and racial variety. We do our best to compensate for this lack with our use of dolls, music, books, pictures, musical instruments, and stories.

For 15 years Stepping Stones has offered a developmental program for children ages three to five. The children enter the program at age three and attend the Tuesday/Thursday Nursery Program. They then move on together to the three day a week Preschool Program.

Walking into the classroom one sees a child centered environment. The walls are decorated with children's art and our family collages. Child-sized tables and chairs, playhouse, loft, easel, shelves holding educational and creative learning materials are accessible to the children. A second room invites quieter exploration with a large library, shelves of cooperative games, puzzles, and learning activities. The rooms are set up in such a way as to make it easy for the children to locate and return the materials they use. The play yard is spacious with items of nonprescribed play materials such as boxes, boards, and cloths. Swings, sand box, jungle gym, wagons, and scooters are available. The school's bunny, Floppy, is housed under the branches of a large cedar tree. Altogether, this is an inviting and child friendly environment.

We sincerely believe that children are best able to develop their unique potential in a small, nurturing environment. Our primary goal is to help the child develop a positive self regard. We place emphasis on emotional growth and the development of social skills. Within this framework, we provide opportunities for creative experiences and developmentally appropriate learning experiences.

SELF ESTEEM

We believe that when children feel good about themselves, they more easily develop into socially responsible and self confident individuals. We adhere to the humanistic philosophy of Dr. Carl Rogers and have a deep and sincere respect for the child as an individual. Through careful observation, we become sensitive to each child's needs and feelings. We communicate love, acceptance, and respect, and use genuine expressions of praise. We are careful to offer real choices and provide real responsibilities to help the child become self confident and independent. We set reasonable and consistent limits so that the child feels safe while learning respect for others and for the environment.

Early Childhood Lab School
Orange Coast College
Costa Mesa, California

PURPOSE

The Early Childhood Lab School is part of the Early Childhood Education Department at Orange Coast College. The purpose of the Lab School is to provide a setting in which college students may observe and learn to be teachers of infants, toddlers, and preschool children. The director and teachers in the program have been selected because they have an especially strong background of education and experience in early childhood education. They exhibit a standard of positive adult-child interactions for students to model and from which parents may draw support. Parents may observe their children through one-way mirrors.

Children in this model program benefit by having the best quality staff to supervise and provide for age-appropriate activities. The staff offers each child the best of quality care, with a focus on warm, nurturing, individualized attention to help the child reach his or her full potential in all areas of development.

PHILOSOPHY

The individual needs and interests of the children must be the base for determining the design of the play space and for development of curriculum.

- ◆ The children are able to choose freely from a wide range of play and learning experiences.
- ◆ The fostering of curiosity and creative exploration of quality materials provides a foundation for cognitive development.
- ◆ The program encourages the development of strong self esteem and feeling of competence.

PROGRAM

The Lab School serves children from nine months to five years of age.

Parents may enroll their children for a maximum of two and one-half hours per day, for two, three, or five days per week.

Curriculum is designed to nurture young children and to stimulate their language, physical, cognitive, and creative development, and to encourage positive self esteem and social interaction. The curriculum is designed to meet the individual needs and interests of each child, emphasizing the building of the autonomy and problem-solving abilities in the following areas:

- ◆ Music and Movement
- ◆ Physical and Natural Science
- ◆ Language Arts
- ◆ Cooking
- ◆ Gross and Fine Motor Coordination
- ◆ Creative Play
- ◆ Dramatic Play
- ◆ Walking Excursions of the Campus

Mary McLeod Bethune School
Philadelphia, Pennsylvania
by Karel Kilimnik

Bethune School is named after the well-known and respected African-American educator, Mary McLeod Bethune. Her pride and commitment to educating Black children permeates the school. There are over 900 children in kindergarten through fifth grade. Most of the children are African-American but about 10% are Latino, with a majority being Puerto Rican.

Built a little over 25 years ago, this round two-story building was originally designed to be an open classroom school. However, all the open spaces have been bricked up, creating two pod areas on each floor. The building includes a health suite, music suite (with practice rooms), science lab, and large art room.

The school is located in an economically depressed neighborhood although we are within walking distance of several large and well-known hospitals. We have five sponsors, including Temple University's College of Allied Health Professions, National Council of Negro Women, and the Bethune-Cookman College Alumnae Association.

The school has a tutoring program, extra-curricular clubs, and English-as-a-Second-Language classes. Our Home-School Coordinator organizes workshops for parents as well as doing home visits.

Applications

Children's Peace Camps
by Susan Hopkins

Children's Peace Camps are being developed throughout our nation and have proven to be very successful in meeting the following goals for children:

1. To teach concepts of peace, equality, and justice at developmentally appropriate levels.
2. To encourage the development of high self esteem, empowerment, critical thinking skills, and the ability to initiate change (activism).
3. To encourage respect for the environment and the interdependence of all living things.
4. To introduce peaceful conflict resolution skills and alternatives to war play.

5. To provide an opportunity for children of diverse ethnic and class backgrounds to create comfortable, empathic relationships with one another.
6. To facilitate in children an understanding of their humanness and the different ways they are human.
7. To provide a relaxing, yet energizing camp atmosphere for the campers and their families.

To meet these goals, the children's Peace Camp programs are developed by the community in which the camp is held. A local site committee is selected, and that committee does the work of defining the needs of that community and how Peace Camp can best meet those needs. Collaboration with various community agencies and businesses creates commitment and involvement. For example, the Santa Cruz camp provides all camp lunches and snacks to campers from supplies donated by local businesses and prepared by volunteers. The ideas and solutions are endless — only limited by the imagination and funds!

At Peace Camp young children learn tools to help create a safer world. Safety and respect for self, others, and the environment are explored and practiced using skills in conflict management and community building implemented with an anti-bias focus and action-oriented strategies.

The Peace Camp program *weaves* together activities which promote:

◆ *The anti-bias perspective:* awareness of self and group identity, developing empathic relationships, critical thinking about stereotypes, and taking action.

◆ *Emergent curriculum:* developed around issues about which children express interest. The "Teachable Moment" is an opportunity to expand children's learning based upon child-initiated action.

◆ *Community-building focus on skills and democratic practice:* empowerment, conflict management, choice-making, shared power, cooperation, inclusion, trust, "Agreements," consensus process (not voting — finding unity).

Camps have developed unique strategies to incorporate the previously mentioned goals and program elements. Each one has defined the needs for the community being served and then created a program incorporating the goals, but focusing specifically on certain outcomes.

For example, one camp was created because of some concerns expressed by a parent of a first grader about the potential development of racial prejudice. The local Peace and Justice Resource Center was approached and they suggested organizing a children's Peace Camp through the schools. By bringing several classes of children together from different schools to make friends and learn the skills of peace-making, the hope was that the potential prejudice which can result from ignorance would not develop. The teachers from three classes, at three different schools, met together for two days of training at the local police department which had violence prevention funds. Then camp was held at a local church, not at any of the schools involved. The children had been looking forward to coming and making new friends. Activities included making peace quilts, cooperative games, music, discussions, and learning to view the world through "goofy goggles" – glasses made by the children using different colored cellophane. The children were grouped prior to camp by their teachers to achieve maximum diversity in their small *home groups*. In some cases, the children had never heard Spanish being spoken; all discussions were held in both Spanish and English. Discussions focused initially on setting up the "Agreements" for Peace Camp – these are written by the children in the home groups and explain how people are treated at camp with the goals of safety and respect in mind. Groups also worked on skills such as conflict management through defining conflict and then role playing various methods to work through it. Two third graders enjoyed the process so much that they invented their own conflicts to resolve, solved the problems, and then came and told the teachers of their successes. They were so proud of themselves and had a very real sense of accomplishment.

Although the same basic Peace Camp goals are integrated into all the programs, camps do have their unique themes. Recently, a camp in Southern California had the theme of advocacy: of speaking out and *Making Our Voices Heard*. In addition to the usual activities, music included a visiting women's drumming group, and crafts involved making origami cranes to send to the Children's Peace Statue in New Mexico. The children could *make their voices heard* by writing letters to government officials about issues of concern to them, create bumper stickers and pins, and develop a drama to act out "The Rosa Parks Story." One of the children wrote a letter to President Clinton about having no more wars. She gave her letter to the teacher and asked her to mail it. The teacher, upon seeing who it was addressed to, asked her if she thought the President would read it. The child answered, "Well, he ought to remember me – I wrote to him last year too!" Peace Camp can empower children to speak out – to use their voices to make their needs known.

The Peace Camps all include community building skills as a basis for their programs. Music, rituals, and traditions play a part in developing a feeling of belonging to a group and the community. Several of the camps have t-shirts which have a peace dove logo and state PEACE CAMP boldly. Each year they are a different color. Children and adults look forward to receiving their new shirts each year. I remember the day that the Fullerton camp was starting its fourth year and distributing t-shirts. They were gray that year, having been black, then beige, then turquoise the previous years. Nick, who had been with us since the beginning year of camp, was handed a gray shirt. He said, in his biggest six year old voice, "You know that I'm really a black t-shirt kid." Those t-shirts obviously play a role in building the traditions, that sense of community and belonging, which is so important to a peaceful world.

Peace Camp is mostly about making and being friends. It's about the skills of working together to accomplish tasks. It's about solving problems so everyone who has a stake in the issue is included. It's about having opportunities to be with people you might not otherwise know, and learning to enjoy what they have to offer. It's so very much about building community and including everyone. Peace Camp is fun! Peace Camp is creative! And, mostly, Peace Camp is the people who come to make it such a special opportunity for all who want to participate!

Peace Camp Song
by Ann Johnson

CHORUS:
Peace Camp, Peace Camp.
It's how I want to be.
Peaceful with my friends,
And with my family.

VERSES:

    1. Sometimes it's hard,
    To find the peaceful way.
    But I will try,
    To live it every day.

    2. I want to have,
    Peace in my heart.
    I know it's good,
    I know that it's smart.

    3. Give me the gift,
    Of peace in my life.
    Without any war,
    Without any strife.

State College Friends School
State College, Pennsylvania

PROGRAM AND PHILOSOPHY

Guided by the Quaker values of equality, community, simplicity, and harmony, teachers at Friends School encourage personal responsibility in an atmosphere of trust and respect. Silent reflection plays a central role in school life. Teachers actively affirm the importance of all faiths — and special emphasis is given to teaching nonviolent ways of responding to conflict.

The Mystery of Meeting for Worship
by Lee Quinby
Adapted and used with permission

The purpose of Meeting for Worship can be explained in relatively simple terms: We gather in silence to seek a deeper understanding of what lies in our hearts, greater awareness of the spirituality of life, and a clearer sense of direction for our lives.

Achieving these goals is far from simple, however. Perhaps the best way of describing how we do that is to address the questions that parents ask most often: What happens in Meeting? How do we make the silence meaningful for the students? What role does Meeting play in the educational program?

WHAT HAPPENS IN MEETING?

Meeting for Worship takes place once each week, and lasts anywhere from 20 minutes to half an hour. (Visitors are always welcome.) It officially starts as the children begin sitting and the first of them settle into silence. It only takes a few people with their eyes closed to set the right tone.

As soon as the children have settled into silence, one of the children reads a query that encourages everyone to reflect on some aspect of their life that they might not think about otherwise. The children all have an opportunity to participate in planning the query at some point in the year. Topics might include friendship, loss, the joy of giving, life changes of all kinds, world hunger, and care for the earth.

Each class takes a turn at creating the weekly query and closing Meeting for Worship. A query suggestion box encourages children to offer appropriate questions as they come to mind.

Some examples — Kindergarten and First Grade:

1. What can you do when you don't like the game all your friends are playing?
2. What are the things that scare you?
3. What are the things that worry you?
4. How can you play with one friend without hurting the feelings of another friend?
5. What do you enjoy doing alone? What do you hate doing alone?
6. Do you remember your first day of school? How did you feel? What did you do?
7. Sometimes it is hard to tell right from wrong. Has that ever happened to you? What did you do?
8. We give to other people in many ways and for many reasons. Why do we sometimes give to other people, even though we may not get something back?

HOW DO WE MAKE THE SILENCE MEANINGFUL FOR CHILDREN?

Physical analogies often help convey the spirit of Meeting for Worship. Early in the school year, after the youngest students have experienced their first few Meetings, I like to visit their classroom with a sealed jar filled with sand and water. After shaking it vigorously, so that everyone can see the cloudy swirling mixture, I tell them, "This is like the start of Meeting when everyone is still moving around."

Then we place the jar in the middle of circle to observe what happens. As we watch, the sand eventually settles and the water starts clearing.

I tell the children, "It takes a while, but every grain of sand finds a resting place. If you close your eyes in Meeting, and let your imagination take over, you can also find a good place to rest your busy mind. By the end of Meeting, your thoughts and feelings may become clearer, like the water in this jar when the sand has settled."

Teacher Cynthia Potter leads an exercise called "Building a Silence" that challenges students to pass a lighted candle around the circle in darkness and silence. The candle represents the unique spirit of each individual that deserves our loving respect. As the candle moves from hand to hand, each child feels the strong affirmation of others during his or her brief moment in the light.

WHAT ROLE DOES MEETING PLAY IN THE EDUCATIONAL PROGRAM?

We know our students will cope better with the challenges of living in a complex world if they learn to use silent reflection as a way to regain a sense of balance and perspective. Friends School parents often see this learning at surprising moments.

Six year old Matthew was playing in a swimming pool and panicked when he accidentally swallowed some water. His mother took him to the side of the pool and suggested that he try to calm himself. She was amazed to see him close his eyes and begin using a deep breathing technique he had learned at school. At one point, he opened his eyes and explained, "I need to get peaceful."

Aside from fostering personal growth, Meeting for Worship helps maintain a climate of trust and respect in the school. Instead of relying on rewards and punishments to guide positive behavior (which only achieves temporary compliance anyway), we focus on encouraging a feeling of community and emphasizing personal responsibility. In Meeting, we look for the best in ourselves and each other, believing that such an awareness should guide moral action.

The regular practice of silent worship also creates a strong sense of community. The spirit of Meeting often seems to fill the school,

creating an ambiance of love and compassion that brings out the best in everyone. Each Meeting is actually a special kind of celebration, with the silent gathering of friends, the anticipation of an inspiring query or message, and the affirming handshake afterwards.

Issues and Obstacles in Dealing with Culturally Diverse Populations
by Anarella Cellitti

Anarella came to the United States of America about 15 years ago from Venezuela and is currently a professor teaching Child Development at Texas A & M University, Kingsville. She also does therapy and testing of children. She shares her thoughts about the differences she perceives among the dominant society in the USA and other cultures.

The relationships among people of different cultures are dictated by several factors which include but are not restricted to: World View, Family Values and Relationships, Time Orientation, Preferred Mode of Activity, Nature of Man, and Locus of Control and Responsibility.

WORLD VIEW

One's perception of the world is based on socioeconomic status, history, society's values of one's own culture, status based on belonging to the group (migrant versus born in the country), and also legal status (legal versus illegal immigrants). On these premises we know that "minorities" in the USA have a different world view due to history and practices of the dominant culture. Racism, Injustice, alienation, and discrimination are (and historically have been) part of the daily experiences of many. In contrast, most Anglo-Americans perceive their country as just, with equal opportunity for the hard workers, and in a way open to many.

The issue of socioeconomic status is important since the degree of financial security and level of education are going to influence the perception of a person. For poor, uneducated, illegal "minorities," their world will be completely different than "minority" people who are educated and hold better financial means. Many people believe that if you work hard enough, become acculturated enough, speak English well enough, you will be guaranteed equal treatment. For many people this world view is not true and does not represent the USA experiences of many poor and nondominant cultural individuals.

FAMILY VALUES AND RELATIONSHIPS

There is a great body of knowledge that points to the strong family ties that exist among African-Americans, Native-Americans, Asian-Americans, and Hispanic-Americans and their families. Many of these "minority" groups believe that the family unit (or tribe) is more important than the individual. Goals which are in opposition or disapproved by the family groups (or tribe) are not pursued. The emphasis is inter-dependency rather than independence which may cause conflict with school, counseling, and social values. School promotes individual achievement; counseling promotes emotional independence and at times people with strong family orientations are perceived as DEPEN-DENT, ENMESHED, and DYSFUNCTIONAL. At times the goal of the therapist in making the individual too separate moves the client from these "SICK" relationships and puts the client at risk of alienation. The same holds true for school activities based on competition. On the issue of discipline and assertiveness by the child: in some cultural/ethnic groups children are expected to submit to authority without complaint. Children are supposed to be seen and not heard; direct confrontation (even if it is done appropriately) is not tolerated. There-fore, practices that focus on being assertive, direct eye contact, request-ing attention, challenging the way of authority will put children at risk of being punished and outcast by their groups.

TIME ORIENTATION

For many Anglo-Americans time orientation is present and future in contrast to many cultures in which the past is most important. For example, for Asian and Hispanic-Americans the past holds much greater value. The traditions of family and groups are very important and grant NO violations. If these traditions get violated, a social price will have to be paid. The role of the elderly is important regarding the socioeconomic status of the individuals. Advice, comfort, reassurance is sought by the younger individuals from their elderly. In addition, care is provided for the elderly regarding the individual level of comfort. Therefore, many individuals will care for their elderly in what is per-ceived by others to be at the expense of individual fulfillment.

It is common information that Anglo-Americans are the one group that does focus on the future. Therefore, planning for career goals, retirement, and family is an activity that is encouraged and considered in those families, in contrast with many other groups which live in the present orientation. At times these time zones are in conflict with well-intentioned adults who want the adolescent child to plan and prepare for a different time zone.

PREFERRED MODE OF ACTIVITY

Differences do exist as to what people "should" be doing. For many Native and Hispanic-Americans, the emphasis is in "being" with someone or the object or experience. For Anglo, Asian, and African-Americans, the emphasis is in "doing." There is an understanding that if you are not "doing" something, time is ill spent. Relationships are formed and maintained in doing things together rather than just being together.

NATURE OF MAN

Again differences exist with Anglo and African-Americans perceiving humans as good and bad while the Asian, Hispanic, and Native-Americans hold a perception of goodness. These beliefs will influence levels of trust, discipline techniques, and intimacy. Individuals who believe that human beings are by nature "good" will tend to be more trusting, helpful, and cooperative. Individuals who believe that humans are both "good and bad" will tend to be more guarded in their interactions with others. In the first case, individuals do not have to earn trust since people are perceived as good, therefore they will not harm others. That position is not held by the second group in which trust needs to be earned by the loyalty and behaviors of the individuals. Regarding discipline, when parents believe that children are normally good by nature, the expectations are that children will normally do what is appropriate, and guidance by parents will focus on developing that inner "goodness." On the contrary, if children are perceived as "bad," the purpose of discipline is to penalize and eliminate the "badness." Many religious groups hold the theory that children are evil and need to be treated harshly in order to change the evil nature of man.

RELATIONSHIPS

Differences have already been discussed in relationships to family, elderly, and authority. In general other groups hold relationships more important than the Anglo-Americans. At work getting along is more relevant than getting the job done. If relationships are not working well, then distress at work and school can occur.

Other components which are important to include are LOCUS OF CONTROL and LOCUS OF RESPONSIBILITY.

LOCUS OF CONTROL

How much control one has in the outcomes of one's life events is also known as personal control. In mainstream American culture it is commonly believed that the individual alone is responsible for his/her fate: that you can make it or not in America if you apply yourself enough; that this is the land of opportunity for the taker, the assertive, the go-getter. Unfortunately that is a myth. In many cases (particularly "minorities") social elements influence and impede the acquisition of education, jobs, homes, and so on. Many Anglo-Americans do have an internal locus of control but many "minorities" have an external locus of control. Individuals who have faced external limiting situations by the environment understand that issues of power, gender, social status, language performance, immigration laws, and politics are limiting the conditions of their lives.

LOCUS OF RESPONSIBILITY

Also we need to examine the issue of locus of responsibility to define who is responsible for the events affecting one's life: either oneself or social factors. Internal and external responsibility are related to the previous issue of control. Basically the point is who is responsible for oneself: individual members for themselves, or groups and government. This issue is very clear in relating to child care. Who is responsible: the parents or the government? Again the dichotomy exists. Many believe it is the individual and many believe that it is the group, that the community and country have a responsibility to its members. Many Anglo-Americans believe that individuals are responsible for themselves, and many "minorities" emphasize the group and the government.

We all hear discussions regarding welfare, child care, senior citizens, and veterans. Unfortunately for the poor, uneducated, and marginal individuals, the government most often intervenes in their lives to penalize or when there is a tragedy; for example, when child abuse or neglect is reported. The government intervenes when there is a crisis

and no responsibility is taken earlier for educational or financial help. A punitive approach makes the social integration of certain individuals difficult. Mistrust of agencies and services, apathy toward interventions, and resistance to disclosed information are a few of the problems faced by individuals who get caught in this philosophical maze.

Hearing from a Newcomer to Our Land

LuAnne Venham, a teacher at the Orange Coast College Early Childhood Lab School in California, received the following letter from one of her adult student teachers. The teacher speaks through a Persona Doll to build enough trust in herself to communicate her feelings to LuAnne about coming to a strange land, learning new customs, and learning to teach all over again. Speaking through the doll gave her the courage she needed to share her thoughts and make herself heard.

Costa Mesa California

Dear LuAnne,

When I start to write a letter to introduce myself to you, it takes me hours to think what I suppose to write and how to explain the difficulty I have to get help from you. Maybe by borrowing your Persona Doll, it is easy for me to come up with the story about a woman named Nga Duong who came from Vietnam six years ago with her husband and two sons and one daughter. Being a teacher a long time in her country, she wishes that someday she could be a teacher to work with children in the United States too. By taking Early Childhood Education class, she hopes that her dream will come true. In each class she takes, she works very hard to get through it. Because English is her second language, she feels nervous at the beginning of every class. She always needs help from teachers as well as from friends. Please support her as a member of teaching team in our class.

Since I come from Vietnam with different culture and language, it is difficult for me to support children through play. Some games, flannel board stories, and songs are familiar with most American students but with me those are new. I try to learn them by observing adults playing with children, asking to have copy of stories or songs to sing and to memorize them. I always find something new to learn each day coming to class. I learn from adults as well as from children. My foreign accent also makes me to work very hard to be successful in

Hearing Everyone's Voice

295

group-time, to intervene or to guide children through play. To have me in your class is to have a child with special needs that requires the teacher a lot of burdensome duties. I will try the best I can to learn in your class. Your advice will help me grow in this field. I appreciate all your support.

Sincerely,
Nga Duong

Hints for Stress Reduction

Reducing the Stress in Living
by Dolores Mohammed Garcia

Dolores writes briefly about her childhood, her background, and her current professional life to help put her thoughts in perspective for readers.

I was raised on a fruit and dairy ranch in Newcastle, California. I have six brothers and two sisters. I remember at an early age taking responsibility by having to do my share of helping and doing tasks.

My father was born in Afghanistan and my mother was born in Mexico. Two different cultures, two different philosophies of life. My father taught me to believe in myself and if I fell down (failed) at anything I tried, I had two choices: (1) I could lay there and not get up and blame others for failing; or (2) take responsibility, pick myself up, and try again. Risks were opportunities to grow and learn. He also taught me to "Walk Proud." He said, "Don't lie down in the face of prejudice — look them in the eye."

My environment was full of love, my mom gave lots of hugs and love. My father did not hug but I knew he loved me. My mother sold eggs to pay for piano lessons and my father believed in education and did everything he could to assist finances in paying for our college educations.

As an adult, I further enriched my life by getting involved with the Head Start program. I enrolled my three and four year old daughters in the program and I also became involved. This program helped balance me out. The major goal for Head Start is to guide and instill a positive self image for the parent and the child. Head Start succeeded in this.

I have a Business degree background and an AA Degree. I was hired as a Secretary/Bookkeeper, and three years later as a Head Start Director. In two years I was promoted to Executive Director, the position I currently hold. I have worked for the agency for 30 years.

To me, life is like a scale and you need to balance your physical and mental states of mind. If you do not take care of emotional turmoil within you, it will eventually come out in a physical illness. I will be addressing "feelings" inside the mind and body, and how to "center" yourself in order to gain control of situations.

PHYSICAL HEALTH   MENTAL HEALTH

Visualize when you are well . . .   Visualize when you are well . . .

Visualize when you are sick . . .   Visualize when you are sick . . .

Are You in Balance?

Please list some things that make you happy:

Please list some things that make you unhappy:

Now, take each of the above and tell how you feel:

When behavior becomes bizarre and out of control, take an inventory of your personal and professional life and see where you are unbalanced.

FEELINGS WHICH CAN UNBALANCE YOUR LIFE:

— FEAR —
This powerful emotion can keep you from acting and can cause serious problems.

— ANGER —

People who hold in anger are bound for trouble. Anger, jealousy, hatred, anxiety, and other strong emotions can drain your energy. They may not hurt the person that they are aimed at, but they certainly take their toll on you.

— IMPATIENCE —

If others do not meet your standards, you make yourself take the heat.

— LONELINESS —

Love is a great healer. If you feel isolated, sad, or depressed, think about how you might express love.

— CHRONIC WORRY —

Worry may show a lack of confidence in yourself.

— INABILITY TO RELAX —

Being on the go all the time leads to exhaustion.

— RIGIDITY —

Perfectionists are often frustrated because the world cannot live up to their high expectations.

When things seem to be out of balance, questions to ask yourself:
1. What can YOU do about a situation on a short term basis?
2. Can YOU change the situation?
3. If YOU make the choice not to change it, then *accept it,* and *let it go!*
4. Once YOU make a decision, you will feel that YOU have control.
Remember: When behavior is unbalanced and out of control, it is neither GOOD nor BAD, but you may endanger your relationships with others.

IF YOU ARE IN A "LOSE-LOSE" SITUATION:

Some common choices:
◆   Accept — with feelings in turmoil.
◆   Challenge aggressively — an attempt to be honest and share feelings. The other person may not listen or may get upset.

◆ Halfway let go — acceptance of "the way it is," but anger may still be carried. Then the negative feelings begin to cultivate over and over again within yourself until they destroy you emotionally.

But, is this healthy???
NO!

How do you take all of the above and turn them around? It is twofold. You need the help of others. You CANNOT do it alone.

First Step: Awareness.

Second Step: You have to want to change and to accept that there is a problem.

Third Step: Seek help and guidance. Find a friend, minister, counselor, whoever you trust.

Fourth Step: Continue to grow, to learn, to let go. Accept and balance yourself.

Accept that only you, yourself, can grow and change. Erase the old video tape and create a new one using the ideas suggested here. And remember: You cannot change or control any other human being. You cannot make your mate or children behave or act the way you want them to, just to meet your expectations. Believe me, they will resist and challenge you in other ways!

Thoughts from Tom Hunter on "Keeping Alive"

Although these suggestions were created for teachers, parents can easily adapt them to their family lives.

1. Be aware of your own "sense of delight."
   What do you get a kick out of? Make sure you get lots of opportunities to do these things often.

2. What are you good at?
   Make a list and keep adding to it. Read it often.

3. How do you watch and listen to children?
   Store up what you see and hear and then use children's interests and concerns to interact with them.

4. Work on whatever gets in the way of your relationships.
   What is it? "I may not be able to fix it, make it go away, or heal the pain, but together we can get through it."

5. What are you learning?
   "When we think of ourselves as learners rather than teachers, we are better with kids."

6. What do you do to nurture yourself?
   How do you cherish and honor yourself?
   What gifts do you give to you?

7. Are you working on what you believe?
   What are your visions? Dreams? Beliefs?
   What are you passionate about?
   Be grounded in a clear idea of why you are doing what you do.

8. Who do you surround yourself with?
   Who makes up your community?
   Who nourishes you?

9. And finally, "may the memories wrap their arms around you."

Training Resources

HANDOUTS for Use in Workshop Sessions Devoted to Implementing Democratic Practice with Young Children

CONTENTS:

◆ Building Connections: Peace, Anti-Bias, and Democratic Practice
◆ Strategies to Build Community Through Democratic Practice
◆ Connecting Democratic Practice Principles Chart
◆ Ways to Promote Caring Communities Through Democratic Practice: Seven Principles
◆ Communication
◆ Skit for Identifying "Roadblocks to Communication"
◆ "Agreements"
◆ Active Listening Practice
◆ Observation and Democratic Strategies Worksheet
◆ Steps to Managing Conflict
◆ Peace Table
◆ Thoughts from Tom Hunter on "Keeping Alive"

Building Connections:
Peace, Anti-Bias, and Democratic Practice

The time is right to look at ways to define and promote appropriate democratic processes in our work with young children. When we think about the developmental needs of children and how best to prepare them to live effectively in a democracy, the connections among peace education, the anti-bias perspective, and democratic practice must be integrated. The overlap and connections are apparent as shown in the following chart. The chart connects the goals of education for peace, anti-bias perspective, and democratic practice in developmentally appropriate ways for young children. The chart may be read across as well as down.

PEACE EDUCATION	ANTI-BIAS PERSPECTIVE	DEMOCRATIC PRACTICE
Self Awareness	Identity: One's self and group	Self Identity and Responsibility
Awareness of Others	Groups: Similarities and differences	Safety and Trust
Cultural Understanding	Awareness of Bias and Stereotypes	Cherishing Diversity
Conflict Management	Empathic Relationships	Shared Power and Decision Making
Creative Thinking	Critical Thinking	Problem Solving and Choices
Love of Nature	Action/Advocacy	Shared Resources

Used with permission, *Hearing Everyone's Voice*, edited by Hopkins.

Strategies to Build Community Through Democratic Practice

There are a number of strategies which can be implemented at home and at school to promote the goal of developing children's skills in speaking out and participating in a democratic society. Use of these strategies will promote a caring community; that is, inclusion of all members. The power structures in our relationships with each other will be addressed as we explore and practice the seven principles of democratic practice.

The development of the democratic principles can be supported through careful thought and planning. Strategies include ways for children and adults to be recognized, listened to, and heard in a variety of ways. When real HEARING happens, people are affirmed in their own value and worth. HIGH SELF ESTEEM and identity within their community develops.

People who feel valued are more able to TRUST; they feel confident that they can share and be open with others. They feel SAFE. They trust that their vulnerabilities will not be exploited. Therefore, TAKING RESPONSIBILITY for one's own actions, and the risks involved, follows naturally.

CHERISHING DIVERSITY is one of the great pleasures in life if one is comfortable with oneself and can accept that people will be different. Respect, in spite of, and perhaps because of, our differences is essential. Finding common ground is important, but so is valuing diversity of thought, ideas, customs, and even values. Enjoying both our samenesses and our differences gives opportunities for creativity as ideas are shared and explored. By welcoming and including those in our lives who are different, we can grow and develop in ways we never dreamed possible.

SHARING CONTROL AND AUTHORITY are basic to practicing inclusion if we are to hear from others. When the control and power are held by one person or group, others may not have opportunities to bring their unique ideas forward. DECISIONS made with thorough input from others will naturally become broader and deeper in scope. CHOICES will be explored and PROBLEM SOLVING will have creative input with a variety of ideas. We deserve to hear from each other; we all have so much to offer.

SHARING RESOURCES and RESPECTFUL HELPING of others naturally follow sharing control in the development of caring communities. If we are willing to share power with others, i.e. adults including children in goal setting and problem solving, etc., then it follows that such willingness would also include being willing to offer assistance, aid, and resources for caring about one another. Issues around respectful helping are complex.

Used with permission, *Hearing Everyone's Voice*, edited by Hopkins.

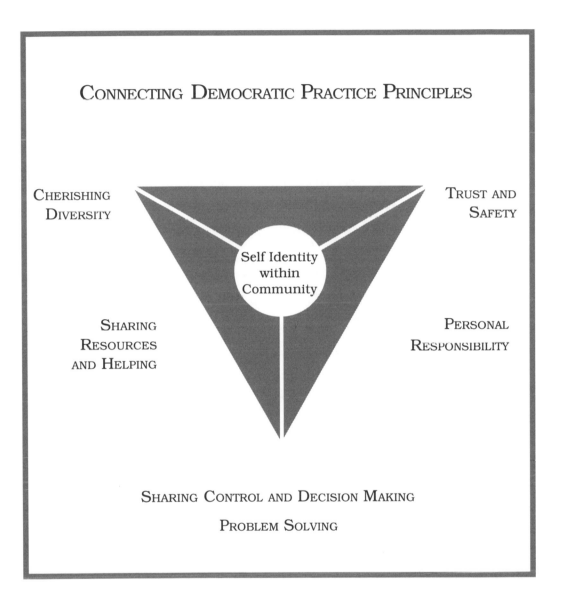

CONNECTING DEMOCRATIC PRACTICE PRINCIPLES

CHERISHING
DIVERSITY

TRUST AND
SAFETY

Self Identity
within
Community

SHARING
RESOURCES
AND HELPING

PERSONAL
RESPONSIBILITY

SHARING CONTROL AND DECISION MAKING

PROBLEM SOLVING

Used with permission, *Hearing Everyone's Voice*, edited by Hopkins.

Ways to Promote Caring Communities Through Democratic Practice: Seven Principles

How do we make these principles appropriate to the needs and development of all members of our community?

DEVELOP SELF IDENTITY WITHIN THE COMMUNITY. Adults will . . .

◆ include photographic likenesses of all children and families in the group in the classroom decor.

◆

◆

ESTABLISH TRUST AND SAFETY. Adults will . . .

◆ affirm children and adults as unique, special people without judging/praising them.

◆

◆

TAKE RESPONSIBILITY FOR YOUR OWN ACTIONS. Adults will . . .

◆ model "mistake-making behavior" and what they can do about the mistake.

◆

◆

CHERISH DIVERSITY: RESPECT FOR AND INCLUSION OF SAME
AND DIFFERENT. Adults will . . .
- ◆ promote enthusiasm for likenesses and differences in ideas.

- ◆

- ◆

SHARE CONTROL AND DECISION MAKING. Adults will . . .
- ◆ work with the children to create classroom "Agreements" about
  how to keep our classroom community safe and respectful.
- ◆

- ◆

PROMOTE PROBLEM SOLVING AND CHOICES. Adults will . . .
- ◆ facilitate children and adults working to solve their own
  problems.
- ◆

- ◆

SHARE RESOURCES AND HELP OTHERS. Adults will . . .
- ◆ model cooperation, working together behavior with children,
  parents, and co-workers.
- ◆

- ◆

Used with permission, *Hearing Everyone's Voice*, edited by Hopkins.

Communication is the weaving together of the message from the sender with the perceptions of the message by the receiver. These perceptions may be influenced by culture, fears, biases, anger, as well as other feelings which may dominate and get in the way of real "hearing." Then misunderstandings may occur. We all have continuous personal work to do to understand ourselves so that our own issues will not dominate and prevent us from being able to really "hear" the messages from others. To listen with respect and a deep commitment to understand provides an environment of safety and love.

ROADBLOCKS TO COMMUNICATION

Sometimes we do and say things which keep other people from sharing and being open with us. It is important for us to be aware of the ways that we block other people from expressing what they feel. We call this blocking "roadblocks." Roadblocks come in a variety of shapes and sizes. Many of them are things that we do with our bodies, like not looking at a person, crossing our arms across our chests, pointing our fingers. Our facial expressions can also roadblock someone's feelings, if we scowl, yawn, laugh at someone, or make faces. And tone of voice can also be a roadblock.

GIVING ADVICE

Suggestions of solutions communicate to other people that you are superior and they are inferior. It communicates lack of confidence in their ability to work things out for themselves. It also encourages dependency and lack of ability to think for oneself. This is true even when people ask for advice. It is most helpful to support the person in discovering his/her own best solutions through resources such as problem solving and experimenting.

Logical arguments may follow giving advice. People seldom like to be shown they are wrong. Often they will defend their position to the bitter end and will end up learning nothing. Defensiveness, resentment, and feelings of inadequacy are often the results.

Interpreting, telling people what their problem is communicates that you have things all figured out. This is threatening, frustrating, and insulting and may bring about feelings of embarrassment, resentment, and anger. If it is so easy for you to figure out, why couldn't they?

Moralizing (shoulds, shouldn'ts, oughts, musts) makes people feel that their judgment is not to be trusted. Instead, they always accept what others say as right rather than evaluating for themselves.

JUDGING

Judging makes others feel inadequate, inferior, stupid, and bad. People need support, not our judgments. Commenting specifically, especially *describing,* on the kinds of things people do well is more helpful than judgments. Descriptions are more likely to be nonjudgmental than general praise.

Praising often embarrasses people and makes them uncomfortable. They also know that if they can be judged positively, they can be judged negatively as well.

RELATING FEELINGS

Reassuring and sympathizing tells people you want them to stop feeling the way they do. This makes them feel unaccepted. People often reassure and sympathize when they, themselves, are uncomfortable with the feelings of another person. If the feelings do make you uncomfortable, make a mental note to consider why they do and perhaps you can gain some personal insight.

Distracting and humoring communicates to people that you are not interested, or are uncomfortable with, reject, or don't respect their feelings. Kidding about an important feeling does not open communication and provide support. Problems put off are seldom problems solved. People want to be heard and understood respectfully.

These roadblocks are not roadblocks if nobody has a problem or feeling they are trying to express. They do become roadblocks when a person is hurting, and we respond to him/her in these ways. It's a long, hard process to learn when not to respond with a roadblock. Nobody says it is easy. But if we can all learn to cut down on the amount of blocking we do, we will find that our children, as well as our family and friends, will feel like talking to us more often about the important things in their lives. If we can learn to listen to feelings without roadblocking, we help people to feel more accepted and understood. We'll be better able to *hear everyone's voice.*

Used with permission, *Hearing Everyone's Voice*, edited by Hopkins.

Skit for Identifying "Roadblocks to Communication"
by Ann Johnson

Characters: Kathleen — Teacher Director
Susan — Teacher
Ann — Family Services Advocate and Narrator

ANN: We have a little skit to help in the process of identifying "Roadblocks to Communication." The setting is a double classroom setting for preschool. Kathleen is the Teacher Director. I am the Family Services Advocate and the Narrator. Susan is the Teacher. We will also be modeling some roadblocks to effective communication. Please refer to your list of Roadblocks handout because we will be stopping the skit periodically to ask you to identify the roadblocks you are seeing. Our skit starts on a hot spring day. The children from the afternoon class have just gone home.

(Susan and Kathleen are waving good-bye to the last of the families, saying "Good-bye," "See you tomorrow," etc. They then move to center stage and plop down into two chairs.)

SUSAN: I can't believe how hot it is.
KATHLEEN: The kids were sure ornery today.
SUSAN: It's this heat, and it's only April.
KATHLEEN: I've got a feeling that summer is going to start early this
     year. I hate the hot weather!
SUSAN: Didn't you put a maintenance request in for air conditioning?
KATHLEEN: That was months ago. They told me to put it on my wish
     list and you know what that means. (Both teachers laugh.) I'd like
     to see one of those people from the office spend a day in this hot
     classroom dealing with these kids! (Both teachers laugh.)
SUSAN: And the parents. Did you hear what "so and so" said at the
     snack table?
ANN: STOP — Time Out! (Addressing the audience) I think we've got
     some problems here. Help me to identify the Roadblocks to Com-
     munication and Problem Solving. What's getting in the way here?
     (Create a list of Roadblocks used with the group.)

DISCUSSION UTILIZING FLIP CHART

ANN: Let's give them another chance.
(Susan and Kathleen are waving good-bye to the last of the families saying "Good-bye," "See you tomorrow," etc. They move to center stage and plop down into two chairs.)

SUSAN: I can't believe how hot it is.
KATHLEEN: This heat really makes me ornery.
SUSAN: Me too. I can see how it effects the children and parents also. Didn't you put in a maintenance request for air conditioning?
KATHLEEN: You're right, I did. That was months ago.
SUSAN: It wasn't hot then.
KATHLEEN: I wonder if it was included on the program improvement grant. I think I'll call the office and find out.
SUSAN: That's a great idea. I'm going to get some ice water, do you want some? (Susan stands up and pretends to get some water.)
KATHLEEN: Thanks, that's just what I need. (Kathleen stands up and follows Susan.) I think I'll call our regional supervisor too, maybe she will have a suggestion.
ANN: Time out! (Addressing the audience) Doesn't that sound much better? Let's look at the Roadblocks we identified earlier to see if they were eliminated.

DISCUSSION USING THE PREVIOUS LIST ON THE FLIP CHART:
CROSS OUT THOSE ROADBLOCKS ELIMINATED.

Used with permission, *Hearing Everyone's Voice*, edited by Hopkins

"Agreements"

One of the most effective ways to share authority and control with others is to jointly establish "Agreements" as to how you want to maintain safety and respect as you work, live, and play together in community. The foundation pieces are safety and respect, but the specific behaviors can be defined by the people in the community. Even young children can, with support in small groups, create their own "Agreements." It is useful to discuss with children *how we want to be together to create a safe and respectful community or family* and to frame the behaviors in the following way:

SAFETY

"WHAT WILL I SEE?"	"WHAT WILL I HEAR?"
"I will see people cleaning up."	"I will hear people using words, not hitting."

RESPECT (KINDNESS)

"WHAT WILL I SEE?"	"WHAT WILL I HEAR?"
"People sharing." "Paying attention."	"Thank you." "Please." "You're cool."

The "Agreements" are written with all participants in the community or family present and giving input, perhaps going around to hear each, one at a time. All can share in the development of the Agreements — everyone given opportunities to speak to each Agreement. If the children in the group speak more than one common language, the languages represented should also be included in the writing. The Agreements can be written on large pieces of paper and posted in the classroom or at home. All participants sign the Agreements. They can be referred to as needed for reminders, or to adapt and change as the needs of the participants change. A constructivist approach to the process will help the Agreements evolve and grow with the community. A caution here that the Agreements are not a punitive technique; they are a way of building community together and working out how to meet everyone's needs within the setting. This method of including everyone is helpful in family discussions as well as classroom settings.

Used with permission, *Hearing Everyone's Voice*, edited by Hopkins.

Active Listening Practice

These vignettes are to be used in partner work with an observer to comment about process. Each member of the group will have an opportunity to be the talker, the listener, and the observer — assuming time allows. The talker will use this script as a starting point to share feelings, concerns, fears, frustrations, etc. The listener will listen actively, remembering to tune in to the feelings behind the words to react empathetically, and to support the talker in working through the concern, and to avoid the "Roadblocks"! The observer will be watching for continuity of words and body language, how feelings are acknowledged, and how the listener supports the talker without taking over in his/her need to discuss the concern.

VIGNETTE #1
"In a meeting this morning someone said, 'The enrollment process is a mess at the ABC Center.' As the person in charge of enrollment there, I'm really upset and hurt by that comment. In fact I'm feeling so hurt I can't even figure out how to do it differently. If only she had said it more gently, with maybe some ideas for us to discuss; but to just call it all a 'mess,' especially when I've worked so hard on trying to do it well. I'm so discouraged!"

VIGNETTE #2
"'Someone burnt the popcorn and smoked up the whole building!' I know I burned the popcorn. I know it smoked up everything. I can't stand it when people talk about something I did, when they know I did it, without speaking to me directly. It makes me so mad when people do that; I wish they would stop blaming and offer to help instead."

VIGNETTE #3
"I'm thinking about violence and children. . . . I grew up in a home where we were sent to our rooms whenever we didn't obey our parents. We had to stay there for 30 minutes or more and then had to come out and say we were 'sorry.' We had to do what our parents told us, or else! I always felt violated and I don't want to do that to children!"

Used with permission, *Hearing Everyone's Voice*, edited by Hopkins.

Observation and Democratic Strategies Worksheet

As we become more and more careful listeners of children, we are better able to discern their concerns and issues. Children are trying to make sense of the world; they may do it awkwardly, but their efforts can be understood and respected. The following chart looks at some typical behaviors we can observe in children, states a concern the child may be working through, and then suggests some possible strategies to support the child's growth in working through the concern. These strategies are used to promote democratic practice.

Observation	Child's Concern	Democratic Strategies
Observation of child backing away from child who might hit him	fears/safety	◆ Meeting to create safety rules using: • shared power • decision making
Hearing child say "You can't play"	inclusion/exclusion	◆ Group discussion and decisions on when it's okay to say "You can't play"
Observation of two children fighting	getting needs met	◆ Problem solving skill building
Karate chopping Power Rangers	feeling powerful	◆ "Power Helpers"
Child not looking at the adult while creating a picture	adult will tell me what to draw	◆ Adult waits to be invited by child
Sand tray work: buries figures in the sand and then brings them out again	gain understanding of mom coming back	◆ Adult reflects on child's words

Used with permission, *Hearing Everyone's Voice*, edited by Hopkins.

Steps to Managing Conflict

1. DEFUSE ANGER

Anger is such an intense feeling that it must be defused before any negotiation can happen. Supportive, active listening may help, pounding the play dough may help, hugs may help. Using everyday songs in new, simple ways can also help: "Gee I'm mad, skip to my loo. . . ." There are many productive ways to defuse anger; it's important to model and practice them.

2. LISTEN TO PEOPLE'S FEELINGS WITH RESPECT

Help children become aware of their own feelings, as well as those of others, by listening to and reflecting the feelings expressed. Acknowledge and support the feelings; after all, the feelings are real and it is critical that we pay close attention to what the children express to us. Their feelings must be validated. It may, in some situations with older children and adults, be useful to ask the question "What worries or concerns you about this issue or problem?" In some cases, simply identifying the *worries* may clarify the issue enough that there is no need to move into problem solving. And, very often, such identification results in being able to think more objectively about the concerns. The listener takes the role of validating the importance of the concerns expressed. Common ground may also be expressed if possible. Problem solving can then be used as needed to resolve what choices and/or decisions to make.

3. PROBLEM SOLVE

Once anger is defused and feelings are respected, then one can settle into problem solving, as needed. Help by:
- Collecting information from both parties: "What happened?"
- Stating the problem clearly, including everyone's concerns.
- Finding common ground: "Do you both have the same worries or needs?"
- Thinking of solutions so everyone's needs can be met.
- Looking at possible consequences of the solutions.
- Planning the solution and helping to implement as needed.

Used with permission, *Hearing Everyone's Voice*, edited by Hopkins.

The Peace Table, a method of conflict resolution with young children, is one of many ways to take peacemaking from the abstract to the concrete. Problem solving, compromising, and thinking through alternatives are learned skills. As teachers and parents, we must find a way to give them the opportunity to experience the process, be responsible for their actions, and to be a part of the solution.

WHY

There is a need for children to learn problem solving and alternatives to fighting in their lives, from the earliest age possible. Authoritarian methods keep all power, decisions, and enforcement in the hands of adults.

GOALS

To have children view the Peace Table as an opportunity for them to be heard and understood. If this method is used for punishment, it cannot work. The most difficult aspect of the Peace Table process is relinquishing adult power. The Peace Table can become the most freeing experience that can happen for you as a teacher or parent.

THE ONLY RULES

You must touch the table to talk, teachers and parents, too! (Children love it when adults must touch table.) This gives control to the process. If someone says something which has already been said, ask to hear that person's special ideas. We want to encourage lots of thoughts and ideas to be expressed.

HOW

◆ Any table or designated spot, e.g., rock, leaf, handkerchief, can be a Peace Table.

◆ Any place and any time.

◆ Adult acts as the facilitator/moderator.

◆ Children involved in the conflict come to the Peace Table and tell what happened from their point of view. Use of a "Go Around"

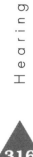

structure works well to hear from everyone. If invited, anyone in the larger group can add to the presenting of the problem.

◆ After the problem has been stated from all points of view, the children of the group are asked to give alternatives on how the problem could have been solved.

◆ At this time, the adult/facilitator needs to accept only real solutions or alternatives, e.g., child says, "They should be nice to each other." Adult/facilitator, "How could they do that?"

◆ Adult/facilitator restates the alternatives but never declares which option they should take or what to do. Adult/facilitator never asks them to say they are sorry or force adult solutions on them.

◆ If an audience gathers, ask Peace Table problem solvers if they feel comfortable with others listening.

TIME AND COMMITMENT
Approximately ten minutes, depending upon the attention span of the children. Some adults may object to stopping activities and calling the group together for a Peace Table because of schedules and time. To make peace a part of children's lives, both a commitment to the concept and a willingness to invest what is necessary to build successful practice are essential.

NOTE
I have used the Peace Table and other methods of teaching peace in my classroom for over five years. After the first of the school year, children call for Peace Table themselves.

Adapted and used with permission, *Discover the World: Empowering Children to Value Themselves, Other and the Earth*, edited by Hopkins and Winters.

Thoughts from Tom Hunter on "Keeping Alive"

Although these suggestions were created for teachers, parents can easily adapt them to their family lives.

1. Be aware of your own "sense of delight."
    What do you get a kick out of? Make sure you get lots of opportunities to do these things often.

2. What are you good at?
    Make a list and keep adding to it. Read it often.

3. How do you watch and listen to children and adults?
    Store up what you see and hear and then use children's interests and concerns to interact with them.

4. Work on whatever gets in the way of your relationships.
    What is it? "I may not be able to fix it, make it go away, or heal the pain, but together we can get through it."

5. What are you learning?
    "When we think of ourselves as learners rather than teachers we are better with kids."

6. What do you do to nurture yourself?
    How do you cherish and honor yourself?
    What "gifts" do you give to you?

7. Are you working on what you believe?
    What are your visions? Dreams? Beliefs?
    What are you passionate about?
    Be grounded in a clear idea of why you are doing what you do.

8. Who do you surround yourself with?
    Who makes up your community?
    Who nourishes you?

9. And finally, "may the memories wrap their arms around you."

Used with permission, *Hearing Everyone's Voice*, edited by Hopkins.

About the Author

As an early childhood educator, I spent the last 20 years of my professional life at Cal State Fullerton Children's Center in Southern California. Ten of those years were spent cherishing the world of four year olds as we shared our days together. The more recent years were focused on the staff of the large, busy campus child care center which employed mostly university students. Throughout all these years, themes of nonviolence and peace education were woven into the curriculum and program development. Skills in communication and problem solving; community building to promote better understanding and living with others; and learning to stand up to injustice — these were all included in our program. The themes also were integrated into a curriculum book on early childhood peace education which was written collaboratively with educators from all over the country.

Currently, I am enjoying the luxury of choosing my own projects. They include advocating for a safe and peaceful world through the work of Concerned Educators Allied for a Safe Environment (CEASE) and the Children's Music Network; the facilitation and organizing of Children's Peace Camps; and working with the California Association for the Education of Young Children (CAEYC) Nonviolence in the Lives of Children Project to implement trainings. Most recently, the editing of our new book, a collaborative effort of many people titled *Hearing Everyone's Voice*, has been one of the most rewarding projects I have ever undertaken. It's a sharing of stories by adults and children who have been and still are struggling with living and being together to better create a democratic society.

"*Hearing Everyone's Voice* is a MUST HAVE resource guide for adults filled with many practical strategies addressing how young people can learn to live together. Through examples of stories, music, poetry, cooperative games, and the integration of the three curriculums — Peace Education, Anti-Bias/Diversity Awareness, and Democratic Practice — one has the rationale plus encouragement to put into practice concepts of social equality. Implementing "Agreements," establishing a Peace Table, and practicing better listening skills are just a few of the many ideas that I will use in my classroom to have everyone's voice heard."

— *Marilyn Pearce*
  First Grade Teacher and Peace Camp Volunteer
  Sacramento California

"As a mother to an infant son and a toddler teacher, the stories shared in this book have inspired me to go beyond helping children develop their vocabulary; they have given me the guidance and strategies needed to help children become empowered through their voices."

— *Heidi A. Smith*
  Mother and Early Childhood Educator
  South Burlington, Vermont

Hearing Everyone's Voice

320

Susan Hopkins

Hearing Everyone's Voice

Educating Young Children for Peace and Democratic Community

Children recognize conflict, injustice, and bias, but they need to be taught how to sort out their concerns and take action to bring about fairness for all. In *Hearing Everyone's Voice*, teachers and parents and children share stories of their struggles to build a democratic community by learning the many ways there are to hear each other given differences in age, ethnicity, gender, culture, and economic background. The perfect guidebook for integrating peace education, anti-bias perspective, and democratic practice into your curriculum.

Published by
Child Care Information Exchange
PO Box 3249
Redmond, WA 98073-3249

ISBN 0-942702-26-3
90000
9 780942 702262